CHUCK D. PIERCE

GOD'S
unfolding
BATTLE
PLAN

A Field Manual for
Advancing the
Kingdom of God

Regal

From Gospel Light
Ventura, California, U.S.A.

Published by Regal Books
From Gospel Light
Ventura, California, U.S.A.

Library of Congress Cataloging-in-Publication Data
Pierce, Chuck D., 1953-
  God's unfolding battle plan : a field manual for advancing the Kingdom of God / by Chuck D. Pierce.
    p. cm.
  ISBN 978-0-8307-4470-1 (trade paper)
  1. Spiritual warfare. 2. Kingdom of God. I. Title.
  BV4509.5.P545 2007
  235'.4—dc22

                                                              2007022110

4 5 6 7 8 9 10 / 10 09 08

Rights for publishing this book in other languages are contracted by Gospel Light Worldwide, the international nonprofit ministry of Gospel Light. For additional information, visit www.gospellightworldwide.org.

Contents

A project like this is never done independently because God didn't make us to do *anything* independently. First, we depend on Him. Second, we depend on others.

Among these, I want to thank my wife, Pam, and my children, who allow me to give so much of my time to the Body of Christ. They know that my heart is that of a warrior and that I am driven to see us walk in victory.

I want to thank Peter and Doris Wagner for being an encouragement to my life and a covering for our ministry.

I want to thank Brian Kooiman, Robert and Linda Heidler, and John Dickson, who assisted me in writing. I have such a wonderful staff at Glory of Zion International Ministries, and I bless them all.

I want to thank Bea Johnson, a lifelong friend from Santa Fe, New Mexico, who played a very great role in helping me research this book.

Finally, I want to give a special thanks to all of the Body of Christ who invest in my prophetic ministry. Without your prayers and support, I could never withstand the war unfolding around me.

Wars Are Always Unfolding

I have a dear friend in Baton Rouge, Louisiana, named Apostle Larry Bizette. We first met in 2003 while I was on a tour of all 50 states to rally the Body of Christ to pray, and I have since returned to his church several times to minister. Larry is a General George C. Patton fanatic—and for good reason. His father, Larry Sr., fought for Patton in the Normandy invasion and was wounded at St. Lo, France, where he saved a friend's life during a battle. Larry Sr. also fought in the Battle of the Bulge and after the war was honored with the Purple Heart, the Four-Leaf Cluster, four Battle Stars, the Bronze Star and the Good Conduct Medal. He is now an active member and honorary elder in his son's church in Baton Rouge.

Larry has always admired his father for laying his life on the line for his country. And when the sixtieth anniversary of the Normandy invasion took place, he traveled with him to France to honor those who changed the course of the world. The trip proved to be more meaningful than he expected, however. Here is Larry's account of what his father revealed to him while there:

On the night of June 12, 1944, my father and his company, with the 29th Infantry Division, arrived at Omaha Beach. They moved about one mile inland and set up camp at approximately 10 P.M. Around midnight, German forces attacked his company of nearly 200 men. The battle raged on through the night until just before daybreak. As the sun came up, the casualties became more visible: There were only 23 men of his company left. Some of his best friends had been killed.

Even though he wasn't a Christian at the time, my dad cried out to the Lord and asked Him why he was still living while others had died. What had he done to escape death? It didn't make sense why he would be spared. For years this cry to the Lord stayed with him, though he never received any understanding about why he survived that night in Normandy.

Years later, in 1978, my father was saved and filled with the Holy Spirit. About three months after his salvation experience, he had a dream. In it, he was brought back to that scene in Normandy, on June 12, 1944. He witnessed the bodies scattered around. He saw himself crying out to God after the battle. But then something miraculous occurred: He saw Jesus standing there near his foxhole. The Lord spoke to my father and told him the reason he was spared that night while others were sacrificed for the cause of freedom: "In your loins was an apostle!" Jesus said. "I saved you because I knew that this leader would go to the nations of the world and advance My kingdom!"

That, of course, was me—Lawrence (Larry) Bizette Jr., born on July 26, 1948. Glory!

There is much in war that we do not understand. War always involves casualties, and, at the same time, divine interventions of which we're unaware. Sometimes war makes no sense to us. Yet war is a part of life. And as we face the unfolding war that lies ahead in both the natural and spiritual realms, it is crucial that we adhere to Paul's words to the people of Ephesus:

Finally, my brethren, be strong in the Lord and in the power of His might. Put on the whole armor of God, that you may be able to stand against the wiles of the devil. For we do not wrestle against flesh and blood, but against principalities, against powers, against the rulers of the darkness of this age, against spiritual hosts of wickedness in the heavenly places. Therefore take up the whole armor of God, that you may be able to withstand in the evil day, and having done all, to stand. Stand therefore, having girded your waist with truth, having put on the breastplate of righteousness, and having shod your feet with the preparation of the gospel of peace (Eph. 6:10-15).

In the midst of conflict, we must learn to stand just as Larry's father did on the rocky shoreline of Normandy. We must stand until we see peace, until the perfect plan of God is manifest. We must stand until evil forces that oppose God's will are pushed back. As long as the Spirit of God is still in the earth realm, He will use His people to stand against the evil that attempts to rule our world.

A Battle Plan from Heaven

I was in a car driving to New Orleans with Larry when he told me his father's story. We were on our way to pray for a city left in ruins by a war of another sort. The wars most of us face today are not between Axis or Allies, North or South, terrorists or dictators. They are often expressed in the earthly realm, yet their origin is always in the spiritual. In fact, as I was driving with Larry, I heard the Spirit of God say to me, *"There will always be wars and rumors of war. There will be many battlefields that unfold in the days ahead. Your future will be determined by how you trust Me on the battlefield. Lean not on your own understanding. In the midst of your conflict, I have a plan! There are some things that are still hidden from you. Trust Me so that in My perfect timing I can manifest why I called you to stand."*

As you read this book, let faith arise in you to stand. God has a plan for His people to triumph in these times (see Dan. 7). His kingdom is everlasting, and He has a strong people who will do great exploits!

Granted, this book is not meant to give you all the answers. In the midst of warfare we never have all the answers. However, we do know that if we will stand and be faithful to the Lord's purposes, we will eventually understand the "whys" of life.

Throughout these pages I have attempted to capture some key issues we will be warring with in the days ahead. By the end of your reading, you should understand:

1. *How to develop an identity and wholeness in Christ that allows you to withstand every looming ploy of the enemy.* This will include how to protect and secure the unique portion that God has for you through His covenant blessings.

2. *The great power of Christ's blood that cleanses us.* The war over blood is one of the great conflicts the Body of Christ must understand in the coming days.

3. *The dichotomy of good and evil that is forming.* We are entering a season of polarization in which we must be trained to discern good and evil (see Heb. 5:14).

4. *How the Church will fellowship in this shifting season.* Though we are moving into a season of decentralized fellowship, we will need to come together to receive God's building plan and model for the future.

5. *The continuing wars between the lines of Ishmael, Isaac/Jacob and Esau.* How do we make sense of the ongoing conflicts in the Middle East and of our connecting roots to that crucial land?

6. *The world trade systems that will emerge under satanic influences.* Lucifer's casting out from heaven involved "the iniquity of [his] trading" (Ezek. 28:18). How are we to deal with "trade iniquities" that have never been overthrown?

7. *The discipline of ruling by night.* By keeping a night watch throughout our spheres of authority, our day will be ordered and light will be extended to us.

8. *Satan's strategies to manipulate times and laws.* There is a law "machine" and an ungodly handshake that God's people must understand.

9. *How to plow so that we develop and cultivate the fields for true harvest.* Our harvest fields have changed drastically, yet we are still called to reap.

10. *The concept of the lampstand.* Is yours burning brightly?

My prayer is that as you delve into these pages your eyes will be opened to the looming conflicts we will encounter in days ahead. May you find both strategy and an assurance of victory for the unfolding war ahead.

Dr. Chuck D. Pierce
Glory of Zion International

The Changing Structures of War

Like it or not, we are at war. Almost a year before the tragic events of 9/11 unfolded, I began prophesying throughout this nation that we as a church were entering into a seven-year season of warfare like none we had seen before. It was not a popular message, yet after that fateful day it became clearer: God was requiring His people to face battles that went beyond retaliating against terrorist attacks or liberating the Iraqi people from a tyrant. These were spiritual battles, to be fought by spiritual warriors. Some wars were to be waged inside our own borders, others on foreign soil.

We are now at the tail end of that seven-year period, and the warfare has continued to escalate in intensity. Yet the question is still the same as it was when this season began: *Are we prepared?*

To wage war—and win—we must have a battle plan. More than 20 years ago God began preparing me for this time of war and revealing to me His plan for the unfolding days. I was not heavily active in prophetic ministry at the time, nor was I looking for some divine strategy from God. But the vision I received from the Lord on December 31, 1985, forever changed my life. I have written about it before in *The Future War of the Church*, but I feel this vision still remains so applicable that it is worth sharing for those who have not heard it.

On New Year's Eve, I opened my Bible to read and pray in preparation for the coming year. As I went before the Lord, I felt a nudging to close my Bible, lay aside my prayer list, and just wait for God to speak to me. As I waited, God indeed began revealing many things to me. I felt

He was showing me how the Church was to prepare for the future.

He began by saying that within 12 years from that time, the government of the Church would change to reflect the pattern given to us when Jesus ascended to heaven. The Lord then said He would release revelation and gifting for new administrative methods that would cause His people to become influential and victorious in the next season of history. In this visitation God showed me three distinct governmental structures on this earth and their importance for the future of society.

1. *The Existing Church Structure*

God first showed me the church as I knew it. At the time, I was a member of a mainline denomination and I really didn't know any other method of doing church. I had always been open to a move of God, but as far as church government was concerned, I knew only the democratic, congregational form of decision-making in church matters. In my vision, that form of church appeared to me as a large building of about 50 stories. Each room in the building was brightly lit and the structure well built, though the building was also flexible. Yet as I watched, the building became more and more rigid and unchangeable. As it grew rigid, the lights grew dim, even though there was still some light emanating from the rooms. The structure began to look more like a prison than a flexible organism of change. And God said, *"I will have an opportune time when many will come out of this church government and begin to flow into another government structure that will arise."*

2. *Adverse Antichrist Governments*

God then showed me two other buildings rising up. The first building was labeled Militant Religious Governments (the "-Isms"). This building was being constructed rapidly and had great strength. I saw rooms that represented religious systems from nations around the world, including the United States. The Lord showed me the effects these religious systems would have on our society in the days ahead. I saw strategy rooms where plans for terrorist activity were being devised. The proposed acts of terrorism were designed to create great fear in the target areas, meant to cause people to convert to these religious systems and to cause wealth that God intended for His kingdom to be withheld and controlled by other religions. I then saw the Lord's heart for those ensnared by and working in these religious systems—He longed to see them released and their trapped gifts liberated for Kingdom purposes.

One key religious system God showed me was Islam, which will have great influence on Earth in the days ahead. (One important note on this point: When I refer to Islam, I am not talking about the Muslim people per se, whom God loves and for whom Jesus died. I am referring, rather, to the religious structure of Islam, which is controlled by satanic principalities and powers.) I saw that Islamic religious forces would be positioned in key places throughout the world. The Islamic religion understands the spiritual principle of treading to gain territory (see Josh. 1:3). First, they march militantly to gain control of territories. Then they establish their authority through war, bloodshed or whatever else may be necessary to maintain and secure the ground they've gained.

In this portion of the vision, there was another smaller building located in front of the -Isms. The smaller building was called Lawlessness. In this building, there were hidden lawless forces linked with secret societies such as the Ku Klux Klan and Freemasonry. I saw the influence of this building begin to result in acts of violence and murder taking place in schools, churches, shopping malls and supermarkets.

The building of Lawlessness was actually connected in form and administration to the religious systems located in the -Isms building behind it. I thought this peculiar at first, but the Lord began to show me that the same type of religious spirit controlled both of these entities. I then saw how the governments of the earth were being influenced by these structures and how some of these governments were trying in vain to resist them with their own strength.

The Lord then showed me what the foundations of these two buildings were made of. Words appeared on their foundations: *mammon, Ashteroth, Jezebel, Ahab, Babylon* and *Baal*. Next to these were anti-Semitic slogans and Hindu philosophies, among others. God said that if we could understand how these structures operated, we would have keys for victory in the future when the structures of the -Isms and Lawlessness would rise up and attempt to gain control.

3. *The Church of the Future*

God then showed me a third picture, of a building filled with light. The Lord called it "My Future Kingdom Authority." The building was very small. It was just beginning to form and was still lacking in size and shape. Even so, the structure was nothing but light (similar to a hologram) and glory.

Several words appeared on its foundation. They were the five ascension gifts listed in Ephesians 4:11 that make up the government of God: apostles, prophets, evangelists, pastors and teachers. God was bringing order to these five gifts and placing them in the foundation. Each time one gift was set in order, the light would increase tremendously.

He said that this order would become very visible over the next 12 years. Once the proper order had been established, He would rapidly transfer His people to the new structure. I saw many leaders from the first building (the Existing Church Structure) move their offices from the old building to this new structure. As they turned out the lights of their offices in the old structure, that building grew darker and much more rigid, and it was unable to withstand the -Isms and Lawlessness. However, the Lord's new structure began to arise, and it had the ability to resist the -Isms and Lawlessness structures and could overcome their governments.

God then said to me: *"This is the government of the Church of the future that will arise and spread My light throughout the world in the latter days. This government will overcome all other governments. When this government is in order, you can then command governments of the earth to come into order. This will be the government that My latter-day blessings will rest on. This will be the government in which My glory will be seen. This will be the government that comes into a double-portion anointing and will dethrone the systems of Babylon on this earth. This government will not be one of compromise but of determined commitment to My purposes."*[1]

A 40-Year Plan in 10-Year Intervals

As you can tell by this vision, God was preparing me—and the rest of the Church—for the future. The precision with which He showed me things was remarkable. This detailed revelation came in 10-year increments, beginning with the coming year, 1986, and including "signposts" that would occur in 1996, 2006, 2016 and 2026. I do not know why God only showed me through 2026, but that is how revelation works: You only see what He is ready to reveal to you.

For instance, the Lord showed me in January 1986 that by the end of January 1996, the government of God would begin to change. You can go back and reread that vision and how it progressed from building to building. Then He showed me that by the end of 2006, His government would be in a new mature state. This meant that a new wineskin would be operating, and the way church had been done from 1966 to 2006 would come to an end. We are seeing this happen. I could document page after page of changes from various authors, but anyone who reads this book will know we are living in a different church era. Peter Wagner has called it the New Apostolic Reformation.

The Lord showed me that by 2006, lawlessness would have many avenues of operation throughout the world. And indeed, we have seen lawlessness arise greatly. By 2016, in an effort to control this chaos, many laws will have been established that will severely restrict our freedom.

Much of what I will cover in chapter 8 regarding the future of specific nations was also revealed to me in this vision. The Lord showed me that there would be a great change in Russia by 2007, and that the Russians would begin to redevelop their plan of world domination. At the time, I had a solid understanding of the former Soviet bloc countries because of my work there throughout the 1980s. Yet I saw that this time they would have to realign with other nations, predominately those in the Middle East. He gave me insight into England and showed me how the one-time driving force of the world would be "bought" by other nations because of its own compromise. There would be a manifestation of this by 2016. (Let me reiterate that I do believe any of this can change by prayer.)

He gave me the greatest understanding about the nation of China. In 1986, He showed me how China would rise to power. He said that by 2006 it would have a greater influence and the eyes of the world would start turning toward this nation. China has now been chosen as the host for the 2008 Summer Olympic Games. He revealed to me that by 2016 this would be the most financially influential nation in the world. By 2026, the Chinese could actually rule the world and Russia would begin to submit to their leading.

When I received this first vision, I was on staff at a denominational church as pastor of Prayer and Benevolence. I went to my pastor and shared what had happened to me. "I really don't understand all of this," he responded, "but I think you should prepare to teach God's people about how to pray so that they are ready to meet the future head-on." I had never really thought about how I would teach a vision. Now it has become a way of life for me.

A Second Vision of the Coming Wars

I am an early riser. In May 1999, I got up early as usual and went downstairs to pray. All of the sudden, it was as if the Lord dropped a blackboard in front of my eyes. On this blackboard He began to write various phrases with His finger: *Anti-Semitism. Militant Islam. Women arising in the future. Increased terrorism. Prayers that outwit the enemy. Prepare for war!* I asked Him what He was showing me. He said, *"This is the future war of the Church."*

His words prompted me to write the prequel to this book, *The Future War of the Church*, in 2001. Since then, we have already entered into a season when more revelation is needed—thus, the spark behind the book you are now reading. We may be nearing the conclusion of a seven-year period of war, but our need to prepare for war is greater than ever.

Part of that preparation is understanding what lies ahead for us both as a corporate Church and as individuals. Because we prophesy in part and prophecy is a process, many times we see a portion of God's revelation and then He begins to refine what we have seen. I believe that is now the case with understanding God's unfolding battle plan for these times. What was delivered to me in part more than two decades ago is now being refined. Therefore, let me present what I believe is a more detailed understanding of the wars we will wage in coming days. I will go into full detail on many of these in the coming chapters of this book. For now, it is important to get a sense of just what we will be standing against as we declare God's reign in this world.

The Mind War
This is essentially a war for *peace*. How we develop our identity in God, how we represent God's kingdom plan in the earth realm, how we strategize for the future according to the Holy Spirit's guidance, how we establish peace and security in the midst of war . . .

victory in this war stems from the Lord having full control over our minds. They are also issues that will create great conflict with societal and philosophical structures, as we will discover in chapter 2. The challenge of today's Church is to transform its way of thinking so that it truly represents God's kingdom in an escalating conflict with the kingdom of darkness. Phrased another way, will the Bride put on her war garment and place her "army boots" on the headship of the enemy in every area of society? Remember, Romans 16:19-20 says, "I want you to be wise in what is good, and simple concerning evil. And the God of peace will crush Satan under your feet shortly."

There is a dichotomy of good and evil that is forming in almost every arena of life. There will be a fine line over how we discern. We must train our senses to discern good and evil. Hebrews 5:14 says, "But solid food belongs to those who are of full age, that is, those who by reason of use have their senses exercised to discern both good and evil." We discern by the Word and the Spirit. That means that the Word of God must come alive again for many of us! This is my greatest concern for the generations that are arising. I do not see the foundation of the Word built within the next generation. Therefore, the enemy will attempt to counterfeit spiritual dynamics. I also see that those who have been involved in cessation theology (which says that God stopped demonstrating His power centuries back) will have a difficult time in days ahead. There will be circumstances that we will only be able to know, see and discern by the Spirit.

Allow me to share a dream that one of my mentors, Lacelia Henderson, had many years ago. The dream has stuck with me through the years, probably because it seems more relevant now than ever!

> In the dream, I had gone with friends (Charles and Charlene) to a cabin they had in the woods. We were dressed for bed when someone knocked at the door. Charlene started to answer the door and I waited in the bedroom. I said I would hide back there while she answered the door. If it was a friend I would come out, and if was not I would jump out the window and run for help.

When she opened the door, these men came in who were dressed in army fatigues. They came in like the Gestapo and took the place by storm [captured it]. In the meantime, I jumped out of the window in my nightgown. When they saw the open window, they knew that I had escaped. Some of them ran outside and got in a vehicle like a Jeep to look for me.

It was very, very dark. I was alone and vulnerable in my nightgown. Their eyes were piercing as they scanned to and fro trying to spot me. When they were not looking my way, I would run from tree to tree. It was all very intense, and I had little time to get behind the next tree before they looked back my way each time.

Finally, I came to a clearing and saw some houses. But I knew that I had to choose the house I ran to carefully. It had to be someone who knew me and trusted me. I knew that once I stepped out into the clearing that I would be spotted. I also knew that when I ran to a house to use the telephone to call for help, I would not have time to explain the situation to get permission to use the telephone. If I took time to explain, I would be caught and stopped by the enemy. Once I got to the house I had to be able to run straight to the phone to make the call for help.[2]

This dream reveals to us the war ahead over discernment. We will have to know when to hide ourselves, when to boldly come forth with a word, when to run, when to fall, when to stand, when to make our way through a crowd, when to embrace revelation (and when not to!), when to be quiet and when to loudly release the sound of the Lord.

The Blood War

In the Church's quest to be received by society, the power of the cross and the overcoming dynamic of Jesus' blood are no longer preached in their fullness. Revival and awakening occur when the Spirit of God comes alive in our blood system, producing a cleansed conscience. The enemy wars with all of his might to keep the consciences of God's people blinded. If he can do this, he can block the anointing that will break his yoke in the earth realm. Because of the world's influences, our conscience struggles to stay pure so that we can see God. That means that in the midst of the war, we must be fervent and disciplined in the battle over our conscience. This is key to our overall victory!

In chapter 3, I will address the various issues surrounding the war over our blood. I see a new breakthrough coming in the spirit realm that will cause the consciences of God's people to be cleansed. That, in turn, will spark many breakthroughs in the realm of healing. This will have to occur because the health care system throughout the world is becoming more corrupted and controlling.

The Time War

Most of us end our day by collapsing on the couch and catching up on our favorite shows, reading a good book or simply chilling out. We've trained ourselves to wind down after an exhausting workday. Unfortunately, most of us have forgotten God's definition of a day—which, in His terms, *begins* with the evening. We have given up the domain of the night by rendering it as the time when darkness of all sorts emerges. I believe the watches of the night are key to reclaiming this time in which God often calls His warriors to stand guard with Him. Chapter 4 explains the concept of the night watch and how it allows God to reorder our day. When we allow His light to shine through every form of darkness, we will see new breakthrough with every dawn. How we learn the discipline of ruling by night will determine how we walk in His presence throughout the day.

The Presence-and-Glory War

Without the presence of God going before us, we are unable to win any war in the earth realm. We must learn how to usher in the presence of God and invite Him to take over our atmosphere. The more we worship, the more we sense the atmosphere of heaven around us, which ushers in God's life-changing glory.

That, in turn, brings societal transformation. The best understanding of how to transform society comes from analyzing the
seven churches that are presented in the book of Revelation. I do
just that in detail in chapter 5. What we will see emerge in the
future are territorial strategies that reflect this model.

We must go beyond trendy "spiritual mapping." We must see
how the government of God in a territory is being established.
Are key anchor churches connecting together? To change society,
I believe we must do three things: First, we have to define our individual or corporate target field or realm of authority. Second, we
have to identify the structure of the enemy that is holding that
area. Third, we have to define how our authority or government
can influence this territory. If a church is vibrant in its assigned
arena, it should be the most influencing structure in that region.
This is a major war for our future.

The Power War

We read in Genesis 1:26-28 that God "created man in His own
image; in the image of God He created him; male and female He
created them. Then God blessed them, and God said to them, 'Be
fruitful and multiply; fill the earth and subdue it; have dominion
over the fish of the sea, over the birds of the air, and over every living thing that moves on the earth.'"

God's plan was for humans to take authority and rule in the
earth realm. I think we all believe this, but most of us hate the
thought of being responsible for how a territory prospers or a land
fails. It's hard enough being responsible for our own families!

God is sovereign. However, in His sovereignty He watches for
us to respond to Him. This is how we exercise our faith: We *act*
rather than sit passively. I am not here to discuss theology or philosophy, but I do believe that in the midst of this season of war we
cannot have a "*que sera, sera,* whatever will be, will be" mentality. We
must be passionate and active in seeking God so that He can empow-
er us to overthrow our enemy. Romans 6:14 clearly says, "Sin shall
not have dominion over you." But do we truly believe that? This
verse means that God never planned for evil to rule and reign over

my life and territory. This also says that I am never to fall into agreement with the antichrist spirit by failing to take a proactive stand against him. I am to take dominion over my enemy!

An interesting note: The antichrist system seems to be forming a great dichotomy between Christians and militant Islam. Those who worship Allah and revere Mohammed believe in the concept of taking dominion. In fact, most have a better understanding of this than those in the Church. Believers, we must change our views about how the government of the Church is meant to be so that we can have a greater influence against evil in the world. If we don't, and if we fail to act, we will be giving over every nation to an antichrist force.

The Wealth War

The goal here in winning this war is not to acquire riches for trendier church buildings, nicer cars or fatter wallets. This is for Kingdom advancement! The world's economic system is not just based on Wall Street or Dow Jones—there are spiritual forces at work that for generations have successfully cut off the supply lines for God's people. In chapter 7, I will explain how the treasurer of this world, Mammon, holds sway over nations' economies. I believe one of the biggest catalysts for war in the coming times will revolve around the transfer of wealth. Will Mammon rule? Or will the people of God understand His plan and position themselves to receive the wealth transfer in the future?

The War of the Nations

Chapter 8 delves into one of the fiercest wars that lie ahead, the war that we will see shifting across the globe. Governments will continue to vie for power. National boundaries will be contested and altered. Strategic alignments will be made according to nations' relationships with Israel. Wars and conflicts will continue to rage, yet we must remember, above all else, that we are Kingdom people. While the earthly kingdoms we live in may rise and fall, our purpose is to establish God's kingdom above all else. We will do well to keep the example of Daniel in mind as we face the days ahead, serving our countries yet depending on the higher purposes and calling of God.

Governments of the world cannot fully change until the government of God here on Earth aligns itself and represents the order of God. That means leaders in the Church must get their act together! I see many denominations or wineskins of the past fading and becoming irrelevant by 2016. There have already been many changes. We have become aware of God's foundational plan of apostles, prophets, evangelists, pastors and teachers. We are learning how to interact with each other. We are letting go of old methods of operation and embracing new ways of worship.

The real war in days ahead will come over how we fellowship. We will have to learn how to operate in decentralized fellowship. In other words, we won't all be going to church every Sunday. That form of worship is changing rapidly. At the same time, corporate worship gatherings in certain territories will break through into new levels of revelation. I am not talking about extra-biblical revelation—the Bible has been canonized; it is the established Word of God. However, I believe there is revelation coming that will cause the Word to become even more applicable for this age, while also giving us strategies to defeat the enemy. Many of what are now corporate warfare worship gatherings will turn into times of travail and the result will be changed nations. As we come together and worship in such settings, we will gain new strategies for how to govern in our spheres of authority.

The Harvest War

The final theater of war will be the war of harvest. Harvest time is when we are at the end of a season, the crops have matured and now there must be a gathering. Revelation 14:15-16 says, "And another angel came out of the temple, crying with a loud voice to Him who sat on the cloud, 'Thrust in Your sickle and reap, for the time has come for You to reap, for the harvest of the earth is ripe.' So He who sat on the cloud thrust in His sickle on the earth, and the earth was reaped."

Harvest is a process. The grain must be cut with a sickle. What has been cut is then gathered into sheaves and taken to the threshing floor, where tools or animals are used for the threshing. The grain is winnowed, tossed into the air, where the wind separates and blows away the chaff from the heavier kernels of the harvest.

The last phase of harvest is when the kernels are shaken in a sieve so that the harvest can be stored. This is the point of the process where the war dynamic of harvest is maturing at this time. We are in a shaking process. What can be shaken will be shaken. The Lord is shaking away the iniquities in our lives, corporate gatherings, cities and nations that would make us less "marketable."

The key to our harvest is the weight of His glory. In the winnowing stage, the weightier kernels do not blow away. In the season ahead there will be many issues that cause us to be tossed to and fro. Without the weight of His glory resting upon us, His people, we will be blown away and will not complete the harvesting process that God has released into the earth.

The harvest is a picture of God's judgment. Jesus used this as a metaphor to make us realize that there will come a time when He gathers those who believe. The harvest has already begun. It began when Jesus first came and now is maturing rapidly. Yet there is a "tug-of-war" in heavenly places over who will control the harvest and bring the resources into the storehouse. Luke 10:2 says, "Therefore pray the Lord of the harvest to send out laborers into His harvest."

Not only are we being harvested, we are the harvesters for the future!

Chapter 1

Becoming a Warrior in a Season of War

D uring a recent trip to Europe, I was able to visit my mother's family's homeland of Luxembourg. Her family descended from the Huguenots, the scrutinized and persecuted Protestant reformers who dared question the Roman Catholic Church during the tumultuous sixteenth century in France. In fact, one of my mother's ancestors married the daughter of the King of France. At the time, the Roman Catholic Church despised the Huguenots for their harsh opposition and pointed criticism of papal hypocrisy. The conflict was so bad that there was a strategy to kill this prince during his wedding celebration. He escaped from France and settled in Luxembourg, and then later, while seeking freedom from persecution, emigrated to the Carolinas here in America.

This was just one of the fascinating pieces of history I discovered while in Luxembourg. It turns out that my mother's royal lineage is full of feuds, scandals, conflicts and wars. Hundreds of years marked by hundreds of wars. Yet with each new story, I was struck by the notion that all of us have similar bloodlines. We all, whether descended from royalty or not, have a history of war in our blood. We are a violent race forever standing on the precipice of conflict. In fact, a group of academics and historians released a report in the early 1990s stating, "Since 3600 BC, the world has known only 292 years of peace. During this period there have been 14,351 wars, large and small, in which 3,640,000,000 people were killed. The value of the destruction inflicted would pay for a golden belt around the earth [97.2 miles] in width and [33 feet] thick.

Since 650 BC, there have also been 1,656 arms races, only 16 of which have not ended in war. The remainder ended in economic collapse."[1] Jesus said that there will always be wars and rumors of war until He returns for a 1,000-year earthly reign.

War is conflict. And in the midst of conflict and seasons of war, warriors must arise. Yet as anyone who has ever fought in battle can attest, simply being a warrior does not guarantee victory against the opponent. It takes skilled warriors to win. We are currently in a season when skilled Kingdom warriors must arise to stand in the gaps where evil reigns in the earth. These warriors must contend for peace and wholeness as the forces of darkness close in with increasing strength and skill.

In such a time of direct conflict, how are we to process the wars and rumors of war that surround us? How do we deal with the warfare of one kingdom against another—both spiritual and physical? With the world around us changing so rapidly, what will the war look like in the future? How can we become mighty warriors in a Kingdom above all earthly kingdoms so that we might establish that Kingdom on Earth? These are just some of the questions we must ask as we move forward and establish God's presence in the days ahead. They are also the questions we will begin to answer throughout this book.

General Plans

While I was in Luxembourg, I also visited the area given by that nation to America to bury its dead from World War II. The memorial site dedicated to those who gave their lives was simultaneously sobering, inspirational and revelatory. Yet for me, one thing stood out.

On this site was the grave of General George S. Patton, one of the greatest leaders among the Allied forces of World War Two. "Old Blood and Guts," as he was nicknamed, was renowned for being harsh in both language and action. He was certainly not the most popular commander among his troops, who under his leadership were forced to adhere to a strict grooming code. And yet these soldiers ultimately respected the hard, humorless general and preferred serving under someone who they believed gave them a better chance of returning home.

As I knelt at Patton's grave, the Lord began revealing to me the connection between such renowned past commanders and our future season of war. He gave me a glimpse of what it would take to win the spiritual war in days ahead, of the types of warriors, the types of leaders and the strategic assignments necessary to defeat the enemies of the future.

We are in a different time than Patton's. We are a different generation. War has changed and the way we battle is completely different. Yet what still remains the same is the importance of strategy. Patton did not enter into any encounter without having a carefully formed plan of attack. In the same manner, we cannot expect to be victorious warriors in the spirit realm—no matter how skilled we are—without first knowing God's plans. The heavenly battlegrounds are no place for lone rangers.

I wrote this book to offer what I believe is the Lord's strategy for facing the unfolding war ahead. We, as God's children, are the deciding factor in this war, and we must understand the times. Second Timothy 2:3-4 says, "You therefore must endure hardship as a good soldier of Jesus Christ. No one engaged in warfare entangles himself with the affairs of this life, that he may please him who enlisted him as a soldier." In the midst of constantly changing times, God can train you for the war ahead.

Whose Side Are You On?

Ask any soldier what matters most when you're on the battlefield and you'll likely get a twofold answer. First, it's crucial to know whose side you are on. Who enlisted you? Who trained you for war? Whose tactics do you adhere to, and whose commands will you follow to death?

As Christians, we are warriors who have been called and enlisted by the Holy God of this universe. We are warriors of the cross. In the heat of battle, we must remind ourselves of these truths about the God who enlisted us: He is the God above all gods. His Son has paid the price for our ultimate victory. Satan's headship has already been broken by the power of the cross. Jesus has already conquered death, hell and the grave. We need not fear death but only resist its sting. The Spirit of God still reigns supreme in the earth to comfort us in the midst of distressing times. He is the only restraining force of evil and is there to give us strategies to overcome every ploy the enemy has set against our lives. The earth belongs to God, and He has a plan linked with the fullness of time. We, His children, might get knocked down, but we will never get knocked out. He is love, and perfect love in us will cast out all fear of the future.

With everything going on in the earth, we must never forget that He is God. We know that He is always in command. Yet if that's the case, why is there so much confusion around us? Why are nations forever in conflict and people groups warring against each other? Why does lawlessness continue to escalate throughout the world? If He is God and has already won the victory, what exactly is our role in the midst of the warfare we encounter on a daily basis?

The truth is, we are fully engaged in a covenant conflict, which means that we are warring to see the blessings of a holy, supreme God spread throughout the earthly realm. Psalm 24:1 declares that the "earth is the LORD's, and the fullness thereof" (*KJV*). God has a plan of fullness for the earth. His desire is for wholeness. Yet the war between God and evil is unfolding, which will determine how His fullness will be manifested in the earth in our generations and those to come.

Know Your Enemy

It's crucial to know whose side you're on when engaged in a battle. But there's another element to warfare that's just as important: Who are you fighting against? Paul answers this question in Ephesians 6:12: "For we do not wrestle against flesh and blood, but against principalities, against powers, against the rulers of the darkness of this age, against spiritual hosts of wickedness in the heavenly places." Our war is and will continue to be with:

1. *Satan* (see Gen. 3:15; 2 Cor. 2:11; Jas. 4:7; 1 Pet. 5:8; 1 John 3:8; Rev. 12:17)
2. *Flesh* (see John 8:44; Rom. 7:23; 1 Cor. 9:25-27; 2 Cor. 12:7; Gal. 5:17; 1 Pet. 2:11)
3. *Those who delight in evil* (see Pss. 38:19; 56:2; 59:3)
4. *The world* (see John 16:33; 1 John 5:4-5)
5. *Death* (see 1 Cor. 15:26; Heb. 2:14-15)

We already know that the headship of Satan has been broken forever. He was defeated the moment Christ rose from the dead and conquered death. Ultimately, we are fighting a war in which we are destined for victory. Why bother, you ask? Because we must contend with the worldly powers, principalities and dominions that continue to withhold the manifest blessings of this age. Satan may be defeated, but he is certainly not going down without a fight. As Christ's representatives on this earth, it is our calling to see His victory through. And that means war!

If we win the war in this generation, the generation that follows will experience blessings. The enemy still believes he has a right to shut the portals of heaven so that we, as God's children, will be confined to a decaying earth realm where death attempts to cast a shadow. Not so! God has made all wisdom available for His children. We can access that wisdom today. We can ascend into heavenly places and gain what is necessary to release in the earth. As blood-bought, redeemed children of a Holy God, we can wield the sword of the Spirit in the earth and declare, "On earth as it is in heaven!" Though the enemy has attempted to prevent God's blessings from manifesting in the earth, we can prepare a way for those blessings to be revealed.

This is a crucial time for believers. We have the opportunity to be as "wise as serpents" (Matt. 10:16) by being like the sons of Issachar. These were men from the renowned tribe in Israel who served as counselors to King David. Scripture records that they were a group "who had understanding of the times" (1 Chron. 12:32).

In the same way, we must discern the times, taking full advantage of the otherworldly wisdom God offers us. When we do, we will be prepared for the unfolding wars of our time.

Entering Into a Season of War

As evidenced by the title, this book is all about discerning the times and, more important, understanding God's unfolding plan for the coming days. We will spend several chapters delving into the details of what I believe is divine, decisive revelation for believers. But for now, it is important that we look to the near past and recognize the greatest emerging force in the end times: the antichrist system.

In October 2000, I prophesied throughout the nation that we were embarking on a season of spiritual warfare like never before. I added that a physical war was imminent and would occur by September 2001. When I communicated this, I met some resistance because it was difficult for people to understand the relationship between spiritual war and physical war.

Many times, what goes on in a spiritual war manifests naturally. Later on, we will discuss this Revelation 12 principle more in-depth. For now, understand that when the Body of Christ at large engages in spiritual warfare, it affects every aspect of natural society: religion, politics (legal and military), economics and education. Therefore, God raises up *worshiping intercessors* in each one of these arenas of power. I believe society is shifting because more people are now interceding. God is raising up an army of intercessors who will contend in the heavenly realm—but many more must be enlisted.

I went on to share that we had entered into a seven-year war season. At the end of that period, we would be prepared to enter all the conflicts ahead with a mind for victory. This is a season in which the Lord is toughening us up. Sometimes we do not understand that the tough circumstances we are in are simply the training tools of God. These circumstances produce a reality of His presence in our lives. They increase spiritual strength within us as we fight against the destructive plans of the enemy to weaken us

in the midst of our trials. Testing produces a testimony, and a testimony overcomes (see Rev. 12:11). During trying circumstances,
God longs for us to draw strength from His greatness. He wants to
be our shield of defense now and forevermore.

Isaiah 41:10 in the *Amplified Bible* says, "Fear not [there is nothing to fear], for I am with you; do not look around you in terror
and be dismayed, for I am your God. I will strengthen and harden
you to difficulties, yes, I will help you; yes, I will hold you up and
retain you with My [victorious] right hand of rightness and justice." Indeed, what have we to fear when it is God who commis-
sions us to fight?

Direct Attack

When I prophesied in 2000 about the coming war season, I knew
that physical attacks were ahead. I shared publicly that I felt the
first attack would be in New York because of its large Jewish population. (At that time, more Jews lived in New York City than in
Israel. Since then, Israel now has more Jewish inhabitants than any
other place in the world.)

The attack in New York City was a physical manifestation of
the new season we entered into. A new type of war had begun, using
everyday tools as weapons. Some would even be willing to lay down
their lives for what they believed. The war of faith had begun!

As three commercial airplanes with suicide pilots approached
the World Trade Center and the Pentagon (with a fourth diverted
plane landing in a Pennsylvania field), the world as we knew it
changed. The resulting crashes and disintegration of the two tow-
ers and the loss of approximately 3,000 lives propelled the United
States—and the rest of the world—into an unprecedented season
of conflict that has escalated over the past seven years.

Exposing the Antichrist System

We all know now that the attacks of 9/11 did not just happen
overnight. Documentaries, commission reports and various other
research prove that the events of that tragic day were long in the
works. Yet what most of these fail to consider is the spiritual force

that has been operating behind the scenes for generations. The antichrist system, while present on this earth for hundreds of years, is now establishing itself through distinct leaders, nations, economic giants and other influences.

I wrote extensively about the antichrist system in *The Future War of the Church*, and I highly recommend it for digging deeper into understanding this end-times opposition. For now, I'll summarize some of the main points for the sake of covering new material in this chapter.

When we speak of the antichrist system, I am not referring to the person of the Antichrist. Instead, the antichrist system is the demonic-based structure that holds as its main mission the destruction of the Body of Christ. Whether or not those involved in this system are aware, it is established to directly attack the Church and prevent Her from advancing the kingdom of God. (For more insight, read 1 John and 2 John.) A couple of clear modern-day examples of the antichrist system are Nazism and Communism, which have seen their rise and fall, yet still linger in our world.

The antichrist system can currently be defined by five distinct operations, each of which has been used to create a lack of blessing within the Church's domain. As I stated in *The Future War of the Church*, "Satan knows full well that the blessings of God cannot rest on a region that is controlled by any of these. The Church, therefore, is going to have to develop a strategy to gain victory over these things in the days ahead if we are to make progress in winning the war for souls."[2] These five elements are:

1. *Anti-Semitism*. As Gentiles, we have been grafted through Christ into the holy lineage of God's covenant nation, Israel. The antichrist system attempts to create a division—a baseless hatred—between the Jewish people and all others who would otherwise stand beside them. Israel is not only God's chosen people, but she also forever stands as a prophetic picture of the Body of Christ. Is it any wonder, then, that Satan abhors this race and has tried to destroy them throughout history? They are,

after all, a reminder of his imminent defeat! At the core of the antichrist spirit is a spirit of anti-Semitism.

2. *Abuse of the prophetic gift.* Just as the Lord has been restoring the prophetic gift to His people in recent years, Satan has raised up a counterfeit to confuse, alienate and destroy. In every region of the world, people turn to "prophetic" voices for guidance. The sad truth is that false prophets now control entire people groups and regions that once adhered to God's voice. The antichrist spirit controlling these prophets is responsible for leading people further from the truth of the gospel. But God has a remnant of prophetic people who need to rise up against the voice of the antichrist and proclaim the truth.

3. *Oppression of women.* We cannot fulfill the Great Commission without men *and* women working side by side. As prophetess Cindy Jacobs writes, "Satan cannot afford to have Eden restored and man and woman standing together as they did in the Garden. This would bring order to the home and order to the Church."[3] As such, the enemy's tactic to keep the Church from winning the war is to cause division between genders. While we argue over what titles women can and cannot have in ministry, the antichrist spirit renders the Body ineffective for complete victory.

4. *Ethnic domination.* Wherever one ethnic group is being dominated by another, the antichrist spirit is in operation. Yet wherever racial reconciliation is occurring, there God is at work. Through His kindness, we are lead to repentance (see Rom. 2:4), even for the sins of generations long past. And repentance, which stokes the fires of revival, creates a spirit in direct opposition to that of oppression and domination, which are energized by an antichrist system.

5. *Sexual perversion.* Point to any society throughout history that has allowed sexual immorality to run ram-
   pant and you will find the antichrist system at work.
   The enemy's desire is to lead people into willful rebellion, wickedness and corruption—all characteristics
   of perversion. As perversion becomes the standard in
   American society, we must understand this is not a
   private issue; this is a demonic structure established
   to invade every facet of our culture while preventing
   God's will from being done.[4]

A War for Every Generation

We witnessed the fruits of the antichrist system on 9/11 and have
continued to see it at work since. This is the primary cause behind
the escalation of wars both physical and spiritual. The truth is, there
has been war in every generation. Some have lived through two
World Wars. They know the pain and glory of victory. Others have
lived through conflicts such as Korea and Vietnam. They know the
pain and power of defeat.

We now have a generation that has known the war of the
desert. In 1991, the Gulf War became a reality and a tyrant was
exposed. My children were small then, and I still remember them
crying as we watched the Baghdad bombings on television. "Iraq"
has since become a household word. Operation Freedom has now
raged on for several years. The tyrant has been removed, but the
conflict still rages. In fact, it is a rare day that some portion of the
Middle East isn't the top story in the news.

We are at a unique stage in our world's history. At this time,
everyone in America has experienced and been part of some conflict that falls under the definition of war. If you are reading this
book and live in another nation, you likely have a similar war-
influenced history. Remember, war is in our bloodline.

However, I am still not sure that the Body of Christ understands
the real war around us. After a couple of decades spent awakening
from our slumber, we now have an awareness of the need for

spiritual warfare. Yet tragically, we often are clueless when it comes to *who* or *what* we are fighting.

Because you are reading this book, it's safe to say you are not clueless as to the enemy of our times. Most likely you have done your part in contending against the powers of our age for years, and your desire in reading this book is to increase your understanding. If that is the case, I honor you as an astute warrior. Yet every warrior, no matter how skilled or knowledgeable, knows his or her limitations. We cannot fight this battle—and win—without the entire Body of Christ alongside us. For that reason, it is crucial that we *all* understand the real war that we are fighting.

Life Matters

Despite what the media and culture say, the ultimate war of our times is not about oil, land or nuclear power. It is not about terrorism and homeland security. The real war of our time concerns one thing: *life*.

God places each of us in a specific time and space where we are meant to experience life to its fullest. Acts 17:24-27 puts it this way:

> God, who made the world and everything in it, since He is Lord of heaven and earth, does not dwell in temples made with hands. Nor is He worshiped with men's hands, as though He needed anything, since He gives to all life, breath, and all things. And He has made from one blood every nation of men to dwell on all the face of the earth, and has determined their preappointed times and the boundaries of their dwellings, so that they should seek the Lord, in the hope that they might grope for Him and find Him, though He is not far from each one of us.

In this age we must fight to keep those God-appointed times and boundaries. Each day we live is a life-or-death matter. I know that sounds dramatic, but it is true. Every day we fight against the forces that seek to steal pieces of our existence bit by bit. Some days the battle seems minor; on others we war for our very next breath. Our culture would have us believe that life can be compartmentalized and ordered—some areas are worth dying for, while others can fall by the wayside if they do not meet our moral criteria of importance. This is why people can fight for environmentalism, stem cell research or human rights yet turn around and justify abortion. We value life—at least when it is convenient for us.

But life involves the whole person. Life is not just our physical surroundings or our emotional well-being; it is a spiritual matter as well, for every human being. Natural life has a beginning, but it really has no end. By that I mean that our Maker has established us as eternal beings. Yes, our natural bodies will pass away with the withering of the trees. But our spiritual beings will remain.

There are three aspects to our spiritual beings. The first and most important is endless *communion* with the God who created us and gave us His Son to redeem us from our self-imposed prison. "He who has the Son has life; he who does not have the Son of God does not have life" (1 John 5:12). Through Jesus we can enter boldly into God's dwelling place. We have direct access to His throne room. There is often, however, a war to get into this place, which we will discuss later.

The second dynamic of our spiritual being is our *testimony*. How we overcome our tests in life produces a testimony that has impact not only in the natural realm, but even more so in the spiritual. As we rely on the mind of Christ rather than on our own understanding, we can testify to His truth. As we find strength in Him rather than our own abilities or fortitude, we bear witness to His power. Abundant life involves discovering the infinite attributes of God and aligning with them through our testimony. And each time we speak out our testimony, we overcome the enemy and seal our abundant life (see Rev. 12:11).

Intuition is the third facet of our spiritual existence. We are shaped in the spiritual realm according to how we perceive or discern good and evil. When we intuitively display the mind of God, we walk in victory. As our intuition alerts us to the schemes of Satan before they come to pass, we have the opportunity to thwart the enemy and conquer territory both in the heavens and on Earth.

That is why there is such a war both over and around us. We are created to have endless union and fellowship with God. Satan wants to create eternal separation from God. Therefore, he wars daily to separate us from God and cause our communion with our Maker to cease.

Strategies for War

Not only is there a war over our very existence, but there is also a war over the manner of life we live. How we live in the place and time in which we have been established determines our manner of life. Satan wants to keep us in poverty and infirmity. He wants to relegate our spiritual existence to barren religion, and he wants to steal every ounce of joy and purpose we have in life. If it were up to him, we would never know abundance, health or freedom in worship.

But God! Our Maker has another plan for us, a destiny in Him. Jesus expresses this in John 10:10: "I have come that they may have life, and that they may have it more abundantly." Considering that we live in a time of war, is this abundance even possible? And if so, how?

Throughout the rest of this book, we will unfold what I believe is God's plan for believers to live abundantly in the midst of the storm. For now, allow me to offer three general strategies as our answer to these warring times:

1. Praise Your Way Through Every Obstacle

War is violent. The mere mention of the word invokes thoughts of artillery and bloodshed. By the same token, we are called by God to be violent in the spirit realm. Matthew 11:12 says, "And from the days of John the Baptist until now the kingdom of heaven suffers violence, and the violent take it by force." So how are we to be violent in the spirit?

Praise. Merely declaring the name of God causes a violent reaction from the enemy. When we praise, we yield a mighty weapon in the heavenlies. We are living in violent times, so praise violently! Worshiping warriors will overcome mountainous obstacles during these times simply by pressing into the high places that the enemy has erected. Abortion, pornography, human slave trafficking, divorce—these are the demonic establishments brought down in part by the double-edged sword of praise (see Ps. 149:6).

The *NIV* translation of Jesus' words in Matthew reads, "The kingdom of heaven has been forcefully advancing, and forceful men lay hold of it." The *American Dictionary of the English Language* describes "violence" as a "vehement, forcible, or destructive action, often involving infringement, outrage, or assault."[5] We are to be violent with our praise, assaulting and destroying the works of the enemy in the process. Talk about warfare!

There is more to the revelation of violent praise, though. "Praise" comes from a Latin word meaning "value" or "price." To give praise to God is to proclaim His merit or worth in every situation. You can shout "Glory!" You can release blessing! Your heart can express thanksgiving! By the Jewish calendar, 5765 is the year of *Samehk Hei*, which embodies the expression of "hallelujah" or "praise the Lord." In other words, this is the year we must bring praise and the acknowledgement of God into every circumstance of our lives. If we do this, God will enthrone Himself in the midst of our circumstances, and He will take on any strategy the enemy uses to bind, block and captivate us.

Praise can be given through many means, as long as it is a natural heart expression and not an outward show (see Matt. 15:8). The most common in a modern-day church setting is through music, both instrumental and vocal (see Ps. 150:3-5). Paul specifically mentions singing psalms, hymns and spiritual songs in the corporate worship setting (see Col. 3:16). Yet worshiping warriors know there are many other everyday ways to declare the name of the Lord: offering sacrifices (see Lev. 7:13), physical movement (see 2 Sam. 6:14), silence and meditation (see Ps. 77:11-12), testimony (see Ps. 66:16), prayer (see Phil. 4:6) and living a holy life (see 1 Pet. 1:3-9). Praise also includes spontaneous outbursts of thanksgiving in response to a redemptive act of God (see Exod. 15; Judg. 5; 1 Sam. 2;

Luke 1:46-55,67-79). Each of these expressions of praise can become violent when you are determined to advance in God's kingdom plan.

One final note concerning praise: During this season of war, many of us have gone through various trials so that we could learn how to bring God's victorious sound from heaven into our atmospheres. How we establish this atmosphere of victory around us sets our course for the future. This is a season of victorious sound. Keep in mind, new songs and sounds will break old cycles and cause us to advance, enlarge and define our boundaries for days ahead.

2. Be Ye Not Passive

This goes hand in hand with violent praise. Too many Christians have resigned to living defeated lives because of their misunderstanding of what it means to love peace. They equate peacefulness with passivity and avoid stirring the waters at any cost. Jesus commanded us to turn the cheek, but He never once told us to be passive. Passivity and peacefulness are two different things. Passivity causes us to *pass up* the God-appointed opportunity to declare Him victorious over the enemy. Ultimately, it renders us ineffective to war against the enemies of God—which we are called to do!

The opposite of being passive is praising violently. And throughout Scripture we see examples of God's chosen people, the Israelites, spurning a passive response in favor of expressing violent praise. Moses and Miriam both sang and danced when they passed out of Egypt. (Miriam was 90 years old when she lead the congregation in dancing!) The Israelites expressed violent praise at Jericho, resulting in the demolition of an entire city. Gideon expressed violent praise over the Midianites. Paul and Silas expressed violent praise that broke them out of prison.

You have the opportunity to take the same actions—and yield the same bondage-breaking results! Don't worry about what to say, just let your heart respond to God. Psalm 81:10 says, "I am the LORD your God, who brought you out of the land of Egypt; open your mouth wide, and I will fill it." Not only will the chains break off and the captives be set free as you praise violently, you will also release the roar of the Lord that has been held captive in God's people.

Allow me to explain. God's sound permeates from heaven and orders much of what goes on in the earthly realm. When He is ready to bring restoration to Earth, He releases His sound. And Scripture repeatedly indicates that Judah, meaning "praise," goes first. Who leads this praise? No less than Christ, the Lion of Judah (see Rev. 5:5). The Lion of Judah roars! As ambassadors of Christ, that roar of God is within us.

Amos 3 tells us that when the roar of the Lord goes forth, a prophetic mantle falls. Joel 2:28 paints a picture of what this covering looks like: "Your sons and daughters shall prophesy, your old men shall dream dreams, your young men shall see visions." The Spirit of the Lord longs to be voiced through such a prophetic mantle. Let that begin with the roar of the Lord announcing both His arrival and His praise. As you shake off passivity and roar with a holy roar, allow the Lord to loose those things that lie deep within you. Let Him break hidden grief that has kept your joy capped. Open the gates for Him to release blessings from within.

3. Change the Atmosphere and Occupy the Land

Praise literally creates a different atmosphere around us because the Lord comes down and inhabits our worship (see Ps. 22:3). He, the God of the universe, dwells in the midst of our praising Him. It's not hard to imagine, then, why this changes our measure of faith and gives us strength to grab hold of the inheritance He has for us.

Did you know that you have a portion specifically allotted to you from God? The word "inheritance" means "my portion." We all have a portion. We have all been given a space, territory or arena in which we have been granted authority. How we steward that space is key to our success in the spirit realm. In fact, the climate of our domain reflects our relationship with the Lord. Therefore, our chief desire should be for the presence of the Holy God to occupy our inheritance.

In Deuteronomy 1:8 and 8:1, we read: "See, I have set the land before you; go in and possess the land which the LORD swore to your fathers—to Abraham, Isaac, and Jacob—to give to them and their descendants after them . . . Every commandment which I command you today you must be careful to observe, that you may live and multiply, and go in and possess the land of which the LORD swore to your fathers."

When we occupy something, we take possession of it or keep it in our possession. In Luke 21:19 we are called to possess our souls. In warring against the enemies of this age, we must learn how to occupy and possess. When we possess the portion that God has for each of us, we become whole, fulfilled and full of peace. This is what we are actually warring to accomplish! We must be a people who settle for nothing less than the abundance the Lord has for us.

Wage War on Both Fronts

We war as an army, as the people of God. Yet we also war as individual soldiers, commissioned by our heavenly Father to possess the land He has given each of us. In these crucial times, you will find it necessary to know how to wage war on *both* fronts. Let violent praise be a standard. Resist the enemy's plans to draw you into passivity. And learn how to enter into any situation and allow the high praises of God to change the atmosphere. He has a battle plan that will pave the way for you to possess your inheritance.

So take a deep breath, and let's enter into the unfolding war ahead. You are God's warrior for the future!

CHAPTER 2

The Mind War
Critical Times Require Critical Thinking

Every family has its "thing"—that pastime or event that draws its members together. I happen to have a house full of bowlers. Since they were young, I have taken each of my sons to the alley and encouraged them to bowl. We have countless stories of classic clashes on the lanes. It's always been a fun thing that we've done as a family.

But there's a problem. My sons have all excelled way beyond my ability. One of them is a pro bowler, and a couple of the others have won key bowling tournaments. I have been bowling for 40 years. But recently when comparing one son's 220 average with my 150 average, I had to ask, *What does he know that I don't?* Obviously what he is doing is working better than what I've done for four decades. Would I be willing to learn in a new way to transform my game? Better yet, am I too old to learn something new? Can the way I have thrown the ball for 40 years actually change?

These are simple questions, yet they are also profound when applied beyond bowling. For every process of moving into a new dimension, change is necessary. Mindsets have to be altered. Old patterns must make way for new ones. Ultimately, we need to think differently. In the last chapter, we identified the current season of war that the Body of Christ is in. As warriors called by God, we are to contend with the enemies of our time that seek to thwart any advancement of the kingdom of God. As we unfold God's battle plan for these days, we can apply divine strategy to enforce the victory.

With every strategy comes tactics. And in this chapter, we will cover one of the primary tactics that must be applied by any believer who desires to move into greater victory: critical thinking.

Time to Think

If I ever hope to become a bowler on a par with my sons, I will have to change my approach to the game. Sure, I can tweak my techniques, alter my form a bit and see immediate results. But if I truly want to enter their league, I'll need an overhaul on how I see the game. My outlook has been great for 40 years, yet to get even better like my sons, I must adopt a new perspective. The same is true for our approach to the war ahead of us as believers. The war is unfolding, but are we expanding the way we think? Contrary to popular belief, you *can* teach an old dog new tricks. (I'm living proof of this!)

Recently the Lord visited me while I was in my office preparing to speak at our church's Feast of the Tabernacles celebration. *"In these critical times, you must think critically,"* He said. The statement left a profound mark on me. I knew a few things about the process of critical thinking, but the Lord intended to take me to new depths.

Through the years, I have learned that if you want to teach children to think critically, you do not give them the answers; rather, you give them the questions. When the Lord visited me in my office that day, it was as if I were downloading a file full of questions. They came quickly and in abundance. I wrote as quickly as He impressed them upon me. However, I did not give an answer to any of His questions. I just received them.

As I communed with Him, He showed me that there was an answer for each question, but in order to get the answers, I had to think the way that *He* thought about the questions. If I trusted my own knowledge, I would miss the mark. But if I had *His* thoughts, I would be in harmony with Him and my spirit would bear witness to His Spirit of life.

Getting Critical

In the last chapter we revealed that the emerging war is not about earthly things such as oil or weapons, but about life. We are fighting both for our existence and for abundant life. It is a critical time, one in which we find the enemy advancing on every facet of culture. Yet we should keep in mind that God has a completely different perspective. The Author of all time places each generation in specific periods to bring about His will on the earth. In doing so, He looks for those who will intercede or stand in the gap and mediate between man, the demonic world and Himself. This is our time to do just that. Can we be counted on?

When we are in the "right" time at the "right" place, God extends our horizon line so that we can see into our future. And, thankfully, even when we miss the mark, the Bible says we can "redeem the time" (Eph. 5:16). It is apparent that time is important to God, yet He places a great responsibility on our interpretation of time. Our ability to read the times can be the difference between meeting and missing a divine appointment. It also can be the deciding factor in whether we seize the moment to gain victory in a conflict we are facing.

When we face a critical time—such as now—we must closely examine every situation before proceeding with action. We must think differently. Ultimately, we must be *critical*, which is defined as having "careful and exact evaluation and judgment."[1] Colonel Stephen J. Gerras, PhD, the Director of Leadership and Command Instruction at the US Army War College, has written a paper concerning critical thinking for strategic leaders. He opens the paper with a statement that is necessary for the Body of Christ to grasp on a deeper level during this season of war: "Technological advances alone do not constitute change. The most dramatic advances in military operations over history have been borne of ideas—ideas about war fighting, organization and doctrine. The Army's most critical asset will not be technology. It will be critical thinking."[2]

What Gerras wants the reader to understand is that this season of war is not the same as what we faced during the Cold War, or even Operation Desert Storm for that matter. It is a different time that requires different thinking. When *The Future War of the Church* was released before the tragedy of 9/11, it jarred the Church to alter its thinking about the war ahead. After 9/11, the book was easier to understand because the time had changed. The conflict that once was imminent had become a reality. Concepts that I wrote about in those pages had transitioned from future to present.

Gerras's words obviously apply to soldiers. Those who are fighting in this season, particularly in the Middle East, need to be thoroughly conscientious and painstakingly careful, using all available resources to think through and accomplish the task at hand. But his words go beyond the military. I believe the Body of Christ must also evaluate every resource available to us and think in a different way. This is a time for leadership to adopt critical thinking methods into their leadership strategies. In fact, we all must grasp the power of expanding our brains through critical thinking.

Brain Power

In a special feature in *Discover Magazine*, writer Kathleen McAuliffe makes this fascinating observation:

> At just a puny three pounds, the adult brain encodes our knowledge and skills, joys and regrets, plans for the future . . . even our sense of self. But this is not the same brain with which we first glimpsed the world. The mental landscape of an infant differs strikingly from that of a teenager or an adult. New discoveries shed light on the exotic world of the newborn, explaining why teens are so impulsive, revealing the rewiring that continues well into adulthood and the new neutrons that keep popping up even into our 70s.[3]

Our brain is constantly updating itself. We would be wise to follow its lead and adapt a more flexible and analytical mindset to interpret the times. Allow me for just a moment to expand on this idea. It is important for us to understand the physiological aspect of critical thinking because our brain obviously plays a crucial role in discerning the times. Yet there is more than just processing new information involved here.

American biochemist Albert von Szent-Gyorgyi once said, "Whatever a man does, he must first do in his mind." This isn't just an eloquent quote. Science proves that the simplest movement in a person's body requires an explosion of activity in the brain. Neurons pass electrical messages down our spinal cord and feed information to our nervous system. This information, in turn, triggers muscle cells to contract and create an action.

Victoria Schlesinger, another contributor to *Discover Magazine*, writes:

> The brain consumes 20 percent of the body's oxygen, without which nothing is possible—not even a breath, let alone a movement. With each inhalation, the lungs pull oxygen into the bloodstream and the heart speeds it toward the brain, particularly to areas of activity when they need extra oxygen. Blood rushes to the cerebellum, for example, when a person prepares to swing a baseball bat, a motion that requires muscle and joint coordination. Transported through a fine net of capillaries, oxygen molecules pass from the blood into the sterile gray matter, reaching the neurons with the help of tiny attending glial cells, which outnumber the neurons ten to one. . . . Like a baton in a relay race, the instructions to move must be handed from neuron to neuron. Spidery tentacles called dendrites . . . extend from each neuron body and function like conductive computer cables.[4]

Wow! This is how complex we are. The way we think is directly connected to the way we act. Our body responds to our thoughts. Stated another way, our actions reflect our thinking. Doesn't this inspire you to become passionate in Christ so that your actions reflect your thinking about Him and His love for you? It is an awesome concept.

It is because of this thinking-into-action reality that the enemy tries to develop strongholds within our thinking process to block us from acting like Christ (we will explore this concept later in the chapter). And that's exactly why it is essential for us to develop critical thinking, to discern who or what is attempting to influence our thoughts—and therefore our actions.

Profile of a Thinker

So what exactly is critical thinking? What does it mean to be a critical thinker? A critical thinker processes information through a system of filters. As believers, our primary filter should always be the Holy Spirit, who testifies to and perfectly aligns with the written Word of God. Other filters include our own experiences, feelings, memories, intuition and insights gathered from the past. Thinking critically involves keeping both an open mind to new revelation and adhering to the established safeguards of the mind that have been constructed throughout our years of living. It is, as Colonel Gerras says, a "purposeful, reflective and careful evaluation of information as a way to improve one's judgment."[5] Richard Paul and Linda Elder, who are authors and internationally renowned experts in the field of critical thinking, offer a comprehensive description of a critical thinker:

> A well-cultivated critical thinker raises vital questions and problems, gathers and assesses relevant information, and can effectively interpret it; comes to well-reasoned conclusions and solutions, testing them against relevant criteria and standards; thinks open-mindedly within alternative systems of thought, recognizing and assessing as need be, their assumptions, implications and practical consequences; and communicates effectively with others in figuring out solutions to complex problems.[6]

The people of God must become critical thinkers of this high caliber to succeed in the days ahead. We must be able to hear the Lord as He asks us vital questions that will change the way we think. It is through critical thinking that the Lord will download key strategies to His people. Therefore, the Body of Christ must have the ability to evaluate the relevant data coming from God as He speaks to us from the Word, from revelation and from events in the earth. We must spend time reaching godly reasoned conclusions about these days and then taking the appropriate actions. The Church must have excellent judgment in this hour. The children of Issachar understood the times and knew what Israel was to do (see 1 Chron. 12:32). So must God's people today.

The Questions of the Day

Most people might assume that critical thinking is all about arriving at the right answers. We have an image of what critical thinkers look like: masterminds sitting around a table, brewing over the piles of data strewn everywhere, when—*voila!*—a "critical thought" arrives in the form of an answer to all the world's problems.

Not so. The heart of critical thinking is not in the conclusions but in the process of asking questions. One way in which the Lord causes us to think differently is by asking questions. Consider the many places in Scripture where God asked His servants a question:

- God to Adam
    —"Where are you?" (Gen. 3:9)
    —"Who told you that you were naked?" (Gen. 3:11)
    —"Have you eaten from the tree of which I commanded you that you should not eat?" (Gen. 3:11)

- God to Eve
    —"What is this you have done?" (Gen. 3:13)

- God to Cain
    —"Why are you angry? And why has your countenance fallen?" (Gen. 4:6)

- The Angel of the Lord to Hagar
    —"Where have you come from, and where are you going?" (Gen. 16:8)

- God to Abraham
    —"Where is Sarah your wife?" (Gen. 18:9)

—"Why did Sarah laugh, saying, 'Shall I surely bear a child, since I am old?' Is anything too hard for the Lord?" (Gen. 18:13)

• God to Moses
  —"How long will these people reject Me? And how long will they not believe Me, with all the signs which I have performed among them?" (Num. 14:11)

• God to Joshua after the defeat at Ai
  —"Why do you lie thus on your face?" (Josh. 7:10)

• God to Israel just before Joshua's death
  —"But you have not obeyed My voice. Why have you done this?" (Judg. 2:2)

• God to Gideon
  —"Have I not sent you?" (Judg. 6:14)

• God to Eli
  —"Why do you kick at My sacrifice and My offering which I have commanded in My dwelling place, and honor your sons more than Me, to make yourselves fat with the best of all the offerings of Israel My people?" (1 Sam. 2:29)

• God (through the prophet Samuel) to Saul when he made a sacrifice unlawfully
  —"What have you done? (1 Sam. 13:11)
  —"Has the LORD as great delight in burnt offerings and sacrifices, as in obeying the voice of the LORD?" (1 Sam. 15:22)

• God (through the prophet Nathan) to David
  —"Would you build a house for Me to dwell in?" (2 Sam. 7:5)

  —"Why have you despised the commandment of
  the Lord, to do evil in His sight?" (2 Sam. 12:9)

• God (through Gad) to David after numbering the people
  —"Shall seven years of famine come to you in your
  land? Or shall you flee three months before your
  enemies, while they pursue you? Or shall there be
  three days' plague in your land?" (2 Sam. 24:13)

• God to Solomon in a dream at Gibeon
  —"Ask! What shall I give you?" (1 Kings 3:5)

• God to Elijah in a cave (twice)
  —"What are you doing here, Elijah?" (1 Kings
  19:9,13)

• God to Job (a sample of many questions He asked)
  —"Would you indeed annul My judgment? Would
  you condemn Me that you may be justified?
  Have you an arm like God? Or can you thunder
  with a voice like His?" (Job 40:7-9)
  —"Who has preceded Me, that I should pay him?"
  (Job 41:11)

• God in heaven, heard by Isaiah
  —"Whom shall I send, and who will go for Us?"
  (Isa. 6:8)

• God to the priests
  —"If then I am the Father, where is My honor? If I
  am a Master, where is My reverence?" (Mal. 1:6)
  —"Will a man rob God?" (Mal. 3:8)

• Jesus to the multitudes
  —"You are the salt of the earth; but if the salt loses
  its flavor, how shall it be seasoned?" (Matt. 5:13)

—"Is not life more than food and the body more
than clothing?" (Matt. 6:25)

—"Are you not of more value than [the birds]?
Which of you by worrying can add one cubit to
his statute?" (Matt. 6:26-27)

—"And why do you look at the speck in your brother's eye, but do not consider the plank in your
own eye?" (Matt. 7:3)

—"Or what man is there among you who, if his son
asks for bread, will he give him a stone? Or if he asks
for a fish, will he give him a serpent?" (Matt. 7:9)

- Jesus to His disciples
  —"Why are you fearful, O you of little faith?"
  (Matt. 8:26)

- Jesus to the scribes
  —"Why do you think evil in your hearts?" (Matt. 9:4)

- Jesus to the two blind men
  —"Do you believe that I am able to do this?" (Matt.
  9:28)

- Jesus to Peter
  —"Are you also still without understanding?"
  (Matt. 15:16)
  —"Who do you say that I am?" (Matt. 16:15)
  —"Do you love Me?" (John 21:15-17)

- Jesus to Saul/Paul
  —"Why are you persecuting Me?" (Acts 9:4)

When we examine the teachings and ministry of Jesus, isn't it
interesting that He, having all knowledge as the Son of God, chose
to ask questions rather than just supply all the answers? The Lord
asks us questions to cause us to think differently and critically.

He stirs our minds and prompts us so that we will seek His way.

I believe the Body of Christ is currently being prompted. Our hearts and minds are being stirred to ask a question that echoes through both Haggai 1 and Matthew 16: *What time is it?* Do we truly understand the season of war we are in? And just as important, what should we be doing in response?

Every Question Demands a Response

When we look at all of the questions above—which are only a portion of what is found in the Bible—we can surmise that each one demanded a response. God is still demanding a response today. This is what makes God so real. The Lord has never ceased interacting with His people, and He desires a people willing to gather *His* thoughts, assess *His* ways—and then align with *His* strategies.

That is the essence of critical thinking for the astute believer: aligning with God's thoughts. I believe there are steps each of us can take to get to that point. Following are a few keys to sharpen your mind and develop critical thinking skills:

1. Define your problem and clarify your real concern.
2. Evaluate all the information you have and then pinpoint the missing pieces so that you can develop a complete thought process.
3. Define your traps and biases.
4. Clarify your position and authority.
5. Identify the root causes of the problem you are addressing.
6. Determine what point of view you are using in your analysis.
7. Be willing to shift your perspective at any time.
8. Ask yourself, *Am I limiting my thought processes to only what I know?* Limited thought processes are synonymous with self-righteousness.
9. Identify anything that you are taking for granted in your analysis. Do not allow your assumptions to cause you to be foolish.

10. Check to make sure that you are not making intellectual judgments based on partial truths.
11. Ask yourself, *Have I simplified things to the point that I'm missing out on the major component here?*
12. Avoid being biased or prejudiced in the way you receive, perceive and release information.

I have chosen the Bible as the absolute authority that shapes my entire belief system. Many people adhere to principles in the Bible, but the Bible is far more than principles—it is the Word of life! The Bible is a living Book that helps us understand the existence of God. Not only can we get to *know* God through the Word, we can *hear* Him. His Holy Spirit speaks to us directly through His living, active words. This is our foundation for critical thinking.

With such a foundation, we are able to base every answer to every question we're ever asked on this living Book. Even the ultimate question about why we exist can be answered: for a relationship to a loving God in pursuit of us, who is displayed throughout Scripture. We can approach problems based on how we see God approaching problems in Scripture. In fact, it is by basing our beliefs on the Word that we can agree with Hebrews 11:3: "By faith we understand that the worlds [during the successive ages] were framed (fashioned, put in order, and equipped for their intended purpose) by the word of God, so that what we see was not made out of things which are visible" (*AMP*). No matter how critical things become, we can be a people who think the way God thinks and see our way into victory.

The War Over Your Mind

If we hope to move forward in complete victory, we must transform our minds to think the way God thinks. We must adopt His thoughts for today rather than our own. I am convinced that one of the greatest coming wars will take place on the battlefield of the mind. We must declare His reign on the earth through our personal renewal, starting with our minds.

As you might expect, this renewal always meets opposition. Satan would like nothing more than to keep you in old thought patterns, stale mindsets and worn-out mentalities. In his book *Authority in Prayer: Praying with Power and Purpose*, Dutch Sheets shares the nature of this confrontation:

> Our war is *not* physical. Though Satan uses people to advance his causes, the New Testament makes clear that we are not warring against flesh and blood. Unbelievers, atheists and those who disagree theologically are not our enemies. They are all loved by God, and He wants each of them to be saved. Our real enemies are the powers of darkness waging war against God's kingdom, trying to hinder His purposes on the earth. Make no mistake: Our war with these forces is a war for the soul of a nation and the destinies of millions of people.[7]

The real war is over the transformation of our thought processes. If you are reading this book, your desire is probably to have the mind of God. You want to see His kingdom reign throughout the earth, which means you want to see it in your life and thought processes. And yet we are all on the battlefield each day when it comes to winning the war over our minds. How exactly, then, does the enemy continue to influence us? What are his tactics?

His most powerful means of influence and attack are through strongholds. In Paul's second letter to the Corinthians, the apostle reveals this potent device of Satan, while also mapping out the spiritual warfare that is just as relevant today as it was during his time:

> For though we walk in the flesh, we do not war according to the flesh. For the weapons of our warfare are not carnal but mighty in God for pulling down strongholds, casting down arguments and every high thing that exalts itself against the knowledge of God, bringing every thought into captivity to the obedience of Christ, and being ready to punish all disobedience when your obedience is fulfilled (2 Cor. 10:3-6).

I suggest that you study all of 2 Corinthians 10. Paul's instructions to the Corinthians are the key to victory in our own battles of the mind. When we capture a thought and make it obedient to Christ, we are simply transforming that thought into the way Christ would think. Paul goes on to tell the Corinthians that if they do not bring their thoughts into captivity, their minds will be affected by wrong philosophies and a stronghold will be developed. Simply stated, a stronghold is a thought process that has been constructed and allowed to take up residence. Strongholds can be either good or bad—David often referred to the Lord as his "stronghold." However, when we allow Satan to establish a stronghold in our minds, we protect his way of operation in our lives.

This is not a book about strongholds. Suffice it to say they are one of Satan's most powerful means to render both individuals and entire parts of the Body of Christ ineffective for war. So how do we prevent them and avoid being another soldier taken out of the fight? Paul lets us know in Romans 12:1-2:

> I appeal to you therefore, brethren, and beg of you in view of [all] the mercies of God, to make a decisive dedication of your bodies [presenting all your members and faculties] as a living sacrifice, holy (devoted, consecrated) and well pleasing to God, which is your reasonable (rational, intelligent) service and spiritual worship. Do not be conformed to this world (this age), [fashioned after and adapted to its external, superficial customs], but be transformed (changed) by the [entire] renewal of your mind [by its new ideals and its new attitude], so that you may prove [for yourselves] what is the good and acceptable and perfect will of God, even the thing which is good and acceptable and perfect [in His sight for you] (*AMP*).

Paul's statement to the church in Rome is just as valid today as it was nearly 2,000 years ago. We can become conformed to the world in a heartbeat. In our sinful nature, we are instinctively wired to take on the blueprint of the world's plans, methods and philosophies. Romans 8:6-7 says, "To be carnally minded is death, but to be spiritually minded is life and peace. Because the carnal mind is enmity against God." Our mind inherently wars against the knowledge and thinking processes of God. The sad truth is that we are more likely to come into agreement with anti-God thoughts and antichrist systems than we are to choose God's way.

However, the Lord offers a solution via Paul's words to the Romans. We are called to be transformed. The word "transformation" essentially means to break out of that confined plan and blueprint and enter into a metamorphosis of thinking the same way God thinks. How do we transform? We become more like Him, thinking *His* thoughts and following *His* strategies, by the "renewing of your mind" (Rom. 12:2).

Be forewarned: Just as violent praise evokes imminent conflict (as we discussed in the previous chapter), so too does this spiritual renewal of the mind stir up warfare. Our mind resists receiving new revelation. Many people avoid prophetic revelation entirely. This typically comes through religious spirits convincing us that we don't need to know anything new or that we have already experienced what God has for us. Yet without prophetic revelation we actually go backward. Again, this is probably the most difficult battle we face on an individual level. Will we receive new thoughts that reflect God's way of thinking in this age, or will we settle for our own knowledge and adhere to the world's mindsets?

The encouraging truth is this: If you make it past this war, you can walk in victory in every war ahead.

God Can Change Your Mind!

At this critical juncture in history, the Church is in transition. We must evaluate the present "appointed time" and act appropriately. To do that, I believe God is causing our minds to shift in a new way. It reminds me of what God did to Jeremiah. In chapter 25 of the book of Jeremiah, we find Jeremiah prophesying 70 years of desolation for the Israelites because they would not listen, heed the word of God and change. He didn't bother to temper his words as he foretold Jerusalem's complete destruction. The result? Jeremiah was thrown in prison.

In the next verse (don't you love those gaps of time in Scripture?), we read that the Lord told the prophet to go and buy a piece of land at Anathoth, the very place over which he had prophesied destruction. Because God instructed Jeremiah to do this, the prophet had to think in a new way: "Ah, Lord GOD! Behold, You have made the heavens and the earth by Your great power and outstretched arm. There is nothing too hard for You" (Jer. 32:17). Obeying a command that was so contrary to Jeremiah's own thought process called for some violent praise!

Fast forward a few verses in this same chapter and we find God turning the tables on Jeremiah: "Behold, I am the LORD, the God of all flesh. Is there anything too hard for Me?" (v. 27). It's one thing for you to tell God that there is nothing too hard for Him—it's another thing for God to ask if you *really* believe it! Our thought processes can deceive us, but they cannot escape the reality of God. This is how critical thinking works: It causes us to become responsive to a purpose or goal. If we align our thoughts with God's thoughts, we are assured success in the future.

It's Time to Align!

That leads us to the obvious question: Just how do we align our thoughts with God's? We have already discussed the tactic of renewing our minds, which sets us up for a showdown against our natural, worldly mindset. There are plenty of opponents who would rather not see us walking in union with God's thoughts and plans—Satan and his earthly accomplices, for starters. Yet there is another force at work against us, one that comes from within each of us: our own emotions.

To think differently we must realign our desires and allow the Holy Spirit to rule our emotions. A *desire* is a function of our emotions. In other words, our desires are birthed out of our emotions. Remember that desire, fueled by emotion, is what caused Eve to stray from the mind of God. Satan convinced her that God was holding out on her by not offering her the fruit of every tree in the garden. She was not content with having access to 99.9 percent of the trees in Eden—she wanted them all. This shifted her desire from God to something that God had forbidden.

Desire causes you to seek what is most precious to you, often without regard to the cost. This can be both good and bad. All prayer and communion is a result of desire. Desire is linked with passion—we all burn to embrace something. Desire is also linked with praise and delight. When you feel spiritually dry and are unable to praise, most likely your emotions have been blocked in some way and your desire function is not in operation. If we don't allow the Holy Spirit to overtake our desires, our minds will not function right.

On the negative side, unrestrained desire leads to covetousness, presumption, dwindling vision and overall decay. When desire is not functioning healthily, we enter into hope deferred. And as Proverbs 13:12 says, "Hope deferred will make the heart sick." When the heart is sick, the mind becomes infected. And if we lose our expectation for God to move in our lives, which is a function of desire, we begin to think with a mindset contrary to the way God thinks.

Pictures of Alignment

In critical, stressful times, our emotions can often become bruised and our desires tainted, causing us to lose the strength necessary to resist the enemy's plan. However, God is always in the process of restoring and strengthening. When we rely on His strength and not our own—on *His* thoughts and strategies, not ours—then we can persevere. One of my favorite passages that exemplify this is Genesis 14, which tells the story of Abraham and his nephew, Lot. Lot found himself in a state of crisis: He was captured by five kings. Even though Lot and Abraham had gone their separate ways, Abraham went to war to get Lot back in place and repositioned. Abraham defeated the five kings, rescued Lot and collected the spoils from battle. He then met Melchizedek, the king of Salem and a high priest, who blessed him: "Blessed be Abram of God Most High, possessor of heaven and earth; and blessed be God Most High, who has delivered your enemies into your hand" (vv. 19-20). In reply, Abraham gave him a tithe of all of the spoils of war.

One of the ways to align with God's thoughts is through giving. Notice that immediately after Abraham gave, God called

Himself Abraham's "exceedingly great reward" (Gen. 15:1) and then made a covenant with Abraham that set the course for the future of all nations. God did not take lightly Abraham's giving to Melchizedek (a symbolic precursor to Jesus), nor does He take lightly our giving today. When we align ourselves with God's strategies to go to war and regain what we have lost, and when our response to victory is to give back to the Lord, we begin to see our future ordered.

Another great example of critical thinking in alignment with the Lord's thoughts comes from the life of David. The prophet Samuel anointed David as king over all Israel, yet it was years before the young warrior ascended the throne. In fact, from that point forward, David had to hide from Saul in the wilderness and seemed to face more conflict than anything else. Yet after remaining faithful and in step with God's destiny for him, David was made king 12 years later. His first reign was over two tribes; seven years later, he was made king of all the tribes of Israel.

You might think that after all David had been through, his first assignment might be to get a robe and a throne and rest for a couple of years. But because he was a critical thinker, David was more interested in the Lord's plans than he was in resting on his laurels. And the Lord had bigger plans. David's first move as king was to overthrow the Jebusites, a people who had never been overthrown before. They had established a stronghold in Jerusalem that had never been dealt with from the time God established covenant boundaries with Abraham.

David inquired of the Lord—a characteristic of critical thinking that he displayed throughout his life—and realized that Zion was to finally be the Lord's once more. This was no small feat. Generations before, Joshua and the people of Israel had been commanded by God to annihilate all those who were in their way as they took possession of their promised inheritance. But Joshua 15:63 points out that "as for the Jebusites, the inhabitants of Jerusalem, the children of Judah could not drive them out." This iniquitous people had kept their stronghold for eight generations. And in David's (and God's) eyes, that was eight generations too many.

The Bible condenses the reclaiming of this long-standing stronghold into one brief sentence: "Nevertheless David took the stronghold of Zion" (2 Sam. 5:7).

Keys to Winning the War of the Mind

Without receiving both instruction and strategy from the Lord, David likely would not have had success against the Jebusites. At least four previous generations had tried and met failure. Yet because David sought the Lord's mindset, knowing that victory lies in *His* plans, the Bible barely even describes it as a battle.

If we hope to follow David's example and win the wars of our time—no matter how fortified or long-standing they are—we would be wise to keep in mind the following elements:

1. We must capture our thoughts and think the way God thinks.
2. We must not allow strongholds or thought processes contrary to God's kingdom plans to develop within us.
3. We must be willing to address issues that have never been addressed and overcome.
4. We must have creative leadership methods so that we can enter into areas that have never been penetrated.
5. We must understand our boundaries and exercise our authority within those boundaries.
6. We must know where and with whom we are building.
7. We must be aligned properly. Our functional authority is enhanced when we join with someone who has more authority than we do in the operation of our gift. This is foundational to the transformation in our territory (see Eph. 4).
8. We must review how we are to build for the future. What revelation got us started? What emotions have hindered us? Is anything too hard for the Lord?
9. We must consider who is giving us counsel and who we are giving counsel to.

Wars are not just won with weapons. Any soldier who point-lessly barrels his way through the battlefield with guns blazing will likely find himself another number on the casualty list. Strategy is essential. On the other side of the coin, however, the greatest mas-terminds behind every war can accomplish nothing without those who wield the weapons of war.

As Christians, we have both weapons and strategy—and both are found in the Lord. In this critical time, one of the greatest weapons He has given His Body is critical thinking. We can do more than just react to every situation from an emotional level; we can assess and process using critical thinking. Yet on our own, this amounts to nothing in our fight against the powers of dark-ness. We must find the Lord's strategy by aligning our minds with His. Only then can we face—with assured victory—the wars ahead.

The Blood Wa.
Empowered in Soul and Spirit

Have you ever heard someone say, "That person just has bad blood"? It's as if we explain away someone's misfortunes, poor choices, addictions, sins or overall weaknesses by chalking it up to genetics. "His father was an alcoholic, so what else would you expect from him?" "Her mother divorced when she was young—I give their marriage a couple of years at the most." "Oh, she's always worrying, just like her grandma." Whether intentional or not, we speak of "bad blood" as a curse.

I remember when we adopted our first child, Daniel. He was meant for us. Just as Psalm 68:6 says, "God sets the solitary in families," Daniel was ordained by God to come into our family. Maybe that's why it hit me so hard when my aunt asked me, "Why are you adopting? You have no idea what bad blood and problems you are going to get by adopting this child."

Immediately I felt the Lord lead me to respond to her by saying, "Auntie, his blood can't be any worse than ours. And he sure can't have any more problems than our family has had. The Lord can change him just like He's changed me."

Divine Intervention

I am one of those who come from "bad blood." Our home life was filled with one traumatic event after another, resulting in death and destruction. We were a family that had great potential. My father acquired land from his family, and the future looked bright—but Dad was ensnared by the enemy and lost his life prematurely at age 39. Consequently, the land and three generations' worth of blessings were lost. This left great wounds in both my soul and spirit. And yet as I told my aunt, the Lord performed a miracle in my life.

When I was 18, God sovereignly visited me. I was in a hospital bed on oxygen, having been diagnosed with double pneumonia and an enlarged heart. By God's masterful design, He placed me in a room with a Pentecostal pastor who introduced me to a Person I did not know: the Holy Spirit. I had accepted Christ years before, and yet through this pastor, the Person of Christ suddenly became alive to me. Not only did the Lord seem so real and near to me, but so did His Word. I began to devour Scripture like never before. I remember two passages in particular that spoke to me during those two weeks in the hospital. The first was Proverbs 3:5-10:

> Lean on, trust in, and be confident in the Lord with all your heart and mind and do not rely on your own insight or understanding. In all your ways know, recognize, and acknowledge Him, and He will direct and make straight and plain your paths. Be not wise in your own eyes; reverently fear and worship the Lord and turn [entirely] away from evil. It shall be health to your nerves and sinews, and marrow and moistening to your bones. Honor the Lord with your capital and sufficiency [from righteous labors] and with the firstfruits of all your income. So shall your storage places be filled with plenty, and your vats shall be overflowing with new wine (*AMP*).

I chose to believe what the Bible said: If I would not trust in my own mind, thoughts and wisdom, then my nerves could be healed and my bones and marrow could be filled with life. (I also saw the connection this verse makes between health and giving.)

The next verse God spoke to me was Proverbs 18:14, which says, "The strong spirit of a man sustains him in bodily pain or trouble, but a weak and broken spirit who can raise up or bear?" (*AMP*). Wow! My eyes suddenly opened to a new understanding. With a fresh revelation of how my mind, spirit, health and healing were all connected, I saw that it was possible to withstand the sickness I was facing. If I allowed God to heal me from the inside, I could overcome sicknesses in my body.

In that meeting at the hospital, the Lord showed me the war that was going on inside of me. There was a war with my evil nature. There was a war with sin domination. There was a war concerning my family and all its downfalls and failings. There was a war with my inheritance. There was even a war with my faith—did I really believe the Word of God?

In that divine time I heard the voice of God. As if reverberating through a mountainous cavern, His words rang inside me: *"I can restore what you have lost."* They echoed throughout my entire being, becoming my lifeline. His words even began a process in my re-creation. Almost instantly I could sense a breaking of the power of loss that was being held within my genetic structure. This was the very power creating infirmity and disease within my body.

Exposing a Curse

I never turned back from following the Lord after He met me so powerfully. And yet there was another incident several years later that brought me understanding regarding what we will discuss in this chapter.

Pam and I had been married for five years. I was teaching a Bible study at my place of employment. In the Bible study were five sisters in the Lord who worked for me. One of the women pulled me aside and said there was an individual who she noticed was drawn to me, and that I needed to be careful with my relationship with her. I wasn't aware of anything that was going on, but when I shared this with Pam after getting home from work, she informed me that during our five years of marriage she had noticed I had a stronghold in this area. I was not sure at that time what she meant by stronghold, but I listened to what she was saying.

Pam explained that if I fell to any temptation such as what I described to her that she would take care of me herself. Actually, her exact words were "I will just kill you."

Thinking she was joking, I laughed it off and replied, "Sure, and how will you reconcile that before the Lord?"

With a dead-serious tone, she said, "That's not the best way, so I suggest you get before the Lord and ask Him to remove anything in your life that Satan could get a toehold in."

Now *that* spoke to me. I went and got before the Lord in the bathroom.

One of the things I have always done is read the Bible out loud to the Lord. There in the bathroom I began reading Romans 6 and got to verse 14: "For sin shall not have dominion over you . . ." I stopped abruptly and asked the Lord a question: "Lord, is this a true statement?"

I heard a voice so loudly that I thought there was a person standing in the room with me. *"Yes,"* the voice said.

Seizing the opportunity, I asked another question: "Lord, is this Book completely true?"

His reply was simply, "Yes, obey My Word."

At that moment I knew I did not have to submit to sin anymore. It did not have to be my master. Even though I had never been taught this before in any of the church services I had attended, it resonated within me as truth. And at that moment, a power that had held control over my family was broken. I knew that I never had to do what my dad had done. I knew that I didn't have to fall to the same strategies Satan had used to entice my grandfather away from God's best. I knew that I could walk faithfully before the Lord and remain in faithful covenant with my wife. What had been in my bloodline for generations had now been detected, addressed and broken. My life took a drastic turn from that moment.

The War of the Word

Following that encounter with the Spirit of God, my daily Bible readings and time of prayer took on new meaning. I continued to read the Word just as I had always done since I was 18, covering three to four chapters a day. Yet when I began to read the next morning, the Holy Spirit spoke to me: *"Don't go to the next verse until you believe the one you just read."* God was going to make me a man of faith just like those I read about in Hebrews 11. He was going to make sure His Word penetrated deep into me and brought all my thought processes into alignment with His.

Hebrews 4:12 says:

> For the Word that God speaks is alive and full of power [making it active, operative, energizing, and effective]; it is sharper than any two-edged sword, penetrating to the dividing line of the breath of life (soul) and [the immortal] spirit, and of joints and marrow [of the deepest parts of our nature], exposing and sifting and analyzing and judging the very thoughts and purposes of the heart (*AMP*).

This is one of the most incredible truths I have ever encountered. The Word of God is alive. It is full of power and, like a sword, can divide a person's soul from his or her eternal part, the spirit. As a result of this incredible power, the Word causes our hearts to change. I believe this change is both spiritual and physical. Romans 10:17 says, "So then faith comes by hearing, and hearing by the word of God." Satan's greatest strategy is to stop you from hearing what God has to say to you. He knows that when the voice of God penetrates you, it goes deep into your bone marrow and rearranges the cell structures within your body. He knows it has a powerful effect on the blood flow within your body. When the Word of God successfully penetrates us, when we allow it to be stored in our hearts and develop the way we think, our blood system begins to be purified. The Spirit of God literally begins to invade blood structures.

We will discuss why this is so important in just a bit; for now, it is key to recognize that there is a war going on over command of our bloodline. The forces of darkness are constantly working to prevent spiritual life from entering into our physical being. I believe the enemy's greatest strategy is to separate us from the Word and the love of God. If he can separate us from the Word of God, we lose the power of life working through our life-giving blood system.

What is so important about our blood? And what does it have to do with the Holy Spirit's work in our life?

Allow me to take a moment to explain some things that will be foundational for the rest of this chapter. We know that God is spirit, and yet He is also the designer of every element within our physical world. Therefore, it is safe to say His works traverse every realm of life—physical, spiritual, mental, emotional, and so on. When considering the physical and spiritual elements of blood, the same is true. I apologize in advance if some of this brings back memories of suffering through biology class. But trust me, you will soon see how valuable that information is in relation to the wars—physical and spiritual—that we face today.

Understanding the Blood

Life is in blood. It circulates through the body, supplying life-giving nutrients to each part. Through the circulatory or cardio-vascular system, blood is provided to the organs of the body from cell to cell. The heart, lungs and blood vessels, which include arteries, veins and capillaries, all work together with about five liters of blood (in the average adult body) to create this circle of life flow.

What is important for us to note is that this blood does more than supply physical life. Leviticus 17:11 says, "For the life of the flesh is in the blood . . . the blood makes atonement for the soul." We can already see that blood takes on a spiritual significance for our very soul. But there is still more. Proverbs 23:7 says, "For as he thinks in his heart, so is he." Without taking this verse out of context, we can see that the heart is at least associated with—if not the controller of—our thought processes. Obviously, the brain is where our knowledge is stored, yet this verse indicates that it is not the brain that thinks, but the heart!

I suggest that if the heart thinks, it involves both our developed belief systems and the information accumulated and categorized in our brains. And if that is the case, then our cardiovascular system—which cycles blood to and from the heart—is responsible for the transportation of our thoughts. When the heart pumps blood, it carries a thought system throughout the entire body. In essence, all of our organs are responding to the way our heart thinks.

Let's take this a bit further. As we know, blood can be broken down to a more microscopic level—within each drop of blood are millions of cells, which are the basic building blocks of life. On the outside of each cell is what's called a cell membrane. This is a barrier or boundary that ensures that the information within that cell is contained properly. Think of the cell membrane as a gatekeeper that allows helpful substances to pass inside, while rejecting harmful substances that should not enter the gates of our development.

In the nucleus of each cell are chromosomes, the rod-like structures that contain the main vehicles of genetics—genes. Where these genes originated is a major factor in what kind of cell is produced. For instance, a gene can be *dominant*, meaning that it will always appear in the next generation, even if only one copy of that gene is passed on. On the other hand, a *recessive* gene will only appear in the next generation if both reproducing cells share that same recessive gene.

If I have already lost those of you who skipped out on biology class, let's simplify things using the excellent analogy of authors Linda Tagliaferro and Mark V. Bloom: "If a cell is like the world, then a chromosome is like a country, a section of a chromosome is like a state, a gene is like a small town, and base pairs (As, Cs, Ts and Gs) are like people and houses."[1] These "base pairs" are in fact the cornerstone of every cell's life because when bound together, they make up the most valuable information carried in every cell: DNA. Simply put, DNA (deoxyribonucleic acid) is the code of life. It is the molecular "stuff" that holds hereditary information passed from one generation to another. It is what causes us to look like our family members and links us into the mysteries of heredity.

When cells reproduce, the most crucial thing they pass along is DNA. A single cell becomes two new cells, yet those two new cells carry bits and pieces of the original cell's DNA. This replication process is continually occurring and is essential to the well-being of our entire body. Everything in a good cell must be replicated into a new cell for larger structures or organs to continue in health.

Battles for Blood

For those of you who use the elements of biology on a daily basis, my simplistic explanation of cell life may have been offensive. Trust me, however—it has a point. It is crucial for us to understand the intricate connections that exist within each drop of blood because we must not forget that every connection factors into the war over our blood.

What war? And *why* is there a war over our blood? We have already established that blood contains life. As it stems from the heart, the blood holds the key to our thought processes. Now consider the concept of war: one people group desiring to impress its life force onto another; one nation desiring to be the "dominant" gene to pass on its "information." If we can see this in the natural realm on a grand scale, then why would it not be so on the microcosmic scale?

Our blood shapes the way our minds think. If the mind is not pure, we cannot perceive the will of God and we fall into lust, pride and other elements of sin. Obviously, this is exactly what the enemy wants, which is why he wages war in the first place. When pride enters our bloodstream and we exalt our thoughts above God's, we find ourselves on the side of the enemy rather than on our Maker's side.

Keep in mind that the war is within the blood, but it often proceeds out of our mouths. The war in our hearts will release words that will always create strife in the earth realm. James 4:1-5 says:

> Where do wars and fights come from among you? Do they not come from your desires for pleasure that war in your members? You lust and do not have. You murder and covet and cannot obtain. You fight and war. Yet you do not have because you do not ask. You ask and do not receive, because you ask amiss, that you may spend it on your pleasures. Adulterers and adulteresses! Do you not know that friendship with the world is enmity with God? Whoever therefore wants to be a friend of the world makes himself an enemy of God. Or do you think that the

Scripture says in vain, "The Spirit who dwells in us yearns jealously"?

The war that is within us will manifest outside of us. It can cause families to enter into conflict that spans generations. It can lead entire nations to war, resulting in blood spilled across the earth. Therefore, the whole earth is crying out for God to redeem it.

When Cain and Abel brought their sacrifices before God in Genesis 4, blood was the primary issue. Abel brought a sacrifice of blood, while Cain brought a sacrifice of the land. The latter's was unacceptable. Only through a sacrifice of blood can we please God (thus, the fulfillment of Jesus). God reasoned with Cain over the offering of the fruit of the ground. However, Cain continued to allow his emotions to rule him. His anger and jealousy caused him to open a door of iniquity, which began to rule his future. Anger and jealousy led to murder, and Abel became Cain's sacrifice. Abel's blood then began to cry from the ground.

A Clean Window for Your Conscience

Throughout history, we see blood always connected with war—and for good reason. All fragmentation in your soul comes from the war that has entered into your DNA. Satan "speaks from his own resources" (John 8:44). If he knows that there is something in you that has not come into alignment with God's way of thinking, he will attempt to take that resource back under his domination. His ultimate goal is to vex your spirit so that God's anointing cannot be released through you to change the world around you. For this reason, you must guard against a negative perspective that is the result of a "hardened" (2 Cor. 3:14), "blinded" (2 Cor. 4:4), "corrupt" (2 Tim. 3:8) or "debased" (Rom. 1:28) heart or mind.

Think about perpetually negative people. They see everything from a pessimistic standpoint. Essentially, that means there is something in their blood that has never been energized by God's perspective. Fortunately, Scripture proves that the heart or mind can be renewed (see Rom. 12:2), made pure (see 2 Pet. 3:1), filled with the love of God (see Matt. 22:37; Mark 12:30; Luke 10:27), and implanted with His law, which creates boundaries for our lives (see Heb. 8:10). However, this requires the Holy Spirit's acting upon our minds, which means that we must allow Him to conquer within our very blood stream.

We must rely moment by moment on the Holy Spirit to clear the path for us and redeem our hearts and minds. The diagram below shows how God's Spirit, flowing through our spirits, invades our blood systems to create a clear conscience within us. Perhaps this will give you a picture of how, as Jesus said in Matthew 5:8, the pure in heart can see God.

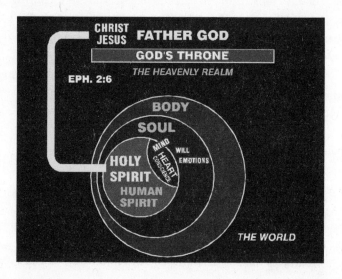

I believe the Lord gave me this diagram to show how the Spirit of God gives us revelation from heaven and connects through the spirit into our own blood system. Matthew 6:22-23 says, "The lamp of the body is the eye. If therefore your eye is good, your whole body will be full of light. But if your eye is bad, your whole body will be full of darkness. If therefore the light that is in you is darkness, how great is that darkness!" When you look at this diagram, you can see that God has developed an "eye" within us.

When the Holy Spirit flows through our blood system, He begins to cleanse our conscience. The conscience is like a window between our soul and spirit. If this window gets dirty, our heart does not perceive the will of God correctly. In the same way, if our conscience is not clear, our spirit does not operate properly.

When we do not allow the Holy Spirit to engage in the war over our flow of blood, our spirit lacks the truth in our very DNA and we will remain in a darkened state. Essentially, we will limit ourselves to the knowledge that we perceive naturally. Yet if our conscience is pure and vibrant before God, we will be able to see God all around us in operation.

We must understand that there is a great war over our conscience. The enemy would love to hold your conscience captive. If he can stop your conscience (or "eye") from seeing God, he can vex your spirit and allow darkness to work within your soul. Instead of you being a light to the world, the world will conform you to its pattern of operation.

The Blood: A Covenant War

If you are still wondering why I am putting such heavy emphasis on blood, look no farther than the Word of God. There we find this mysterious life-giving liquid being the centerpiece of countless passages of Scripture, partially because it played such a major role in the Jewish culture. Blood is the joining element between God and humanity. Hebrews 13:20 says, "Now may the God of peace who brought up our Lord Jesus from the dead, that great Shepherd of the sheep, *through the blood of the everlasting covenant*, make you complete in every good work to do His will" (emphasis added).

Throughout Scripture, blood is closely connected with the concept of the covenant. A covenant wasn't just a haphazard promise. In the Jewish culture, this was a binding contract that established a lifelong bond of fellowship. In the Early Church, the blood covenant connected you to someone who was not related to you by birth. Your possessions became their possessions (see Acts 4). You committed your all to them, even vowing to die for them if necessary.

In the same way that covenants were made between people, they could also be established between individuals and God.

In both cases, the covenant was sealed by the cutting of a sacrificial animal into two parts, as exemplified through God's covenant with Abraham in Genesis 15. In many cases, both parties would walk between the split carcasses, signifying the new blood union between the two. In the Abrahamic covenant, God Himself passed through (see v. 17)—a symbolic precursor of the ultimate fulfillment of this promise through Jesus Christ. Years later, Jeremiah prophesied about the new covenant (see Jer. 31) and spoke of a spiritual cutting that would occur in our hearts, which would allow the Spirit of God to enter our bloodstream, renew our spirit and give us a new spirit. Once again, God's Spirit would go before us and "seal the deal" by walking through the symbolically split pieces of flesh.

Perhaps the greatest—and certainly the most fascinating—thread among these and every covenant made between God and man is this: Jesus Christ was the ultimate fulfillment. Point to any major covenant—God and Noah, God and Abraham, God and Moses, God and David—and you will find Christ as the accomplishment of every promise. His blood triumphs over all.

And to think that blood now cleanses us from the inside out! In *The Power of the Blood*, H. A. Maxwell Whyte writes:

> Jesus was the only begotten of the Father (John 1:14) and His body was formed and fashioned wonderfully in the womb of Mary His mother; but the *life* that was in Jesus Christ came alone from the Father by the Holy Spirit. Therefore, this life which flowed in the veins of the Lord Jesus Christ came from God. No wonder He said "I am the *Life*." God imparted His own life into the bloodstream of Jesus. . . . If we can clearly understand the meaning of the word *atonement*, we have discovered tremendous truth. God has provided a substance by which we can cover things we no longer want; God guarantees not even to see our sins after we reckon by faith that the blood of Jesus has covered them. When God sees blood, He does not see sin.[2]

Christ's blood is our ultimate atonement. It is the surest sign of victory over every power of darkness. Is it any wonder, then, why Satan and his forces work so hard to war over our blood? He knows that with one drop of Jesus' cleansing blood, our very DNA will begin to declare His victory.

At times throughout history, the enemy has even warred over believers' celebration of that sacred blood at Passover. Constantine forbade this celebration, knowing that it was fine for Christians to have the "name" but not the empowerment of the blood of the One they worshiped. Why would such a celebration matter to the enemy? One reason is because he understands God's name as *Jehovah-Rophe*, the God Who Heals. During the Jewish exodus from Egypt, our heavenly Father said He would put none of the diseases from Egypt upon His people (see Deut. 7:15). When you look at this verse in context, you find that He was showing His people a vital truth: If they relied on the Passover lamb completely, disease would not be able to overtake them.

This is why it is important that we always celebrate the Passover lamb. Every time we remember how God brought His people out of Egypt and how Jesus redeemed us through His obedience and the shedding of His blood, I believe our cells cry out in celebration. Worshiping cells are important to our bodily health. When our cells celebrate, they mimic the celebrating nature of the overcoming blood of the Lord Jesus Christ.

Let us not forget, the war will always be over the blood of our Lord and how we worship Him. This threatens an enemy that will continue to gain power in the earth realm. The antichrist force is always against the blood of the Lord Jesus Christ. As the war escalates, we must discern this force and declare the victory of our Lord through His wondrous blood. As John said, "He must increase, but I must decrease" (John 3:30). His Spirit must increase in our blood!

The reason for such opposition against Christ's blood reigning in us is simple: It reminds Satan of his defeat at the cross, and it reminds him of his imminent defeat upon the Lord's return. We must never treat the phrase as cliché: *There is power in the blood!* As one Bible commentary says:

Jesus' blood was entirely "poured out" of His body by
the various ways in which it was shed—His bloody
sweat, the crown of thorns, the scourging, the nails, and
after death the spear, just as the blood was entirely
poured out and extravasated [forced] from the animal
sacrifices of the law. It was *incorruptible* (1 Pet. 1:18-19).
No Scripture states it was again put into the Lord's
body. . . . The blood itself, therefore, continues still in
heaven before God, the perpetual ransom price of "the
eternal covenant" (Heb. 13:20).[3]

Satan hates to be reminded of our blood covenant with God,
so as antichrist forces increase in the blood of humans, they will
attempt to war with anyone who is carrying the life force of Jesus
Christ within them. Make no mistake: We are about to see a major
shift in war. We are moving from an imperialistic warfare, in which
nations and leaders vie for control over land, to a blood warfare
that finds people groups and nations trying to control how each
other worships. This goes hand in hand with Revelation 12:10,
which says, "Then I heard a loud voice saying in heaven, 'Now salvation, and strength, and the kingdom of our God, and the power
of His Christ have come, for the accuser of our brethren, who
accused them before our God day and night, has been cast down.'"
The accuser of the brethren must work with humans, yet God
designed us for His redemptive plan. That means the only hope
the enemy has is to turn us against each other. When this happens and
people come into agreement with the accuser, he can attempt to overcome entire people groups, dominating all those who come under his
thought process.

The Healing War

Obviously, Satan detests the atoning quality of Jesus' blood.
Through it, we are forever redeemed and saved from his fatal sentence upon us. Yet there is another reason the blood will always
meet such opposition: It heals! Jesus said that Satan's desire is "to
steal, and to kill, and to destroy" (John 10:10), which is the opposite

of being whole. The enemy of our soul would like nothing better than to see us crippled with sickness.

Sadly, believers often seem to forget the revitalizing attribute of the blood and instead give into Satan's attacks. The Bible says that if we submit ourselves to God we can resist the devil and he will flee (see Jas. 4:7). Yet one of the biggest problems we have is learning to withstand weakness and infirmity in our lives, both of which can be tools of Satan. Even though Jesus took stripes for our infirmity, we're often caught wearing the prison garb of decaying health and sickness. We must remove the impurities in our lives so that we can walk in divine health. We must learn to break any cycle of infirmity that has developed in our bloodline.

In *God's Now Time*, Rebecca Wagner Sytsema and I wrote extensively about the cycles of infirmity, poverty and religion that Satan inflicts on God's people. A *cycle* is an interval during which a recurring sequence of events happens. A cycle can also be a periodically repeated sequence of events, something that happens over and over at a certain time. It can be linked with a specific time or event and orchestrated supernaturally so that a repeating wound or injustice occurs from generation to generation. Satan loves to keep us going around the same mountain or held in a cyclical pattern. But God has a remedy for iniquity! By embracing the blood and redemptive sacrifice of the Lord Jesus Christ, we can break out of any old patterns.

"Infirmity" is a term that encompasses more than just sickness and disease; it is also related to suffering and sorrow. Matthew 8:16-17 states that Jesus "cast out the spirits with a word, and healed all who were sick, that it might be fulfilled which was spoken by Isaiah the prophet, saying: 'He Himself took our infirmities and bore our sicknesses'" (see also Isa. 53:4). Infirmity can also refer to a disability of one kind or another. It can occur as a result of moral or spiritual defects that cause our will to stray from God, or from the influence of an evil spirit (see Luke 13:11).

Infirmity can also be linked to an overall weakness in our bodies or with anything that created the weakness, such as grief. Romans 15:1 states that those "who are strong ought to bear the weaknesses of those without strength" (*NASB*). This weakness is infirmity. Not only did Christ bear our weaknesses and infirmities, but we are also called to bear the weaknesses and infirmities of our brothers and sisters in the Lord. This is called intercession. Romans 8:26 says, "Likewise the Spirit also helpeth our infirmities: for we know not what we should pray for as we ought: but the Spirit itself maketh intercession for us with groanings which cannot be uttered" (*KJV*). We have been called to intercede for the sick, which allows us to bring someone weaker than ourselves before the Lord. Again, is it any wonder why Satan wars so violently against the blood?

Jesus' Redemptive Plan of Freedom

The Gospels are full of stories about Jesus healing sick people. He dealt with many organic causes of illness, along with those affected by madness, birth defects and infections. The blind, the deaf, the lame and others who suffered approached Him for help, and His response to them was nothing short of revolutionary. You see, in the Hebraic culture of the day, most people believed that illness was the direct consequence of sin (see John 9:1-3). However, Jesus shifted this concept by healing a blind man who had been sick since birth. When Jesus' disciples asked, "Who sinned, this man or his parents, that he was born blind?" Jesus answered that the sickness was not related to the man or his parents, "but that the works of God should be revealed in him" (John 9:3). What an answer! We know that many wrong choices produce consequences that affect our bodies, yet Jesus' reply reiterated His mission of mercy. In essence, He came to extend grace and bring us out from the bondage of sin's punishment and into healing and wholeness. He has the power both to forgive sin and to heal its repercussions (see Matt. 9:1-8; Mark 2:1-12; Luke 5:17-26).

Jesus healed those who suffered from mental illnesses and epilepsy—sicknesses usually associated with demonic powers (see Mark 9:18). The Lord addressed issues of fever and dysentery (see Matt. 8:14-15). Sterility and barrenness were also major issues in biblical times. On several occasions, Jesus used His own saliva as an ointment or anointing (see Mark 7:32-35; 8:22-25; John 9:6-7). I find this fascinating because one of the primary ways DNA is collected for testing is through saliva samples. Jesus took His own saliva, placed it on the eyes of the blind and watched their eyes become whole.

Regardless of the cause of their distress, people found that Jesus could truly help. And today He extends the same healing power through His healing blood, now found in the very DNA of every believer.

Draw a Bloodline

So far in this chapter we have explored my understanding of the war within our bloodstream. We have identified how the real war is over God's Spirit flowing through our blood, which then transforms our minds. If you will recall, we learned in the last chapter how crucial it is in these times to align our minds with Christ's. Taking both wars into consideration, it becomes clear that the enemy is engaged in a fierce battle over our minds, which are controlled by whose DNA is in us: Christ's or the world's. We take on the DNA of Christ by being transformed by the Spirit's blood flowing through us, by the Word of God changing our belief systems and by the Spirit of God bringing us into unity with the mind of Christ so that we can do the Father's will.

However, in this crucial blood war there is a tactical offensive position we can take. Just as troops must draw a line on the battlefield, we must learn to draw a bloodline so that the enemy cannot cross over and entice us to do his will (see 2 Tim. 2:26). Teacher and author Billye Brim explains what this bloodline is all about in her book *The Blood and the Glory*:

> The bloodline began in heaven. . . . [It] was consummated when the manifested Lamb poured out His life in His blood on Calvary's altar. The circle of the blood turned upward again on the third day. Our Lord Jesus Christ arose—triumphant over death, hell and the grave—and carried His own precious blood into the Heavenly Holy of

Holies where it was accepted for man. The resurrected
Lamb closed the circle giving glory to God the Father.
The powerful, redemptive blood is returned to its heavenly terminal. There before the throne of the Living God,
the blood ever speaks "mercy" for man (Heb. 12:24).[4]

Satan's goal is to break the circle or cycle of life that the Father
offers us from His throne. Jesus reconciled us back to the Father and
has given us access to go boldly into the throne room. Yet through
war, Satan tries to break that cycle of life that is offered to each
one of us. When he does that, he creates his own cycle by operating in infirmity, poverty and religion.

But as Christians, we have an all-powerful weapon. When we
use the name of Jesus and rely on the power of His blood, we draw
a bloodline that says to the enemy, "You have no right to cross!"
We must learn this type of warfare in days ahead. It will not only
protect our families and homes, but it will also shelter our bodies
from disease. Jesus drew a bloodline when He went to the cross
and poured out His blood. We must not forget that His same
power is active in us today (see Eph. 1–2).

Breakthroughs on the Horizon

The blood war that is now being waged is a timeless war. Since the
moment he was thrown from the splendors of heaven, Satan has
been trying to entice the blood of humans toward his darkness.
His efforts have only intensified since Christ's victory on the cross,
and today we find him determined to rule the earth.

For that reason, I feel it fitting that I write briefly about what
I believe the Lord has shown me concerning the blood war ahead.

1. *The war with cancer will shift.* The Lord will give His Body
   a new understanding of carcinogens, which are detri-
   mental to our health. We will better understand how to
   rely on Him to resist the aggression and destructive
   forces set against our blood systems. With war escalating

in the earth realm, people's adrenal glands will be overworked, and chronic anxiety could become an epidemic throughout the earth. Stress and anxiety create many cancerous invasions in our bodies, but we will see a drop in breast and prostate cancer because of a move of purity in the Body of Christ in days ahead. God's people will begin to recognize the stress of the world. We will develop a peace in the midst of the storm and rise above this stress.

2. *The fear of pandemic viruses and biological warfare will continue to increase in the world,* but God's people will have confidence that He can cleanse and filter our blood in new ways. I believe that God will have people who create filtering processes that can cleanse a person's blood in less than an hour. Things such as the SARS virus will not create fear worldwide. Not only will God create natural ways to cleanse blood, but He will supernaturally set a blood barrier for His people so that these viruses cannot enter them.

3. *An anointing for healing is going to enter the Body of Christ.* I was ministering in a service recently and it was as if I had X-ray vision. I saw where diseases were in the bodies of those who were sitting in the congregation. I wish that would happen every day! This kind of anointing will become more and more common among the people of God.

4. *The blood-brain barrier will shift in days ahead.* There will be a change in the way the brain operates. Not only will there be breakthroughs in the area of brain technology and progress in Alzheimer's research, but we will also have major breakthrough on how thoughts have been blocked by strongholds. The power of meditation will return to the Body of Christ. This will create a new move of success in the Church.

5. *There is going to be a return to the "natural."* There is already an incredible move in the area of homeopathic healing. As we have developed society, we have lost much understanding about the use of the elements of the land. The Lord will return us to natural ways of healing. Our bodies will respond better to things the Lord put here naturally than to the synthetic drug structure we have depended on.

6. *Because of increased technology in healing, we must be careful not to try to create a "perfect race."* The antichrist system operates out of a humanistic standpoint that seeks perfection in humanity. Many of the same techniques we will see emerge were used in World War Two. We must watch for similar patterns once again. God's people must come to a place where they trust Him—and only Him—to increase their strength and vitality.

7. *With war escalating, casualties will escalate.* Despite a greater number of deaths, I believe there will be great development in God's people coming into a revelation of His Body. The gift of healing will be released as the government of God and the Body of Christ matures into the wineskin for this generation. We must expect God to move through His people as He touches humanity and brings us into an awareness of His reality.

No matter what the future holds, we must always remember: Christ's blood overcomes!

CHAPTER 4

The Time War

Praying to Reorder Your Day

I travel constantly. Typically, I'm away from home about 200 days out of the year. While getting a firsthand look at what God is doing in this nation and around the globe has its obvious upsides, and while I relish my calling to minister to the nations, there is one attribute of my "job description" that I'm less than crazy about: jetlag. I have lost count of the number of times my body's clock has had to be set and reset. Most frequent flyers and hardcore business travelers find ways to adjust to the constant time changes and how that affects their biological clock. And to a degree, so have I—but there are times when my body is stuck in another time zone . . . one that's miles and miles away!

All of our bodies have a biological clock. Our entire physical being—our inner movements, the rise and fall of body temperature, blood pressure, hormones, our sleep and wake cycle—is connected to this biological clock. Because our cells keep time, our bodies operate in cycles and loops. For the most part, our fast-paced modern society tends to ignore these circadian rhythms in an effort to be "more productive." But thankfully, more people are now returning to the art of listening to the body's natural signals and seasons. In fact, the entire medical field of chronobiology, which treats patients according to their coordinating biological rhythms, is becoming more prevalent.

A recent article in *Science Daily* highlighted the discoveries being made in using circadian rhythms to further treatment of diseases: "For example, heart and asthma attacks are more likely to occur at certain times of the day. And certain medications have greater efficiency and lower toxicity depending on what hour they are given."[1] In previous chapters I have mentioned our need to become like the sons of Issachar today, paying attention to and understanding the times (see 1 Chron. 12:32). I believe God is raising up Issachar prophets now who will understand the importance of how God designed our bodies and set within us an internal clock. We must understand that the body's sense of time matters in every phase of life. Our bodies' clocks affect our physical reactions and mental ability. They determine the way we sleep and rise. When we do certain things at a particular time in the day affects our proficiency and productivity. Just as plants respond to day and night, our bodies take cues from the rotation of the planet as it shifts from night to day and one season to another.

As our Maker, God designed us intentionally with a body clock. He knows our most productive times. More important, He knows the best time for us to seek Him, and He knows how to get us in His perfect timing. But unfortunately, when humanity sinned in the Garden and brought the Fall, it affected more than just our spiritual alignment with the Father. Our bodies were thrown askew as well. Now we find a body that resists changes and an internal clock that struggles to control us.

We must be willing to allow God to order our time so that we can seek Him. Jesus displayed this principle when dealing with His disciples during a crucial time in His life. In Matthew 26:40-41, Jesus asked His disciples a question: "Then He came to the disciples and found them sleeping, and said to Peter, 'What! Could you not watch with Me one hour? Watch and pray, lest you enter into temptation. The spirit indeed is willing, but the flesh is weak.'" Indeed, our flesh is very weak. Once a cycle of time begins to control our body's clock, it is difficult to change. We are no different from the disciples.

The thing we must remember, however, is that Jesus faced the same human struggles, temptations, feelings and bodily desires we do. Given the context of His question, we see that He must have been past exhaustion. He was in travail over the redemption of all humanity to the point of sweating blood (see Luke 22:44). It was the middle of the night in the Garden of Gethsemane, and Christ was in the throngs of anguish over our condition and His need to go to the cross for us. Many of us would have prayed for a while and then joined the disciples for a snooze. Others would have slept through the whole night. After all, Jesus knew what was coming— if anyone had a right to catch up on some sleep before the horrible day that would follow, it was He.

Yet Christ ignored His body's clock. He set aside the desires of His own flesh to align with God's will. Jesus' question is just as valid today as it was for the disciples. In times of war and intensity, can your body's clock shift to operate on God's timetable? We are entering into intense times. It is essential to know how to respond to the Father when He calls us to prayer in days ahead. Jesus responded and wanted to know why His disciples could not respond the same way to watch with Him. That is the question I believe He is asking each one of us. We are all called to watch and pray. However, there is something inside us and in the atmosphere that stands against our joining Him for even that one hour He desires. Obviously, we should practice the presence of God all day long. But the real issue for each of us is this: "*Can you watch with Me one hour?*" I believe the Lord is calling us to reorder our day to do just this.

Reordering Our Day

As we order our prayers, the Lord will order our steps. As we spend time in the watch with Him (I'll explain this in a bit), He will begin to reorder the timeframe of our day. "Order" is a mathematical and military term. It is the opposite of confusion. *Order* . . .

- Means "to set in a straight row"
- Is a fixed or definite plan
- Is linked with the law of arrangement and the sequencing of events
- Is a state or condition in which everything is in its right place and functioning properly
- Is a command, direction or instruction
- Is a request or commission

All the functions of society are linked with order: architecture, finance, military, science, theology, grades of angels, ranks of clergy, politics, and the list goes on. Without order, these structural components of society would not work properly nor accomplish their purpose. We need order for every element of life. And as we stand watch as God has called us, He will reorder our day.

The Night Watches

Soldiers keep watch. Bodyguards, bouncers and security guards keep watch. Police officers, FBI agents and other government officials all keep watch. All of these examples involve a similar posture: When we keep watch, we are on high alert. We patrol, protect, keep post and stand guard. In essence, we stand our ground, remaining prepared for whatever comes our way. And if a command comes from higher authority, we are ready to move in an instant.

The same is true when the Lord asks us to keep watch with Him through the night hours. The very word "watch" has always had a military connotation. The Jews in biblical times, as well as the ancient Greeks and Romans, divided the night by military watches instead of hours. Each watch represented the period for which sentinels or pickets remained on duty. This was the "watch in the night" (Ps. 90:4). The Jewish timetable recognized only three watches: the first, or "beginning," watch (see Lam. 2:19), the middle watch (see Judg. 7:19), and the morning watch (see Exod. 14:24; 1 Sam. 11:11). (Note that the biblical day began at sunset [6 P.M.], which put even more importance on watching through the night.) When Rome established supremacy and began to influence the Early Church, the number of watches was increased to four, which were categorized as follows:

- Evening—6 P.M. to 9 P.M.
- Midnight—9 P.M. to 12 A.M.
- Breaking of day (cockcrowing)—12 A.M. to 3 A.M.
- Morning—3 A.M. to 6 A.M.

There is a twofold reason for God's establishment of the watch of the night. First, we must watch for the enemy's activity. Toward the end of this chapter, we will discuss the strategic ways we combat the spiritual forces of darkness while we are on watch. Second, we watch to set the standard for the coming day. As we learn to watch in the timeframes prescribed by the Lord, we will see our "light" part of the day reordered while we increase in efficiency. As we watch with the Lord, we will begin to see how to build for our future. Our alignments and assignments will become clear. We will begin to receive the right counsel we need for our future. Most important, we will develop His mind for increase and multiplication.

Mark 13:35 is explicit in explaining the reason behind our watch, as well as pointing out the various times of watch: "Watch ye therefore: for ye know not when the master of the house cometh, at evening, or at midnight, or at the cockcrowing, or in the morning" (*KJV*). *The Living Bible* puts it this way: "Keep a sharp lookout! For you do not know when I will come, at evening, at midnight, early dawn or late daybreak."

We must be a people who allow the burden of God to guide how we seek Him. Our times are in His hands. We must not be a people who simply seek God when it is convenient for us. A watchman has an assignment from God and a burden to seek His moment-by-moment command. He or she is called to observe how to secure God's purposes in the earth. We must be like the watchmen on the wall described in the Bible, watching for the enemy and announcing what we see.

Restoration of the Watch

Matthew 24:43 says, "But know this, if the goodman of the house had known in what watch the thief would come, he would have watched, and would not have suffered his house to be broken up" (*KJV*). I believe these words of Jesus are some of the most important for us to understand today. Let me paraphrase this Scripture: *If we watch, we will understand the time of visitation of the Lord. We will also recognize the thief when he comes. If we watch, we will not have to be scattered in all directions. We will remain whole.*

This verse has a dispensational connotation, but also a reality for today. Let's briefly examine the meanings behind each watch and how they apply to us now (we'll go into further detail later in the chapter).

The *first (evening) watch* is linked with the call of God on the life of Israel. This is synonymous with God's call on our own lives. If we will enter into the watch, then we will be alert for His time of visitation. Every nation has this open window of visitation from the Lord, just as there is a time of visitation for each one of us. The point is not to miss His calling, no matter what the hour or season.

The *second (midnight) watch* comes when we get scattered. In the verse above, we see that if we do not watch, then we get scattered. If you never develop a personal discipline of watching, then you will find your life being scattered instead of being ordered. The second watch also represents times of Israel's scattering.

The *third (cockcrowing) watch* is linked with the concept of Peter's denial. Instead of watching, Peter hid in fear. The Lord warned Peter that he would deny him three times before the cock crowed. There have been times Israel as a nation has denied the Messiah's coming, and yet the Lord desires that His people be restored to the truth. On a more personal level, if we will watch prior to the crowing of the cock, our faith will be made strong. This third watch represents the trial of our faith.

The *fourth (morning) watch* is the time the Lord reveals His glory. There is a breaking of a new day, an ultimate returning of God's glory to Israel. Even with all of Israel's problems throughout history, she has a wonderful future as a nation. She is God's chosen nation of example. One day all nations will face the decision whether or not to align with and reconcile their relationship with Israel—with eternal consequences. On an individual level, this watch also represents the power of resurrection as we watch with the Lord. If you will continue to watch with Him, then you will experience His glory. Your future will be established.

Reasons for Restoration

God is restoring the apostolic-prophetic alignment of spiritual gifts in the Body of Christ. In Ephesians 4:11-16 and 1 Corinthians 12:28-30, Paul lays out the facets of the Body and discusses how each part plays a unique role. In modern times, the Church has been strong in certain areas but extremely weak in others. Today God is restoring the essential elements of the apostolic and prophetic. In essence, the foundation of the Church is being realigned. Wealth that has been hidden is being uncovered so that the kingdom of God can advance. Instead of being cloistered away in a building, we are recognizing that His kingdom must invade all dimensions of society.

With great advancement of the Kingdom, however, comes great opposition. We must be on watch for our lives, our families, our cities and the nations of the earth. Without the watch, the antichrist system will have a field day during our time of harvest. This is one of the reasons why we must mature in the watch. We are not just watching on behalf of the Church; we are watching on behalf of a Kingdom in conflict, one that is advancing in the earth yet constantly meeting opposition.

On a corporate level, the watches are an integral part of seeing the Tabernacle of David restored in this generation. Just as the nation of Israel spent generations longing for David to restore the Temple during His reign, the Church has continued a similar cry for centuries. Obviously, our desire is now different because Jesus redefined for us what the Temple is. *We* are now the carriers of His presence, not the Ark of the Covenant or some extravagant house of worship. Yet there is still a cry from the Bride of Christ for the full restoration of God's glory. We want Him to inhabit the earth!

The watches also involve personal, daily, significant revelation for each one of us. The Lord promises to restore the years that the canker worm has eaten away (see Joel 2:25). If we will watch, we will see how the thief has entered in and eaten away our blessings. Once we understand what the thief has done, the Bible says that we can call back our losses at up to a sevenfold increase (see Exod. 22:1; Job 42:10; Prov. 6:31).[2]

Without keeping watch, we miss the significant seasons of the Lord in our lives. He visits, but we don't recognize Him. We get scattered and don't know why. We go through times of trial wherein the confession of our faith is crucial, yet we fail to pass the test, just as Peter did. The cock crows and we hide in shame. We are awakened during the night with God attempting to communicate His will for the new day, but in our tiredness we choose to sleep rather than seek.

Praise God for second, third and fourth chances! His grace continues to be extended for us to enter in to a new dimension of communion. That is how much He desires to stand with us during the watch.

Do We Really Understand the Days?

To fully understand the watch, we must come to grips with how much it redefines our concept of the day. For most of us, a normal day goes by with us getting up, rushing to work, dealing with all the cares of the world that come into our path and then coming home to fall exhaustedly and passively into a place of rest. But God has a different plan for our day. Actually, the day *begins* with the watch.

God ordered the day to begin at 6 P.M. with meditation (see Gen. 1; 24:63). He wants us to seek His will and be ready to advance at 6 A.M. into what He is breaking forth in our lives. In other words, from sunset to twilight we should be watching—which includes resting—so that we are ready to prosper throughout our time of light.

The first occurrence of the term "day" in Scripture is in the story of Creation. "Night" was then added to help distinguish the time of light from the time of dark. Yet notice in the following passages what the defining markers of each "day" are: "And God called the light Day, and the darkness He called Night. And the evening and the morning were the first day . . . And God called the firmament Heaven. And the evening and the morning were the second day . . . And the evening and the morning were the third day . . . And the evening and the morning were the fourth day . . . And the evening and the morning were the fifth day . . . And God saw every thing that He had made, and, behold, it was very good. And the evening and the morning were the sixth day" (Gen. 1:5,8,13,19,23,31).

In Western culture, we think the day begins when we get up and enter into the light. (For some of us, that's 6 A.M. For others, it's 10 A.M.!) Yet the biblical concept of the day was the 24-hour period from sunset to sunset. Psalm 104:23 says, "Man goes forth unto his work and to his labor until the evening." Evening is when the biblical day begins. That is a foreign concept for most of us, yet it is declared so by God's appointed time.

I believe in our culture we have viewed "night" differently from God's plan of evening till morning, and we have therefore missed reckoning the day and redeeming time so that we overcome evil and efficiently and effectively prosper. Psalm 90:4 says, "For a thousand years in Your sight are like yesterday when it is past, and like a watch in the night." By understanding God's timeframe according to His Word, we will be more efficient as we go through the time sequence of what we call a day. The truth is that God has a plan for each rotation of the earth. How we react during each rotation "sums up" His benefits and blessings on our behalf. How we seek Him determines how we fill the bowls of incense from our prayers that are poured out into the earth realm (see Rev. 5:8-10).

A Time Beyond

Of course, there is more to the Jewish sense of time than a single day from sunset to sunset. Since Creation, days have made up the weekly division of time, which is a seven-day period—six days for man and the seventh for the Lord, called *Shabbat* (see Matt. 28:1; Lev. 23:15; 25:8; Luke 23:54). My good friend Robert Heidler has written a book called *The Messianic Church Arising: Restoring the Church to our Covenant Roots*, which addresses the fundamental need we all have for this God-appointed day. He writes:

> Interestingly, even though God's instruction concerning *Shabbat* [Sabbath] is widely ignored and misunderstood by Christians, it is a blessing *desperately needed* by all of us in our modern world. We need to see that Sabbath has nothing to do with what day we go to church. The early Christians met daily. But the seventh day was still their Sabbath.[3]

Weeks make up a month, and months, of course, are linked with the moon and its changes in relationship to the earth.[4] Each month there is a blessing to receive. The beginning of the month, *Chodesh*, begins with a Firstfruits celebration, which causes the heavenly-planned blessing to be released (see Num. 10:10; 2 Kings 4:23; Ps. 81:3-7; Isa. 66:23).

Months make up a year, yet this year is different from our modern-day Gregorian calendar year. The Bible was written in alignment with the Hebrew year, which is composed of 12 or 13 months, depending on the lunar correspondence with the solar year. This timeframe is linked with God's pre-appointed feast times, as laid out in Exodus 23 (which, by the way, is an important chapter to understand because God said the feasts should be understood from generation to generation). The official beginning of the year is called *Rosh Hashanah*, which means "the head of the year." This is usually in the seventh month of the Jewish calendar year. The first month of that year revolves around Passover time. The Feast of Ingathering, better known as Pentecost, is the next significant feast, while the Feast of Tabernacles, which is in the Rosh Hashanah timeframe, is a prophetic feast that will be fulfilled in all nations (see Zech. 12–14).

If you haven't already gathered, the concept of time in the Bible differs vastly from our modern-day measurements. I believe that if we become more acquainted with God's order of time, our prayers will not only be more efficient, but we will also understand why God is calling us to come near to Him and visit with Him at certain times. That is why we find David in Psalm 55:17 saying, "Evening, and morning, and at noon, will I pray, and cry aloud: and He shall hear my voice." He knew he must order his prayers in conjunction with God's timeframe. If he did this, he would always have the anointing to break the yoke upon him and overthrow his enemies.

Let Light Overtake Darkness

Just as the Bible is filled with references to various times, God's Word often uses the imagery of light and darkness. Light is a powerful force; so is the dark. Have you ever been afraid of the dark? Many of us were as children, but we outgrew that fear. Yet many of us have yet to overcome our fears associated with the darkness of a troubled past. We have little hope of ever having complete victory over what has already happened yet continues to rule us today. So let me ask you: Have you chosen to leave the darkness of your past and enter into the light of your future? Are you aware that you have a "yet" time to come in your life, and that it really doesn't matter how old you are? Are you aware that there is a hope waiting for you to grab hold of?

Acts 17:26 says, "And He has made from one blood every nation of men to dwell on all the face of the earth, and has determined their preappointed times and the boundaries of their dwellings." God has a pre-appointed time and boundary for you. Do not fear the dark that is in your boundary, whether that darkness lies ahead or is in the past.

"Darkness" can be defined as "the absence of light, error, evil, bad luck or affliction."[5] It is a term synonymous with chaos, disorder, condemnation, ignorance or spiritual blindness. Sometimes, when we experience gloom, sorrow and distress, we say that it is a day of darkness. And then, of course, the Bible uses the word "darkness" to refer to works of Satan and the antichrist system of unfruitful deeds. Isn't it interesting, however, that in the Bible night is never directly connected to darkness other than the physical aspect of a time devoid of light. Therefore, there is no need for us to fear the night. In fact, the night is our opportunity to seek God the most. It is the period when we are not working by daylight, but instead can commune with our Lord and seek His ways. Be willing to seek God in the night so that you can bring the true Light into a time of darkness. Light is the opposite of darkness. Light is synonymous with illumination, clearness or glory. It is equated with knowledge and the release of revelation. Light is also likened with purity. In spiritual terms, we can never forget that the light of God dwells within us. His Word is a light for our path (see Ps. 119:105). That means our path will be ever illuminated, no matter what darkness we have to walk through.

John 8:12 says, "Then Jesus spoke to them again, saying, 'I am the light of the world. He who follows Me shall not walk in darkness, but have the light of life.'" Throughout God's Word, light is directly linked with God. Scripture tells us that *light* . . .

- Came into existence at the decree of God
- Is associated with His presence
- Symbolizes His truth
- Reflects His glory
- Expresses His righteousness
- Can be seen on us
- Brings judgment (see Rom. 13:12; Isa. 60:1-2; 1 John 1:5; Ps. 119:105; John 3:19-21; Eph. 5:8)

Light comes in many forms. It can be natural, artificial, miraculous, spiritual, symbolic and expressive. It is an element that both surprises and brings change. As believers who carry a light within, we are to both seek out and possess light. Yet the real question is, How are we to respond when light dawns on us?

Countless people in the Bible faced the same question. The Christmas story alone includes several individuals dealing with the issues of light: Zacharias, when an angel visited him over Elizabeth's pregnancy to come; Mary, when both an angel of the Lord and the Holy Spirit visited her; Joseph, when an angel of the Lord twice visited him in his dreams; Simeon, when the Lord was brought to be dedicated in the Temple; the wise men, when they followed the light of a spectacular star in the sky; and, of course, the shepherds, when they were privy to both the ever-shining of God's glory *and* a radiant chorus of angelic hosts singing praises to a newborn Savior. God's light is continuous and undeniable. And as these renowned individuals can attest throughout history, His light forever changes a life!

Break the Fear of Darkness and Receive Light!
When God interacts with us, His holy, penetrating light breaks through our barriers of darkness. He overcomes our sin, our shame—any area that lacks light—with His radiance. On a literal

level, to "break" means to "destroy, quench, or deliver."[6] Yet the process of breaking is also linked with intercession. In Dutch Sheets's primer on intercession, *Intercessory Prayer*, he explains the concept of *parach*, which means "to break forth and away from." When we intercede (*paga*), we literally strike or light upon a spiritual dimension. It is an act of breaking forth with light.[7]

In the same way, our faith must break forth. When it does, the light of God breaks through any darkness. Faith overcomes. As the promised bearers of such powerful light, we would be wise to ask God on a regular basis to fill us with His breaking light. And as we heed His call to enter into the watches from this day forth, we will find the light of God radiating through us in a new way.

There is another word, "dawn," which is linked with the breaking of light. How we approach the breaking of a new day is extremely important. Do we approach it with praise? Anticipation? Anxiety? Fatigue? Resistance? This is key. If our day is ordered and we have watched with the Lord as He has called us to, then we will break forth into a new day with His order. When we break forth into a new day, our light will grow brighter and brighter throughout the day (see Prov. 4:18; 2 Pet. 1:19).

Nelson's Illustrated Bible Dictionary references this breaking of dawn as it appears in Scripture:

> The first appearance of light is in the morning as the sun rises (Job 7:4; Isa. 58:10; Acts 27:33). Matthew's account of the resurrection of Christ begins with these words: "Now after the Sabbath, as the first day of the week began to dawn, Mary Magdalene and the other Mary came to see the tomb" (28:1). Matthew also quotes the prophet Isaiah using the figure of the dawn as the beginning of a wonderful new era of hope and promise: "The people who sat in darkness saw a great light" (4:16).[8]

When we watch with the Lord, dawn takes on an entirely new meaning. The sunrise becomes simply an extension of the Light that has already been present through the night!

Entering Into the Watches

Over the years, God has trained me in the prayer room. I enjoy being there as much as any place. I have found God very creative in how He leads us to pray, decree and seek Him. By the same token, there is a unique power and anointing when the corporate Body gathers together specifically to watch with the Lord. In fact, leading corporate prayer watches is my favorite assignment from the Lord.

The remainder of this chapter deals with the specifics of the four watches, but I feel it would be helpful to describe what goes on during a watch. Many of you reading this may be unfamiliar with what a watch is. As an example of what goes on during a watch, here are some notes taken by Linda Heidler during a seven-week corporate prayer watch. Linda is one of the ministers and prayer leaders of our church:

In September 2003, Chuck called us to seven weeks of prayer during the morning watch, at 3 A.M. to 6 A.M. We met every Friday morning beginning September 19 and ending October 31. Chuck said that by praying during this time, we could order the day before the enemy ordered his day. This was an amazing time of revelation as we met with the Lord for those seven weeks.

From the very first meeting, we knew that we were in a different time and place of revelation. One of the first passages the Lord directed us to was Job 38:7, which talks about the morning stars singing together and shouting for joy with the sons of God. We saw that there were certain sounds of heaven and certain songs of heaven that could only be heard in the early morning hours when the morning stars would still be visible.

The Lord began to unfold revelation about how the stars actually release sounds—essentially vibrations that can be heard. These sounds form a song of praise to God as the day breaks. We began to join in with this sound and song, releasing spontaneous praise to God. From there, the Lord opened up a new realm of revelation from Psalm 22:3 about how our praises enthrone Him. As we enthrone Him, His glory comes down among us and creates a covering over us (see Isa. 4:5). From Ezekiel 28 we saw that Lucifer was the "covering" cherub that "sealed the pattern of perfection." We related this to the two cherubs on the Ark of the Covenant. There were cherubs on either side of the Ark, but there was no "covering" cherub. Where there should have been a perfect pattern of three, there were only two. The cherub who was to lead creation in worship and form the covering of glory was not there. Instead, God created man and gave him the place of creating a covering of glory over the land in worship. This covering of His glory was to make our land like the Garden of Eden. The sound of our praises joined with the song of the morning stars would so change the atmosphere of our territory that the land would flourish. Psalm 67:5-7 showed how the land would flourish when God's people praised Him.

During these days of morning watch prayer, Rosh Hashanah began. On Rosh Hashanah, the only requirement is to hear the sound of the *shofar*. This is a call to attention. It is a call to assemble and get your instructions for the next season. It is a call to war and a call to worship. The Lord began to speak to us about the effect of sound on solid objects and how sound will reveal things. We saw that sonar would reveal ships in the water. A sonogram would reveal a baby in the womb. Anything that resisted the path of the sound waves would be revealed.

The Lord said that the sound of the *shofar* would resonate with the sound of heaven, the voice of the Lord. When this sound penetrated into our inner man, it would reveal anything in us that resisted the voice of the Lord. Through this, God would reveal any places in us that would hold us back, weigh us down or otherwise stop us from moving forward in the next year. As we received the sound, it would cause things that were out of alignment to come into alignment with God.

The sound of the shofar would also release hidden wisdom by the voice of the Lord. The sound would reveal deep things of God into our inner man, wisdom to which the powers of darkness could not gain access. It is a sound that causes our spirit man to awaken and hear what God is saying.

The sound of the *shofar* would also reveal structures of the enemy that opposed the plans of God. It would reveal obstacles on our path so that we could find our way through without getting snared. Jericho was a picture of how the sound of the *shofar* brought down an enemy structure that opposed the plan of God.

The sound of the *shofar* is also a sound of worship. As we heard the sound of the *shofar* and began to resonate with it, we would enter into a new realm of heavenly worship.

As we moved from Rosh Hashanah into the Feast of Tabernacles, in addition to having early prayer we were having nightly meetings. As we looked at the schedule, we began to ask the Lord how we were to have the strength to do this. He reminded us of several occasions in Scripture where His people marched all night, then fought all day in order to recover what had been taken from them. In Genesis 14, Abram took the warriors from his household and pursued those who had captured Lot. They marched all night and fought all day and recovered not only Lot, but also all those who had been captured, as well as additional plunder.

In Joshua 10, the Israelites marched all night and fought all day to rescue the Gibeonites. Joshua commanded the sun to stand still so that they could take complete victory. David and his men marched all night to overtake the Amalekites, who had sacked and burned Ziklag in 1 Samuel 30. They recovered everything that had been taken and took plunder from the Amalekites. The last example of this that we saw was Jesus: He prayed through the night so that He could fight all day to gain His inheritance back from the enemy. This caught the devil by surprise with a strategy and wisdom of which he had no knowledge.

The Lord said to position ourselves during the night so that we could fight during the day. If we would position ourselves during the night, then we would be at the right place at the right time for victory in the morning. During this watch, John [Dickson] got the song "We Marched All Night." Also during these weeks of prayer, the Islamic celebration of Ramadan was taking place. We noted that Muslims had many calls to prayer during the day, but none through the night. We declared, "This hour does not belong to the powers of darkness. We will awaken the dawn with worship!"

We prayed to bind the spirit of fear that Islam releases. We prayed against the spirits of legalism and lawlessness that work together to resist the Holy Spirit. We completed these weeks of prayer by driving around our whole city, encircling it with praise as we went. We printed up sheets with the names of God and with the Hebrew words for "praise," and we praised the name of the Lord all around our city. We also had psalms of praise that we read over our city.

These were weeks that none of us will ever forget. We came into a realm of revelation that was just incredible. Through the whole time, we had great participation. The number of people did not drop off as we went through it. God met us every week and it was well worth getting up to hear what He had to say to us week by week.

It is one thing to talk to you about the power of the night watch and try to convince you that it truly will reorder your life. It is another to have someone else testify about just how life-changing it is. In Candi MacAlpine's book *Take Back the Night*, she writes the following:

One day, during my morning time with the Lord, I heard Him say, "Take back the night; it belongs to Me." I did not think too much of it at the moment, but almost a year later, in my quiet time, I was reading Psalm 74. In verse 16 I read, "Both day and night belong to you; you made the starlight and the sun" (*NLT*). It really attracted my attention. After repenting for my disobedience to the word I had previously received from the Lord, I began to research the subject of the night. I was utterly amazed at what treasures began to unfold before my eyes. From this point I began walking through experiences that showed me the value and importance of the entire season of the night. The Lord wanted to redeem His purposes, as stated in His Word. It is from this journey that we begin this journey into the night and into His light. I pray His light will be shed abroad in your hearts and minds, and that you too will take up the call of God in this hour.[9]

You can take back the night! Remember, the day begins at sunset at the first watch. Let the Lord lead you on a journey of watching as you witness all darkness begin to go! Enter into the watch of the Lord.

Let God Reorder Your Day—and Your Steps
Below you will find details about significant events that occurred during each watch presented in the Bible. It is crucial during these times that you understand what each watch means and how each serves a unique purpose. This will help you understand why you are feeling the tug of the Holy Spirit to pray at a certain time.

Obviously, we should pray without ceasing. But there are times when the Lord wants to meet with us for a specific reason. There are times when He wakes us up for an assignment, or simply to be with us. As you reorder your day and pray:

- Expect amazing turns of events in your life!
- Look at issues that have gone before you and expect a 180-degree turnaround.

- Decree that the enemy who has plundered you will be plundered.
- Decree that the power of loss breaks and that you experience a reversal of fortune.
- Get ready to counteract "faith destroyers" that have held you in unbelief.
- Declare that the enemy will not succeed in any attempt to make your faith empty.
- Watch the strategies that have captured you and held you in hard labor break.

The Four Watches

The transition of day to night begins before sunset and lasts till after sunset. The change of night to day begins before sunrise and continues until after sunrise. Because of these two facts, the four watches extend from 6 P.M. to 6 A.M. (see Matt. 14:25; Mark 13:35). Acts 12:4 speaks about four parties of four Roman soldiers (*quaternions*), each of whom had to keep guard during one watch of the night. In the same way, I pray the Lord uses your new understanding of each watch to make you a good soldier in His army.

The First Watch:
The Evening Watch (6 P.M. to 9 P.M.)
During the evening watch, we regroup. Most of us have worked all day and would love to just to chill out during this time. We like eating with our family, perhaps reading a book or watching a TV program—any way we can escape from the day's activity. However, this is a time that we need to "still" ourselves from the world. The oft-cited Psalm 46:10 says, "Be still and know that I am God." There must be a time before we sleep when we quiet our hearts. The evening watch is that time for meditation. Try to find at least 30 minutes when you can meditate before going to bed. From your meditation, find time to release your anxieties to the Lord in prayer.

Genesis 24:63 says, "Isaac went out to meditate in the field in the evening. He lifted his eyes and looked, and there, the camels were coming." In his place of meditation, Isaac saw his future: When he lifted his eyes, there was Eliezer bringing Rebekah back to be his bride. This created the extension of the covenant of Abraham in the earth. When we meditate, we get focused on God's covenant plan. Joshua 1 tells us to "meditate day and night on the words of His mouth" and we will be assured of success. I like to call the evening watch my time of focus, which allows me to start my day with a mentality for success. I have had many anxieties in my past, yet the Lord has used the evening watch to purge me of the fears that would keep me from advancing into His perfect plan. This is the watch that Jesus also pulled aside into, to find His place of quietness. Try to do this before you go to bed each day.[10]

The Second Watch:
The Midnight Watch (9 P.M. to Midnight)

Psalms 119:62 says, "At midnight I will rise to give thanks to You, because of Your righteous judgments." This is a time for thanksgiving. This is also a time of visitation. The midnight watch begins at 9 P.M. and goes to the middle of the night, specifically 12 o'clock. The word "midnight" is often used symbolically of a period of time of intense darkness or extended gloom. Many times we try to sleep during this hour, yet sleep escapes us because of our anxiety. Be sure to remember the power of prayer during this watch.

This is also a time when God deals with our enemies that are trying to keep us from entering into His perfect plan for our lives. It was at midnight that the Lord struck down all the firstborn in the land of Egypt (see Exod. 11:4; 12:29). Obviously, midnight can also refer to the "half of the night." It's interesting to realize that in the period before Israel's exile, it seems midnight was not accurately determined. The night was divided into three watches, the middle one of which included midnight. In New Testament times, however, people used the four-watch division, at which point midnight was accurately determined. In essence, midnight is a defining point.

The Third Watch:

The Breaking of Day (Cockcrowing) Watch (Midnight to 3 A.M.)

What you entered into during the last watch can carry into the third watch. This is a watch when there is much spiritual activity occurring. I believe the majority of dreams from God occur during this time. Most of us equate this watch to Peter's trial that led him to deny His relationship with the Lord. If you are having trouble with doubt, unbelief or the direction of your path, I suggest that you do this watch for 21 days. I especially want to suggest this watch if there is a covenant-breaking spirit in the region where you live (for example, a high frequency of divorce, church splits, unethical business dealings, and the like). Why 21 days? This is the time it took Daniel to break through in prayer and for a principality to let go of the revelation God was releasing to him (see Dan. 10:13-14). I do not have a specific prayer focus for this watch, but the following will help you better understand the significance behind the "cockcrowing" watch.

In the East it was common for a rooster to crow during the night at regular times. This gave rise to the expression "cockcrowing" to indicate a definite portion of time, as seen in Mark 13:35. The Romans called this the last watch of the night. This watch could also be equated to "the break of day," which occurs at about three o'clock, or what is known as *gallicinium*. The Hebrews designated the cockcrowing period with a phrase meaning "the singing of the cock." Within Jewish history, we find no mention of the flight of the hours of the night except the crowing of the cock.[11] "Cockcrowing" was an indefinite hour of the night between midnight and morning, referred to by all the evangelists in their account of Peter's denial (see Matt. 26:34,74; Mark 14:30; Luke 22:34; John 13:38). All other New Testament references, however, describe an actual rooster that crowed. The crowing of a rooster reminded Peter how easy it is to deny the Savior.[12]

The Fourth Watch:

The Morning Watch (3 A.M. to 6 A.M.)

This watch is linked with morning light approaching and the day breaking. Scripture contains several references to the time of this watch:

- Twilight of the morning (see Job 7:4; Ps. 119:147)
- The change from darkness to light (see Job 17:12)
- The approaching of the morning (see Judg. 19:26)
- The eyelids of the morning (see Job 3:9; 41:18, *ASV*)
- The ascent or rise of the morning (see Josh. 6:15, *YLT*)
- The approach of the dawn (see Matt. 28:1; Luke 24:1)

Many of Israel's watches recorded in the Bible were developed so that protection would be established for God's people, and possibly none were more important for this reason than the fourth watch. (For a great study on this watch, read 2 Kings 11.) The fourth watch is the last portion of the night, so we always need to be ready to arise and watch. The word "morning" generally refers to the day and means the hour of dawn or soon after (see Gen. 19:2; 2 Chron. 36:15; Hos. 6:4; Luke 24:22). Ask the Lord to meet you early so that you are prepared for the day ahead.

Prayers of Another Kind

In a physical context, a watch involves remaining alert for any potential intruders, attackers or signs of harm. The same is true when keeping watch in the spiritual realm. However, this does not always directly involve "enemies" of any sort, but rather spiritual forces that stand against the advancement of God's kingdom.

With the conflict of covenants occurring in the earth today, I believe it is important to know the Islamic prayer times as the necessity for watches becomes more obvious. Muslims pray at the following five times each day with the purpose of constantly being reminded of Allah:

- *Fajr* (pre-dawn)—performed before sunrise
- *Dhuhr* (noon)—in the middle of the workday
- *'Asr* (afternoon)—before the end of the workday
- *Maghrib* (sunset)—as the day begins to come to a close
- *Isha'a* (evening)—prior to sleeping

In Muslim communities, people are reminded of the daily prayer times through the "calling of the *adhan*," which is an inspirational call to prayer. As one Islamic website states, "In ancient times, one merely looked at the sun to determine the various times of day for prayer. In more modern times, daily prayer schedules are often printed which precisely pinpoint the beginning of each prayer time."[13]

We must understand that the people of Islam are extremely devoted. Many would rather pray than sleep. This is why they respond to the call of prayer before sunrise. This is also why they are moving with great authority in the earth realm. Wake up, Christians! We represent the one true God who longs to call us to Himself so that His purposes can already be in order before the sun comes up.

Just as Islam is a primary force that believers must be aware of during a watch, so too are the dark powers of witchcraft. For instance, thousands, if not millions, of spells are cast around the world during the night hours, particularly with the onset of various lunar seasons. Many witchcraft ceremonies and expressions stem from the different phases of the moon (such as new moon, waxing moon, waning moon, full moon). Rather than just tacking it up to another "attack of the enemy," we would be wise to recognize the specific cause behind an increase in spiritual warfare during certain lunar cycles. Many things go on during the night, so we must learn to rely on the Holy Spirit. If we are awakened and watch with Him, we will see what we need to counteract with our prayers.

Stay Awake and Alert

This gives you an understanding of why the watches are so important and why the Lord asked the question, *"Can you not watch with me for one hour?"* Remember, in addition to the spiritual forces opposing our watch, our bodies naturally resist our responding to God. With so much pushing against our keeping watch with the Lord, we need His help. We need to recognize the power of communion. I encourage you to make a simple request to the Lord: "Help me to respond to You when You call me." Is God our Creator not greater than the will of our bodies? As a Church, let's get to the point where we can answer His question, *"Can you not watch with me for one hour?"* with a definite *yes*!

I believe that if we will allow the Lord to reorder our day, and if we will get our bodies in sync with Him, then many blessings, including healing and prosperity, will begin to break forth in our lives. I also believe that we will gain knowledge in the night that we need to rule during the day. Darkness will continue to cover the earth. But God's people will rule in the midst of darkness and radiate with His presence.

CHAPTER 5

The Presence-and-Glory War

Is Your Lampstand Burning?

I have always been an irregular sleeper. Some people use the term "light sleeper," but that doesn't exactly fit me. I've never developed good sleep patterns because of the turmoil and trauma that I grew up in. This has had some negative effects on my health, but on the positive side, it's also allowed me to commune with the Lord and keep watch while most people are fast asleep. I'll never forget one night in particular.

Pam had gone to bed at our normal time of 11 P.M., but I continued to stay up to read the Bible and pray. I was immersed in the Word, having a wonderful time with the Lord, when I suddenly felt the Spirit of God come down into the room of our home where I was praying. His presence was tangible. I then heard His voice say an interesting thing to me: *"You can turn Satan into his own fire. When his fiery darts come against you, repel those darts and return them against him."*

Like most anyone would have reacted in that same situation, I was a little stunned. I wasn't exactly sure what God's words meant, but I knew by the Spirit that they had done something within me. At the time, Pam and I were seeing great breakthroughs in our lives personally and in other areas in which we were seeking Him. I had been praying for lost people in our church and they were getting saved. I was being favored in the workplace. Overall, I was learning to prevail in prayer. So even though I wasn't too sure about the meaning of God's words, I knew for certain that He would reveal what I needed to know in time. At about two in the morning, I turned off the lights and went to bed.

Only an hour later, Pam and I were suddenly awakened by our dog, Josh, who had jumped into bed with us and was yapping as if there were a burglar in the house. We sat up and discovered the real source of distress: Standing next to our bed was a presence! To me, the presence had a distinct physical form, dressed like a woman with a man's voice. Pam, however, saw it differently. She said it was a green-like slime form with fiery eyes. (Looking back, this is yet another reminder of how most of us see into the spirit realm but perceive things differently, even though what we perceive is actually the same.)

Almost immediately I said, "Who are you and what gives you the right to be here?"

"I am Ashteroth," the presence replied, "and I have come to take your children." Not your average houseguest, that's for sure!

At that moment, Pam and I had the choice to be gripped with fear over this visitor's presence and its menacing words, or turn to the Lord. We chose His truth. I instantly stood up and said, "In the name of Jesus, you have to leave this house!" Pam and I then began to clap and shout, overwhelmed with joy.

You see, up to that point in our lives, we were barren. We had been seeking God for children but were unable to conceive. It was disheartening, yet we trusted the Lord. This force had come and announced the will of darkness to take our children. But instead of us falling to the ploy of the enemy and submitting in fear and con-fusion, we rejoiced. Why would we be happy over this presence? Because what this evil force was really announcing was that we were going to have children! Yes, there would be a war over the children, but I knew the Lord well enough to know that once we had chil-dren I could trust Him to keep what He had blessed us with.

There was another element to this encounter that dramatical-ly changed our lives. When I commanded this force to leave our house, I was also declaring that any familial spirit that had been in our bloodlines and had been sent against us would now have to fully let go and remove itself from our sphere of authority. The change was instant—as crazy as it sounds, the room actually lit up. God's presence so flooded our bedroom that it became as bright as day. When we resisted evil, His glory came in and overtook our atmosphere.

Stake Your Claim

The incident that night revealed a level of warfare we had never been in before, but that was not the most important thing. The main point was that God's manifest presence was now free to rule this particular area of our lives. And what was revealed was a truth that is key to this chapter: Once evil is confronted in our atmosphere, then God's presence has the liberty to replace evil with glory.

Did you catch that? We'll discuss it further throughout this chapter, but for now I want to make sure you understand the basic concept. God's desire is to flood this earth with His glory. Habakkuk 2:14 says, "For the earth will be filled with the knowledge of the glory of the LORD, as the waters cover the sea." The thing that prevents God's glory from doing so is the evil in this world, and this is the essence of the presence-and-glory war we will discuss in this chapter. There is a fierce war that wages over occupying the atmosphere of this earth. Neighborhoods, cities, regions, nations, continents—each has atmospheric boundaries that have either been declared for the purposes of darkness or for housing God's glory. If we read Habakkuk 2:14 with this understanding, we see that the Lord already has a plan to remove evil that is blocking His presence and glory from invading the entire earth realm. His Word declares that "the earth *will be* filled" (emphasis added), which means that the plan of fullness He has for the earth *must be* manifested.

It also means that in the midst of our conflicts, we must never forget that God has a plan for our lives. Many times darkness wants to rule through fear to stop us from entering into the ultimate plan the Lord has for us. We must never forget that His plan is good. In chapter 2, we discussed the account from the book of Jeremiah in which God asked the prophet to stake his claim on the future by buying a field that was about to go into desolation. What I didn't mention was how in the midst of all the darkness that was surrounding Jerusalem, Jeremiah prophesied that God would eventually restore Israel and Judah, and a remnant would be saved. If we stray from the Lord, He offers a way to bring us back and restore His plan for us. He has a future of prosperity for us. Jeremiah 31:23-33 says:

> Thus says the LORD of hosts, the God of Israel: "They shall again use this speech in the land of Judah and in its cities, when I bring back their captivity: 'The LORD bless you, O home of justice, and mountain of holiness!' And there shall dwell in Judah itself, and in all its cities together, farmers and those going out with flocks. For I have satiated the weary soul, and I have replenished every sorrowful soul." After this I awoke and looked around, and my sleep was sweet to me. "Behold, the days are coming, says the LORD, that I will sow the house of Israel and the house of Judah with the seed of man and the seed of beast. And it shall come to pass, that as I have watched over them to pluck up, to break down, to throw down, to destroy, and to afflict, so I will watch over them to build and to plant . . . Behold, the days are coming that I will make a new covenant . . . not according to the covenant I made with their fathers . . . but this is the covenant that I will make with the house of Israel . . . I will put My law in their minds and write on their hearts and I will be their God and they shall be My people."

Once Jeremiah staked his claim on the future, it really didn't matter that there was darkness that would attempt to overcome his land—because God had a plan. If we trust Him in the midst of our warfare and obey Him to do the faith acts He requires of us, God will secure our future even in the midst of war. Jeremiah 33:3 says, "Call to Me and I will answer you and show you great and mighty things, fenced in and hidden, which you do not know [do not distinguish and recognize, have knowledge of and understand]" (AMP). Because God has a great future for us, we can shout loudly and get His attention in the midst of our warfare so that He shows us things we could not normally see. In the midst of whatever haziness presents itself in the now, He will show us our future. Most of us are used to watching out for what we presently have and what is dear to us. But we must also watch after our future.

With His Presence Comes Vision

We can neither watch *after* nor *for* the future if we do not have the presence of the Lord. It is His presence that allows us to see into our future. Sadly, many Christians get nervous when talking about seeing into the future. We give this the same stigma associated with fortune-tellers and palm readers. Let me say this as clearly as I know how: God's people must have foresight! We must have vision for what lies ahead, or we will be unprepared. And in these times, preparation and readiness are essential.

The enemy can only mimic the truth. This has always been the case. We find plenty of people in the Bible who were able to predict the future, yet they had aligned themselves with the enemy. How much more, then, is the God of all truth willing to reveal His plans for the future to His own children? Prophecy—which is simply the testimony of Jesus' reign in the coming days—is all about vision. And in the presence of God, there is perfect vision. Habakkuk 2:1-4 says:

> I will stand my watch and set myself on the rampart, and watch to see what He will say to me, and what I will answer when I am corrected. Then the LORD answered me and said: "Write the vision and make it plain on tablets, that he may run who reads it. For the vision is yet for an appointed time; but at the end it will speak, and it will not lie. Though it tarries, wait for it; because it will surely come, it will not tarry. Behold the proud, his soul is not upright in him; but the just shall live by his faith."

When we live in the Spirit and see by the Spirit, we gain vision for our future. Not only does God reorder our time, but He also positions us in a place so that He can extend the horizon line of heaven and cause us to "see" what He sees. This is what makes us a prophetic people. Acts 17:24-27 says:

God, who made the world and everything in it, since He is Lord of heaven and earth, does not dwell in temples made with hands. Nor is He worshiped with men's hands, as though He needed anything, since He gives to all life, breath, and all things. And He has made from one blood every nation of men to dwell on all the face of the earth, and has determined their preappointed times and the boundaries of their dwellings, so that they should seek the Lord, in the hope that they might grope for Him and find Him, though He is not far from each one of us.

When we are at the right place at the right time, the Lord "pro-horizons" us, or extends our horizon line so that we can see farther than ever before. We are not a people limited to the finite space that we are in. We are a people filled with vision. We can *sense* His presence, *feel* His presence, *see* His presence and *move in* His presence.

As I mentioned before, God has promised to cover the earth with His glory (see Hab. 2:14). I believe this was His original intent when He planted the Garden and gave it to the human race. He wanted us to cultivate that garden and live in communion with Him so that He could give us a vision of how to effectively invade the whole earth with His presence. However, when we listened to the enemy, our perfect communion was broken with God and our vision became hindered.

The same principle applies today. If we adhere to the plans of Satan rather than listening to God's voice, we limit God's presence from moving through us and increasing our boundaries. Because of this, there is a huge war raging over His presence. The enemy does all he can to prevent us from seeing what the Lord wants us to see. Satan longs for us not to have vision for our future. Remember, without a vision, we perish (see Prov. 29:18).

Seeing What Is on the Horizon

When Pam and I had our encounter with the enemy's forces that night, it left us with a vision for the future. We knew that what the enemy had planned for harm, God meant for good (see Exod. 50:20).

And so we began to cry out for our children. Two years later, we received our first child, Daniel. Two years after that, Pam was healed and we conceived our second child, Rebekah.

One of the primary reasons God allows us to see into the future is for the benefit of the generations who are arising. We must prepare the way for God's best in the lives of those who will follow. The Lord doesn't give us glimpses just to titillate us or make us long for better days ahead. The vision of God—which we all need—always has a divine purpose.

Another reason God supplies prophetic vision, one we've already hinted at, is simply for strategy. We cannot be victorious against the forces of darkness that rule our world without the precise, perfect plans of the Lord. Here are some directives that I believe are important for each of us to trust the Lord for in days ahead:

1. *Ask for* three *generations to agree prophetically over what God has said.* This reflects the tri-generational nature of our God—that He was the God of Abraham, Isaac and Jacob. It also aligns with Isaiah 59:21, where we find God pronouncing a covenant that His word will be in the mouths of three generations. When this happens, He will unlock the heavens and manifest His presence in the earth.

2. *Trust that He will expand your borders and redefine your sphere of authority.* When this happens, you will see people running to find out what you are about. The Lord will secure your inheritance of souls won for Him. There came a time when Naomi said to Ruth, "Daughter, how shall I secure your inheritance? Not only do you have a future, but you can begin now to secure it!" (see Ruth 3:1-4).

3. *See your storehouse as full.* Before you can do that, however, you must *define your storehouse.* What areas of provision has God established in your life? Let Him show

them to you, and ask Him how to fill them. He will give you the strategy.

4. *Don't allow your past to rule you.* God can take situations from the past and bring them into the present so that you can reconcile your own mistakes and failures. When your past is reconciled, your future is unlocked.

5. *Believe that you can defeat your enemy!* See your enemy. See his headship broken over your life. Do not be afraid to discover how his voice has ruled your bloodline. Remember Jesus! The cross broke the headship of Satan. Drive a stake through his headship and you will begin to hear what God has for your future.

6. *Never forget that you have been given the ability to connect heaven and Earth.* Let the Lord teach you to pray today, "Thy will in heaven, come to earth!"

7. *Watch for your divine connections.* They are on your path already. Success means that the Lord has positioned help on the way ahead. When you see a divine connection that God has placed on your path, watch Him develop that covenant relationship to help you establish your future.

These seven points are crucial to our success in the coming wars. They also emphasize the need for God's presence to be stronger than ever in our lives. Remember, when we establish His presence, we force out every power of darkness. His glory always overcomes!

A Change in the Air

Do we really understand this presence-and-glory war that is being fought? A better way to approach this may be from an understanding of the atmosphere. According to the *American Dictionary of the English Language*, the atmosphere is the whole mass of fluid, consisting of air, aqueous and other vapors, that surrounds Earth.[1]

The word is rooted in the interaction between vapor and Earth's sphere. Vapor consists of the fumes, moist floating substance or invisible elastic fluid that encompasses Earth's sphere. The Bible even refers to this in Psalm 39:5 when it says, "Certainly every man at his best state is but vapor." Yet when most of us speak of "the atmosphere," we're referring to a generic sense of an airborne aura surrounding us.

What does the atmosphere have to do with a war over God's presence? Actually, everything. We have an atmosphere about us that affects the way the earth operates. The atmosphere we carry affects the land we walk on. The more we are in union with God and His purpose for the earth, the more we create a right atmosphere around us.

To usher in God's presence requires a change in the atmosphere, and we are assigned the task of bringing this about! The Bible establishes that Satan is the god of this world, the "prince of the power of the air" (Eph. 2:2). Yet how is this so if Psalm 24:1 says, "The earth is the Lord's, and all its fullness"? First, we must understand the terms used in those two verses. The Greek word for "earth" is *topos*, while the word for "world" is *cosmos*. This means that any structure that protrudes or is above the *topos* is subject to warfare. Second, we must realize the Bible establishes that there are three heavens. God and all His heavenly beings dwell in the third heaven. Satan, as the ruler of the air, attempts to rule from the second heaven to illegally legislate in the first heaven—that place where we physically stand above the earth.

Apostle Kim Daniels, in her book *Give It Back*, explains it this way:

Ephesians 2:2 describes the assignment of the prince of the power of the air. One name for the Greek god of the second heaven is Zeus. The second heaven is the demonic headquarters that is strategically set up to control people like puppets on a string. In the spirit, that is exactly how it looks—like a puppet show! Every human being is connected to either the second or third heaven. People who are bound by second heaven activity are connected to the second heaven by demonic stings. The hydra is the god of recurring curses and is also seated in the heavens. It is one of the constellations or groups of stars that abide in the heavens. The power of the air (or unconscious cycles) is a subliminal bondage, which is controlled from the air. This spirit hides behind the cover of natural habits, and its victims never suspect that they are under its control. Before people are delivered from addictions and habits, demonic strings must be cut in the spirit to sever their alliances with the second heaven. After this, ground-level deliverance can take place.[2]

We must determine who is in charge of our atmosphere. Are we going to legislate God's rule in our atmosphere or will our enemy control it? This is one of our greatest warfare dynamics to understand. In *Authority in Prayer*, Dutch Sheets writes:

Where God and Satan are concerned, the issue has never been power, including control of the earth. God is all-powerful . . . it is always a question of authority. The same is true with us and our struggle with the kingdom of darkness. Satan didn't gain any power at the Fall and didn't lose any at the cross. His power or ability didn't change at either event. His authority, or the right to use his power, did. In fact, though Christians often state otherwise, Scripture nowhere says that Christ delivered us from or dealt with Satan's power at Calvary. He dealt with Satan's authority.[3]

We must learn to legislate our realm of authority, while understanding that it is not the same thing as wielding power. Our realm of authority includes both heaven and Earth. That is what makes up our atmosphere. Jesus broke Satan's headship and removed his legal authority at the cross. He then overcame death, hell and the grave. He liberated the captives. However, we must keep Satan's power neutralized and defeated in the place in the earth where God has called us to be His stewards. That is what Elijah did when he commanded the heavens to withhold rain for three and a half years (see 1 Kings 17). Then, knowing it was God's perfect time for rain, he birthed a cloud into his atmosphere. The atmosphere was then filled with rain.

Is a Curse Working in Your Midst?

Satan has a million different ways in which he tries to extend his dominion of the air. This chapter is not dedicated to identifying all those opposing tactics, but I do feel it necessary to highlight one in particular: curses. Passed down through time, curses work with iniquitous patterns that have developed in our bloodline. Let's look at how curses play a major role in our reclaiming the atmosphere around us.

Though it seems almost too simple, one of the ways that you can detect a curse is by recognizing the absence of God's glory or presence. According to *The Encyclopedia of Jewish Myth, Magic and Mysticism*, a curse is a "verbal invocation to bring harm, evil or detriment on another. More than a threat or a wish, a curse is assumed to have the power to make the desired harm a reality."[4] Curses result from not hearing God's voice or from receiving another voice that is contrary to God's plan for your life. Curses will agree with internal deficiencies within us, such as rebellion, lust or any other sin of the flesh. Derek Prince wrote a wonderful book called *Blessings or Curses: You Can Choose*. In his analysis of Deuteronomy 28, he says there are seven main categories that curses deal with. They are:

1. Mental and/or emotional breakdown
2. Repeated or chronic sicknesses (especially if hereditary)
3. Barrenness, a tendency to miscarry or related female problems
4. Breakdown of marriage or family alienation
5. Continuing financial insufficiency
6. Being "accident-prone"
7. A history of suicides and unnatural or untimely deaths[5]

Because I teach so much on breaking old cycles, I want to be sure that you recognize that curses can be timed and sequenced so that they reoccur from generation to generation. This will continue to take place until the iniquitous pattern in a bloodline or the iniquitous violation on a piece of land has been addressed. I have much experience with both of these patterns. In fact, my wife jokes that I'm qualified to teach on demonic powers all over the world because my family had all of them in operation! Many of those curses operated on the land that we owned. I won't tell all of those stories here, but I will say this: The Lord took me through a 30-year process going back and forth to places where iniquitous defilements occurred in our family. He then would have me repent and release His presence to replace the working of evil. I read many books on cleansing the land and discovered that there are four major areas of iniquity that cause curses to have a right to operate in a land: covenant breaking, idolatry or blood sacrifice, illegal bloodshed, and sexual immorality.

Many Christian leaders make light of the concept of curses. I do not want to do that. I do believe that curses are conditional. I am well aware that they can come through words, timing and astrological influences, or magical incantations and actions. More important, however, curses can be broken.

A man once approached me who was from a denominational background. The group he worked with had bought a new piece of land to build a school and ministry on. When he and some of his coworkers were walking on the land, they got to a place where everyone immediately sensed a change in the atmosphere. Every hair on his body seemed to stand up. He asked me what that meant.

"When that happens, it means you have discerned a presence of evil," I answered. "It is the Holy Spirit manifesting in you with the gift of discerning evil spirits." He then asked me what he should do and how he should pray. I said, "Well, first of all, you pray until all the hair on your body goes down! That means you have commanded the presence of evil to let go of the place where you are standing and the atmosphere has been cleansed." The group later found several places where satanic sacrifices had been made on their land.

Planning for the Presence

Many of us need to reclaim territories just like this group did. While this can certainly involve claiming victory over the dark history behind a piece of physical land, more often than not it involves cleaning out areas of our lives in which God's glory is not fully seen. We must become people of His presence, consumed with His habitation throughout every inch of our atmosphere.

King David was such a person. Despite making some major mistakes during his reign, David loved the presence of God and had a heart that was turned after God. He was always willing to rely on God to salvage his failures and restore him.

In 2 Samuel 6, we find an account of how David first attempted to bring the Ark of the Covenant into Jerusalem, where he lived. His desire was pure: He wanted the presence of God to surround his life. Yet his execution was flawed and left one of his men dead. As a result, David feared transporting the Ark to his house and instead left it at the home of Obed-Edom. Scripture says, "And the Lord blessed Obed-Edom and all his household," and this was relayed to David.

What is interesting is that this Hebrew word for "blessed" is *barak*, which at its root means "to kneel." Jeff A. Benner, on his Ancient Hebrew Research Center website, gives an understanding of this word as, "Yahweh (he who exists) will kneel before you presenting gifts."[6] The Ark was only with Obed-Edom for three months, yet there was a discernible change in his situation that caused others to recognize that he was being blessed, that Yahweh was presenting him with gifts—all because of the presence of the Ark!

The mistake wasn't in David's heart or in his lack of preparation. David had already built a site for the Ark. He had established a special place for God's presence to dwell. No, the lesson David learned was simply this: *How we invite the presence of God and how we honor His presence are very important.* David serves as a wonderful example because although he made a great mistake, he discovered how to properly bring the Ark to the City of David. He then entered a "series of conquests which greatly extended and strengthened his kingdom (2 Sam. 8). In a few years, the whole territory from the

Euphrates to the river of Egypt, and from Gaza on the west to Thapsacus on the east, was under his sway (2 Sam. 8:3-13; 10)."[7]

According to Leen and Kathleen Ritmeyer in *From Sinai to Jerusalem: The Wanderings of the Holy Ark*, the Ark was placed right next to David's palace, in his yard.[8] Living on his property, *in his backyard*, was the God who brought him gifts! The Tabernacle of David would have remained there for about 30 years. I believe this is what gave David great credibility in war. What an incredible principle! When we have the presence of God in our homes, the gifts of God are bestowed abundantly on our lives and we are successful in war.

However, I also believe this is why David was judged so severely when he didn't go to war and fell into passivity, lust, manipulation and murder after coveting Bathsheba. When we commit open sin while in God's presence, our problems escalate. This is why it is more disastrous when a minister hides a lifestyle of sin than for an everyday Christian to do so. Obviously, sin is sin, but the influence that we have from the presence of God in our midst is not to be taken lightly. I believe we are more accountable when we are aware of God's presence in our midst and we do not act accordingly.

John Dickson, a fellow minister and friend of mine who co-authored *The Worship Warrior* with me, writes the following about David:

What was unique about the Tabernacle of David was that it was a heavenly paradigm in an earthly setting. When David brought in the Ark, there was already a Tabernacle specifically designed to house it: The tabernacle of Moses was just down the road in Gibeon (see 2 Chron. 1:4-5). But God said of David that He would "carry out My program fully" (Acts 13:22, *AMP*) and so we find David setting up a different kind of tent on Zion's hill with no brazen altar, no laver, no lampstand, no altar of incense, no table of show bread and—most importantly—no veil. The worshippers entered the very presence of God face-to-face, just like they did in heaven. The way they worshipped was also just like in heaven: With no forms or rituals, they sang and danced and prophesied and warred before the Lord as the minions of heaven are seen doing in the book of Revelation.

There in that Tabernacle on Zion's hill, God enthroned Himself on their praises (see Ps. 22:3) and from that throne He stretched forth His scepter (see Ps. 110:1-3), issued His commands (see Ps. 133:3), declared His blessings (see Ps. 128:5; 134:3), heard the prayers of the destitute (see Ps. 102:17) and punished His enemies (see Isa. 66:6). That word *enthroned* implies in the Hebrew that God not only came to sit as judge, but also to stay or to dwell—even to marry. God was not going to leave once His "work" was done. He had found a suitable dwelling place for His presence to continually dwell on earth. Psalm 132 says "For the LORD has chosen Zion; He has desired it for His habitation. This is My resting place forever; here I will dwell, for I have desired it" (Ps. 132:13-14, *NASB*). In David's Tabernacle, God was in the midst of continual praises. It was just like His holy hill, by the same name, in heaven. As a matter of fact, Psalm 78 says that God built His sanctuary on Mount Zion "like the heights" (Ps. 78:67-69) or just like it was built in heaven. God's presence, which was continually manifested in heaven, was now continually manifested on the earth. His people could come into that small tent and experience that presence just like the inhabitants of heaven. How wonderful![9]

Throughout the Bible, we see that God is enthroned in praise. We glorify Him through our worship. That is why praise and worship are essential to experiencing God's glory. Praise is that element of celebration that can transport us into the throne room of God. Once we are in the throne room at His feet, the only suitable response is to worship and adore Him. As we worship Him in that intimate place, He begins to reveal His glory to us. God is looking for true worshipers who will worship "in spirit and truth" (John 4:24), and as He finds those worshipers, they are able to experience the reality of heaven, which is God's glory.

The Lights Went Out, But the Lamp Was Lit!

Throughout the Bible, God's glory is often seen in terms of radiant light. In his well-known introduction, Gospel-writer John describes Christ as "the Light which gives light to every man coming into the world" (1:9). In Revelation, the same apostle describes the New Jerusalem as having "no need of the sun or of the moon to shine in it, for the glory of God illuminated it. The Lamb is its light" (21:23). Jesus declared Himself "the light of the world" (John 8:12).

What is often just as interesting to me is that Christ crowned those of us who follow Him with the very same title. In Matthew 5:14-15, He said of believers, "You are the light of the world. A city that is set on a hill cannot be hidden. Nor do they light a lamp and put it under a basket, but on a lampstand, and it gives light to all who are in the house." In the remainder of this chapter, I want to delve into the deeper meaning of this vivid imagery of lights and lampstands. Allow me to start by offering a wonderful illustration of the importance God places on His Son—and us—being the light of the world.

I travel all over the country and usually find myself in Houston several times a year. In November 2002, I was ministering at the Worship Convivium in Houston, hosted by Lora Allison. I had been sharing a message on my heart from Jeremiah 1:11-12, which is part of Jeremiah's initiation as a watchman prophet. In those verses, the Lord asks Jeremiah an important question: *"What do you see?"* This would be crucial to our meetings that week.

Friday morning when we came to the meeting, I shared with Lora that I felt the Lord was going to do something new and we would have to follow Him to experience what He wanted. After the first song in worship, I felt I was to stand up and give a teaching instruction over what God was saying and how it related to what we were singing. I then made a declaration that God was going to transform Houston, but it would be in His way.

I sat down after about 15 minutes of speaking and we started to worship again. Suddenly, the whole place went pitch black, with no electricity for instruments, lights, sound or anything else plugged

in. (A *transformer* had blown in the Houston area where we were having the meeting.) Almost immediately the Lord said, *"Let Me lead you
into the sound I have."*

I stood up and asked the question to the whole group: "What
do you see?" Of course, we saw darkness. Then someone brought
in a lampstand or menorah with seven candles lit. I responded by
saying to the Lord, "Lord, I see your lampstand in the midst of
the darkness."

So the Lord said, *"Yes, darkness is coming upon the earth, but I am
lighting a lamp in the midst of the darkness. This will be a season where those
with My light will shine brightly. This will also be a season of removing. I will
remove My lampstand from certain churches, cities, states and nations."*

I went on and prophesied for another hour. During this time,
God added each sound that He wanted to bring forth. It was one
of the most incredible gatherings I've ever been in. It was as if the
whole place knew when to dance. The violin knew exactly when to
play, the drums when to beat, the horns when to resound and the
singers when to come out front and sing prophetically. It was def-
initely a "transforming" time.

Yet the words we received that day still ring true today: The
Lord will continue to move us out of the soulish realm of worship
that we are presently operating in. The methods and mindsets
concerning worship are changing. And in the midst of our darkness, the Lord will send for the light that will guide us.

Is Your Lampstand Burning?

Prophetically, I believe it is crucial for us to understand the lampstand. This simple device is one of the key items that God is using
to teach us about both the general future as well as the specific
warfare we face ahead with the powers of darkness. In the book
God's Lamp, Man's Light, theologian John D. Garr states:

> Because of the extreme attention to detail given to the
> design of the menorah, it is clear that it is more a symbolic
> form, a work of art, rather than a mere cultic apparatus. Moses
> was instructed by God to "make a lampstand of pure gold.

The lampstand and its base and its share are to be made of hammered work . . . six branches shall go out from its sides; three branches of the lampstand from its one side, and three branches of the lampstand from its other side." The menorah is a concrete symbol of God himself, the source of light. Its central lamp is called by the Jews *ner Elohim* (the lamp of God). David exclaimed, "You are my lamp, O Lord; the Lord turns my darkness into light," thereby identifying God with the menorah as He who illuminates the darkness. The Psalmist observed that God "wraps himself in light as with a garment." Rather than bedeck Himself in the brilliant colors associated with the pagan deities of the ancient world, God clothes Himself in pure white light as a mantle. God's divine presence, the *Shekinah*, was manifested as a "fiery light." When Ezekiel saw the temple, the earth shone with God's glory, the same glory that the prophets saw as "fire." God's majesty illuminated the temple as the fiery light of a golden lamp. The sages noted that the "Holy one, blessed be he, was constrained to dwell with mortals in the light of a lamp . . . and so a 'pure menorah' came down from heaven."[10]

Sadly, many Christians don't understand the significance of the menorah. In our modern world, we have lost much of the understanding of artifacts in the Bible, along with its sacred symbols and elements. Because of this, we have lost spiritual understanding as well. Garr goes on to say:

The truth is that the menorah is God's lamp, as Scripture clearly declares: "The lamp of God . . . in the temple of the Lord, where the ark of God was." The menorah is not merely the Jewish candlestick or the tabernacle lampstand or the temple candelabrum. It is "God's lamp." It belongs to all of God's people, both Jews and Christians. Its rich symbolism is appropriate to both faith communities, representing God's light radiating into man's world, the power of vision and insight that comes to believers in God, both Jew and Gentile, through God's Word. The Word of God is like a light that shines in a dark place, clearly pointing the way. It channels the path of the just toward the "day star" who arises in the hearts of believers. It dispels the darkness, the confusion, the ignorance, the fear, the superstition and the dangers inherent in human existence. In spite of the ominous obscurity of the human situation, one small ray from the Eternal Word dispels the darkness, brings clarity of purpose and unmistakably marks the way to the tree of life so clearly that no one who walks in that light will stumble.[11]

The lampstand or menorah actually symbolizes salvation through the Word of God. His sevenfold Spirit (a menorah has seven candles) is offered to us to bring us stability into our lives and link us into the eternal flame that is burning in His throne room. When we fail to understand this concept of the lampstand, we rob ourselves of God's glory as we war against powers and principalities.

Psalm 119:105 says the "word of God is a lamp to [our] feet." As the living Word, the anointed One and the Messiah, Jesus can do nothing less than reflect God's glory. Both Jesus and God's written Word illuminate our lamp. And when our lamp is illuminated, we cannot be overcome by principalities and powers. When the Word of God is manifesting within our lives, the light of God shines through us and dispels the darkness.

With God's lampstand burning in us, we truly become a light to the world. Many mountains come into our path as we walk through this life. Much warfare occurs around us, but we need to keep our lamp burning brightly. If we do that, we will be able to shout "Grace! Grace!" to every mountain, and the power of light in the sound of our voices will cause the mountain to fall.

The Seven Churches of Revelation

The Lord has given us keys to victory during these times of darkness. I believe one of those keys is found in Revelation 1. There, the apostle John sees a vision of seven golden lampstands. In context,

I believe these are seven menorahs, that is, these are seven "seven-branched" lampstands. The Lord then tells John that these seven lampstands represent seven churches.

What are these seven churches? First, we know that they were *literal* churches. John lists seven of the churches that existed in his day in the Roman province of Asia. But it's clear that these churches are more than just seven churches chosen at random. They are called *the* seven churches—in some way, these seven churches represent *all* of the Church! Some have suggested that these seven churches represent seven eras of Church history, that each of the seven churches pictures a different historical time period, beginning with Ephesus as the Early Church and ending with lukewarm Laodicea as the Church today. The problem with that interpretation is that it doesn't work.

The "eras of Church history" interpretation might sound convincing to Christians living in America, where many churches match the description of the lukewarm Laodiceans. But the American Church is only a fraction of the Church worldwide. In places such as China or Africa, major segments of the Church today are filled with life and power in the midst of severe persecution. The fact is, the majority of the Church today worldwide is not Laodicean.

I believe a better explanation of these seven churches is that they represent seven *kinds* of churches. These church types exist in every age of history, although at certain times and in certain places, each tends to be more representative than the others. That means that *every* church—and *every* Christian—is to be found somewhere among these seven churches. In these seven churches, we see all the different strategies Satan uses to keep God's people from fulfilling their call. But in each we also hear a word from Jesus. He is walking among the lampstands, tending to each one, and offering instructions to each church for how to become a brightly burning lampstand.

I am fortunate enough to minister with Robert Heidler, one of the most profoundly straightforward theologians I know. I believe Robert's incredible teaching on the seven churches of Revelation is vital for us today if we are to continue to pray for transformation in our regions. The seven churches represent regions—they are lampstands in a region, the menorah lights of a region. Each has an array of characteristics—some good, some bad. That is why the Lord commended each church and then revealed any weak point that needed to be addressed for these churches. Below is an analysis of each church, compiled from Robert's audio series, *How Is Your Lampstand Burning: Understanding the Seven Churches of Revelation*. Review your region and see how the lamp of God is burning.

Ephesus: The Church That Lost Its Fervent Love

The first church is the church at Ephesus, which represents the church that has departed from its first love. Ephesus had been a brightly burning lampstand. Jesus commended those in the Ephesian church for seven things.

- Their living faith (their deeds)
- Their diligence (their toil)
- Their standards (they did not tolerate evil)
- Their discernment (they tested apostles to see who was true)
- Their perseverance (they kept going despite opposition)
- Their endurance (they were in it for the long haul)
- Their strength (they had not grown weary)

But the Ephesian church had a problem: Somehow, in the midst of all their work, they had lost the *love* of God they had once known. They still did a lot of good things, but the fervent love that once motivated them was no longer there. The result was that their lampstand had begun to go out! Because of this, Jesus gave them a warning: "Repent! . . . Or I will come and remove your lampstand out of its place." All the work in the world counts for nothing if you've lost your love!

Jesus then showed them the path to restoration. To regain what they had lost, they needed to do three things:

1. Remember from where they had fallen.
2. Repent to change their direction.
3. Do the deeds they did at first.

Smyrna: The Persecuted Church

Smyrna was a large and prosperous city, a seat of learning and culture. The Smyrnans were proud of their city and had a fanatical loyalty to Rome. Within this culture, the highest form of worship was worshiping the Roman Emperor, and the Smyrnans had no tolerance for those who would not worship the Emperor. As a result, the church there suffered for its faith. In Mark 10:29-30, Jesus promised that along with many blessings, we would receive persecutions. The church at Smyrna had experienced that persecution and was about to go through more.

But Jesus had a promise for His persecuted church: "Do not fear any of those things which you are about to suffer. . . . He who overcomes shall not be hurt by the second death" (Rev. 2:10-11). Jesus assured them that while they may face suffering and even physical death, they had eternal life. Essentially, His message to Smyrna was, "In the midst of persecution, *be faithful!*" Jesus identified Himself to them as the One "who was dead, and came to life" (v. 8). He was reminding them that death is not the end—if you are faithful, you will receive a victor's crown! Even if you suffer in this life, it's worth it to follow Jesus. Even if you die for your faith, you still have won!

Pergamos: The Unfaithful Church

Pergamos was a center of paganism. On the hill above the city was the Pergamos acropolis, crowded with pagan temples. The most striking feature of the acropolis was a huge temple, shaped like a giant throne. It was the altar to Zeus, ruler of all the Greek gods.

Jesus' message to the church in Pergamos began with: "I know your works, and where you dwell, where Satan's throne is" (v. 13). False gods are demons, which means the worship of false gods is the worship of demons. Zeus, as the ruler of false gods, represented the head of all demons, Satan—which means that above the city of Pergamos was a huge throne dedicated to the devil! Jesus later added that their city was "where Satan dwells." As the worship of God brings God's presence, so the worship of Zeus had caused Pergamos to be a place where Satan's presence dwelt in a discernable way. This church was called to stand in a hard place, and Jesus immediately acknowledged that they had held fast to His Name.

Unfortunately for them, Jesus also had some issues with their current state. He told them that they had fallen into the trap of the Nicolaitans. These were false teachers who perverted the idea of freedom in Christ. They taught that since we are free in Christ, why should we invite persecution by being legalistic? Their view was, "Pagan gods are nothing! They don't exist! It doesn't hurt to eat at a pagan feast. It doesn't hurt to put incense on an altar."

The Christians at Pergamos had been seduced by this teaching. They compromised with the pagan world, even joining in feasts given to honor demons! Jesus compared this to the trap set for Israel by Balaam (see Num. 22–24). If joining in pagan feasts was the equivalent of fornication, to be seduced by the world is adultery. As a result, Jesus gave this church a harsh warning: "Repent, or else I will come to you quickly and will fight against them with the sword of My mouth" (v. 16). Thankfully, Jesus also promised a reward to those who would repent.

Thyatira: The Church Invaded by a Religious Spirit

Thyatira was a city known for its purple dye and fabrics. It was home to corporate guilds of potters, tanners, weavers, dyers and robe makers. To hold membership in these guilds, it was necessary to feast at the temple of Apollo. Guild business dinners were held there and were usually followed by orgies. Obviously, this made it difficult for Christians to prosper in Thyatira.

Jesus' issue with the church was this: "You allow that woman Jezebel, who calls herself a prophetess, to teach and seduce My servants to commit sexual immorality and eat things sacrificed to idols" (v. 20). The main problem at Thyatira was that the church tolerated the teachings of a false prophetess. An influential woman in the church had identified herself as a prophet and justified the practice of fornication, idol worship and eating of meat sacrificed to idols. We can presume this false teaching was welcomed because it allowed church members to join the guilds. Yet it is interesting that Jesus never said exactly *what* this

woman's teaching was, He simply identified the spirit behind it—
that of Jezebel!

In certain church circles, the term "Jezebel" is tossed around
frequently nowadays. The problem is, many believers do not accurately understand the Jezebel spirit. A Jezebel spirit is not a "female"
spirit—in fact, many men have a Jezebel spirit. It does not always
work behind the scenes. What actually characterizes a Jezebel spirit
is that it is always religious. A Jezebel spirit seeks a position of
influence among God's people so that it can promote a false system of religion. Here are some characteristics:

- A Jezebel spirit seeks to draw God's people into *false
  religion*—any kind!
- It operates through control, false teaching, manipulation and intimidation.
- It often identifies itself as a defender of the faith and
  promotes false prophets.
- It opposes the Holy Spirit and all of His manifestations.
- It hates the true prophetic word and persecutes God's
  prophets.

A Jezebel spirit is a mean spirit. It shows no mercy. In this passage, Jesus personally decreed judgment on Jezebel. To those who
had not followed her, He had a word of encouragement: "Hold fast
until I come!" Thyatira was a good church. It did not have a lot of
problems—apart from Jezebel! Simply put, Jesus was saying, "Deal
with her and you'll do great! Keep moving forward!"

Sardis: The Comfortable Church

Sardis was one of the most pleasant places to live in the ancient
world. It was a center of worldwide trade and one of the most afflu-
ent cities in the world. Life was easy in Sardis. Even in the pagan
world, Sardis had a reputation for materialism and decadence. The
pagans there were extremely accepting and didn't care if you worshiped their gods or not—they just wanted to make money and
have a good time.

The church in Sardis was also comfortable. There is no mention of persecution or opposition whatsoever, no issue of false teaching or heresy. They were contented and well-off—yet Jesus had nothing good to say about this church! He told them, "I know your works, that you have a name that you are alive, but you are dead" (3:1). Ouch! In other words, Jesus was saying, "You have an appearance of life; you *look* good. You are doing lots of good things—but there's no *life*!"

The church at Sardis was the Church of the Living Dead. They had become too attached to the world. They loved all the luxuries Sardis had to offer and their hearts were captured by the affluence of the city. Jesus' exhortation to the church at Sardis was to *wake up*! (Sardis was not all dead, but it was losing strength fast.) "Strengthen the things which remain, that are ready to die, for I have not found your works perfect before God" (v. 2). He then told the people, "Remember therefore how you have received and heard; hold fast and repent" (v. 3). They didn't need a new message; they needed to hold on to what they received, turn back and get on the right path.

Jesus warned the Sardites that He would come to examine His church. The word He used actually suggests an audit. If they would stay as they were, they would forfeit their destiny. But if they woke up and overcame, they would take their part in ministry among His priests, and He would confess them before the Father and all the angels.

Philadelphia: The Church of God's Favor

Philadelphia was located on the Royal Road, the main east-west trade route into the interior of Asia. Because of this, it was built as a missionary city. It was designed as a showplace for Greek civilization in Asia to spread Greek language, culture and religion to the barbarians of the East. In fact, it had so many temples it was known as "little Athens."

In AD 17, a massive earthquake struck and the city was literally destroyed overnight. Emperor Tiberius rebuilt the city and restored its beauty, but massive aftershocks continued to hit the city for decades. The result was that the majority of its people lived in the surrounding countryside. Few were brave enough to live in the shaky city.

The Philadelphia church had experienced shaking also. They had been through seasons of persecution. They had been through a hard season, and they felt weakened. But Jesus had a word for them—the most positive word given to any of the seven churches. He told them, "You have suffered for your faith, but you persevered . . . and that's something very important to God. You kept My Word and did not deny My Name. You endured patiently. And because you have remained steadfast, God has opened up a door for you that no one can close." In short, Philadelphia had passed the test and, as a result, now had a golden opportunity.

For the Philadelphians, this included an open door to their city. They had been falsely accused, and their reputation in the city had been tarnished. Yet Jesus promised vindication. He said that even their enemies would acknowledge that God was with them. Their open door was also one to the entire world. Philadelphia was called to be a missionary city. Through the Church, Philadelphia would begin to fulfill its destiny as a gateway to the world.

Philadelphia indeed became a gateway city for the gospel. We know from history that missionaries went out on the Royal Road that ran through Philadelphia and established thriving churches in Persia, India and even as far as China.

Laodicea: The Lukewarm Church

Laodicea was a major trade center and banking capital. It was built on the crossroads of several trade routes, and its banking system and the many caravans that came through made it a wealthy city. It was also an important medical center. Built at the foot of a volcanic mountain known for its hot mineral springs, the city had many health spas where the sick came for treatment. Jesus described His relationship with this church in Revelation 3:20: "Behold, I stand at the door and knock. If anyone hears My voice and opens the door, I will come in to him and dine with him, and he with Me."

That's probably the most famous verse in Revelation. We frequently talk about Jesus "knocking on the door" of an unbeliever's heart. Yet few Christians really understand this verse. In its context, Jesus wasn't knocking on an unbeliever's heart—He was knocking on the door of His Church! It's important that we understand this picture. The second and third chapters of Revelation show Jesus moving from church to church. He is tending His lamps to keep them burning brightly. He comes to each one to correct and encourage—but when he comes to Laodicea, *He can't get in!*

Other churches had problems, but Laodicea had gone a step farther. Something about the church at Laodicea shut the door against Jesus coming into their church. Jesus described the problem in Laodicea with one word: *lukewarm.*

If anyone understood what it meant to be lukewarm, it was the Laodiceans. The hot springs up on the mountain were wonderful for the health spas, but by the time the hot water flowed through the aqueducts to the city, it cooled off. The city's water was lukewarm mineral water, and it was considered almost undrinkable. In fact, it was nauseating! Jesus said to the believers of Laodicea, "Your church is like your water!" He then added a surprising twist: "I wish you were cold or hot."

To be cold is to reject Jesus, yet Jesus can deal with rejection. If you are cold to Him, it just means you have never known His love. The truth is, there is great hope for those who are cold. When they see who He really is, they can quickly change from cold to hot. On the other extreme, to be hot is to be on fire for Jesus. Madly and passionately in love. That's what Jesus is looking for! That's what He deserves! He gave Himself completely for us, and He wants us to give our hearts completely to Him.

The Laodiceans were neither cold nor hot. They were lukewarm—about as middle-of-the-road as you can get. They didn't oppose Jesus, but they weren't excited about Him either. They were indifferent to the One who gave His life for them.

To that attitude, Jesus' response was harsher than any of His others to the churches: "I will vomit you out of My mouth" (3:16).

Vomiting is a violent involuntary reaction to something that is totally unpalatable. It is a knee-jerk, natural response that requires no thinking. And here Jesus is saying, "Lukewarm Christianity makes me want to puke!" That's what kept the door closed for Jesus. He couldn't come into a church like that.

But Jesus did not give up on Laodicea. He was still knocking at the door, calling out for someone to open it. In fact, the Lord had high hopes for it: "If you will open the door, I will come in!" Their solution was to gain a new perspective on life. They thought they were rich and needed nothing. Jesus' response? "[You] do not know that you are wretched, miserable, poor, blind and naked—I counsel you to buy from Me gold refined in the fire, that you may be rich; and white garments, that you may be clothed, that the shame of your nakedness may not be revealed; and anoint your eyes with eye salve, that you may see" (vv. 17-18).

Jesus wanted the Laodiceans to see their need and come to Him as their source. He promised that if they would open the door to His presence, He would be faithful to come in. They would feast with Him! Not only would they feast with Him, but Revelation 3:21 guarantees that if they would overcome in the battle before them, they would also gain a place on His throne.

Jesus' word to Laodicea was simply this: "It's a battle to break out of the lukewarm. But if you overcome, You will gain great authority in the earth. *You will reign with Me!*"[12]

When I cannot hear God, or revelation seems to be blocked, I have learned to do two things. First, I always ask God what I should give. I find that if I obey God in giving after the pattern He created for us in redemption, then things around me will begin to move in a new way. Faith will begin to rise, and I will see what I need to see.

Second, I read John's Revelation of the seven churches and I ask God, "What church am I?" If I am in intercession, then I ask, "What church am I dealing with?" This always points me to my lampstand first to see if it is burning brightly. Remember, Jesus said that before we deal with our brother's sin, we must first examine our own shortcomings (see Matt. 7:3). So it is when we search for a reason behind the absence of His voice or revelation.

This also allows me to see how powerful the fire is burning in the atmosphere of the group with which I am worshiping. I always feel that the group or ministry where I have been assigned reflects one of the churches mentioned above. This gives me great insight for how to pray.

War Is Coming into My Atmosphere

On Saturday, April 14, 2007, Tricia Miller, a friend of mine from Tyler, Texas, sent me the details of a dream that she felt was a word from the Lord. Not only do I agree with her, but also I can't think of a better way to capture the heart of this chapter than sharing it as I conclude my thoughts on the presence-and-glory war. The dream began with Tricia in a hotel, where she was preparing to go to a retreat of the apostolic network that she is part of. Here is the rest as told by Tricia:

> I was very agitated and confused. I could not get anything done. Then two ladies came into my room and began to take over. When I asked what they were doing in my room, they responded that they were going to wait in my room until their room was ready next door. I became so frustrated that I left the room and began to drive down the highway. Suddenly I realized that I was almost to the meeting place but was still not ready, so I made a U-turn under an overpass. The next thing I knew I was walking through a store or place of business releasing the glory of the Lord. An old woman came up behind me and was screaming at me to not do that. She was yelling, "You don't have a right to do that! I don't want that done in this place!" Still, I continued. She then began to call for her husband to stop me when I exited the building.
>
> I drove again and came to the meeting, which was in an old church building painted white and with a steeple. I was still in that state of frustration and agitation. The group was doing normal meeting things, and I became so agitated

that I left the meeting and went outside. My thought was, "I can't do this!"

When I got outside, I saw large wheat fields in front of me. I looked up and saw about 20 to 30 enemy planes coming closer. [In the dream, these looked like World War Two planes.] They began to drop bombs and shoot machine guns at the fields. I turned, went back inside and was trying to get to the apostolic leader to let him know that we were in trouble. I could hardly make it; I was crawling and pushing with all my strength to get to him. When I finally reached him, I told him what was happening outside and that we were in trouble. He had the people break up in prayer groups. I remember seeing his wife and another leader that I was familiar with in the room.

I was still in that state of frustration, but by now I had realized that the reason I was feeling this way was because the Holy Spirit was showing me what was coming. I went back outside and was watching the bombing when the planes turned and started toward us. I was going to run back into the building but realized if I did, they would see me and shoot me. So I crouched down while they flew over. I then ran in the building to tell everyone to get out. At this point I woke up from my dream.

As I've said throughout this book, the Body of Christ has entered into a season of war. We've discussed the wars over our minds, our blood and our time. Now we've examined the crucial fight that is occurring over the atmosphere. Will the forces of darkness occupy our territories, or will God's glory finally flood the earth?

Sadly, the Body of Christ is also in a place of frustration. We have the appearance of getting many things accomplished, yet in reality we are not getting anything done because things are changing so quickly. Our busyness, if we do not keep it in check, is crowding out our efforts to see God's presence established in our territories. On an individual level, it has become more difficult to find our abiding place in Him because people keep interrupting our time of preparation.

This season, I see the glory of God getting released in the marketplace before He manifests Himself in the Church. But notice in this dream that the harvest fields were being attacked. We have not defined our harvest fields, nor have we gathered the harvest that is before us. Therefore, the enemy is attacking the harvest field. This dream even seems to imply the reason: The current Body of Christ, as well as its leadership, is gathering without understanding the atmosphere around us. We are failing to recognize both the harvest fields in our reach and how the war is escalating in our midst.

I believe that the leaders of today's Church, if they were fully aware of the war that is at hand, would be ready to call the Body to prayer. However, it is almost as if we have to be under attack before we call the spiritual army into battle. We must be prepared! Nevertheless, the Lord is telling those who are His prophetic watchmen for this hour to be a protection to the present gathering. We must stand watch in His perfect timing, awaiting His signal. And when we see those forces approaching, we must cry loudly, signaling the battle cry, so that the Body will be alerted to the war in the harvest fields.

CHAPTER 6

The Power War

Who Are You in Agreement With?

I like power. I am sure you enjoy a bit of it, too. In our world, having power is seen as a good thing—it means that you are not weak, that you have control over certain things. Since the beginning of time, the quest for power has been at the heart of virtually every conflict. Satan fell because he wanted more of God's power for himself. Humanity fell for basically the same reason. Nations have fallen and continue to fall in the ever-shifting balance of power throughout this world.

As an all-powerful God, our heavenly Father is the author and creator of power. Therefore, it is perfect and good within itself. The problem with power is when it falls into the wrong hands—or hands that become corrupted by its allure. We characterize such people as "drunk with power," "power-hungry" or having an "insatiable lust for power." Yet these are often the people who change the course of history.

We are currently in a time in our nation when certain individuals are vying for the power to shape our history. One of the strongest fights for such influence is now taking place in our courtrooms. Author Mark Sutton agrees with this assessment in *Walk Through the Wall, America*, an eye-opening, key prophetic book for this hour. One of Sutton's many excellent points is that our judicial system is quickly becoming out of control with its leading figures' unrelenting, unchecked pursuit of power and authority. "By making constitutional law, federal judges can bypass democracy and, in many respects, rule America from the judicial bench," Sutton writes. "Some federal judges have repeatedly and without any fear of consequences effectively amended the U.S. Constitution for more than 50 years. The resulting judge-made constitutional amendments are an unconstitutional act, because judges are not permitted by the Constitution to make constitutional law."[1]

How are federal judges getting away with this? The checks and balances system on which our American government is based keeps Congress's and the president's power in check via the U.S. Supreme Court. However, there are very few checks in place to keep judges from redefining and amending some of the core elements of our nation's laws, which is especially likely when legislation is poorly written. Judges must clarify and interpret laws, and when laws are ambiguous, judges sometimes make decisions that rightfully belong to the Legislative Branch (which represents the people). The Executive Branch has the power to appoint judges, but it is extremely difficult to remove a judge once he or she has been sworn in. This means that if a handful of judges begin to overreach their Constitutional powers, there is little that can be done to stop them.

A perfect example, as Sutton points out, is what is now termed the "separation of church and state." Today, the majority of people in our society simply accept this as a Constitutional doctrine: Government and religion must be kept separate. The fact of the matter is that our nation's forefathers consistently melded the two. "The Establishment Clause of the First Amendment was designed to, among other things, *prevent the new federal government from interfering* with the religious practices of the state and local governments," Sutton writes. "In 1947, the Establishment Clause was altered to mean, in many respects, the opposite of what was originally meant. According to the U.S. Supreme Court, the Establishment Clause now means that *the federal government must interfere* with most interfaces between religion and state governments."[2]

This is just one example of how laws have drifted from God's purpose and been used against God's kingdom plans. Our society has almost removed the concept of God-consciousness from its midst through changing laws in this time. As frightening as this sounds, it reminds me of God's words in Isaiah 1:

Your country is desolate, your cities are burned with fire; strangers devour your land in your presence; and it is des-

olate, as overthrown by strangers. So the daughter of
Zion is left as a booth in a vineyard, as a hut in a garden of
cucumbers, as a besieged city. Unless the LORD of hosts had
left to us a very small remnant, we would have become like
Sodom, we would have been made like Gomorrah. . . . "To
what purpose is the multitude of your sacrifices to Me? . . .
Come now, and let us reason together," says the LORD. . . .
"I will restore your judges as at the first, and your counselors as at the beginning" (vv. 7-9,11,18,26).

This is not a gloom-and-doom chapter, though it might feel
that way from how it has begun. My point is not to discourage
you, but to emphasize the relevance and immediacy of the war
that we will discuss in this chapter. I believe that one of the greatest battles in this and many other nations is for judges who rule
the judicial system to have an awakening of who the ultimate
Judge of the earth is.

And yet that fight, as crucial as it is, is but one of the battles in
a war that has raged for millennia. This is the power war. Or stated a better way, this is the war *over* power. Since the Fall, Satan has
used his limited power to entice countless people into fighting
this war. History has shown us climactic glimpses of this through
such antichrist figures as Hitler and Herod. Yet possibly the most
destructive weapon the enemy has used is religion. Later in this
chapter we will discuss how religion has partnered with governments to come against God's plans.

God is represented by us, His people. Therefore, the way we
exercise our authority in God and demonstrate His power through
us determines how He rules in the earth. Most of us are fully aware
that there is a relentless opposition that stands against us taking
such dominion, yet it is critical for every believer to grasp just how
strong this fight is—and why. We are not only fighting for authority, power, cities or even nations; we are fighting for souls, for a
heavenly Kingdom. How we take dominion in the future and influence the world with our Kingdom perspective is key to unlocking
the harvest.

Find the Ancient Path

I recently had a dream. In it, the Ancient of Days took me by the hand and led me to a three-by-five-foot box made of a pearl-like substance that shimmered like gold. In the box were approximately 300 tightly rolled maps or blueprints standing on end. The Lord told me to choose the ones I wanted. I chose three, and when I unfurled them, I found that they were ancient maps of places in the earth realm. One was a blueprint of my ancestral lineage—where my family came from and the lands that they belonged to. The Ancient of Days then spoke to me and said, *"I am ready to unseal revelation that I have been holding since ancient times. When you return to the ancient paths, you will move forward to unlock treasures for your future."*

When I awoke, I thought of two passages. The first was Jeremiah 18:15: "Yet My people have forgotten Me; they burn incense to false gods, they have been caused to stumble in their ways and in the ancient roads, to walk in bypaths, in a way not graded and built up [not on a highway]" (*AMP*). In the context of this verse we find that the people of God had forsaken the living waters offered them, and their cisterns had begun to leak. This would keep them from having water in the desert. Therefore, they were prevented from uncovering the desert treasures they otherwise could have had access to. The Lord was calling them to return to the ancient paths from which they had lost their way, the highways that held all of the blessings He had for them.

I believe the Ancient of Days was saying the same thing to me: *"I am returning My people to a place of recovery. They will recover what they missed when they deviated from My paths and My highway. I am remembering now what has never been accomplished. I am offering My people the blueprint to return, uncover and recover the hidden treasures that they have never gained access to."*

The ancient paths will lead us into the future.

Wisdom from the Ancient of Days

The second passage I thought of after waking from my dream was Daniel 7. In this key chapter for our times, we find that Daniel had a revelation of God's everlasting reigning power. "I watched till thrones were put in place, and the Ancient of Days was seated. . . . and behold, One like the Son of Man, coming with the clouds of heaven! He came to the Ancient of Days . . .   Then to Him was given dominion and glory and a kingdom, that all peoples, nations, and languages should serve Him. His dominion is an everlasting dominion, which shall not pass away, and His kingdom the one which shall not be destroyed" (vv. 9,13-14).

God's power can never be in doubt. The Ancient of Days is named so for His rule over all time. His name implies dignity, endurance, judgment and wisdom. As the Ancient of Days, He releases ancient wisdom for present-day victory. First Corinthians 2:6-10, a passage that has revolutionized my prayer life, speaks of this:

> We speak wisdom among those who are mature, yet not the wisdom of the age, nor the rulers of this age, who are coming to nothing. But we speak the wisdom of God in a mystery, the hidden wisdom which God ordained before the ages for our glory, which none of the rulers of this age knew, for had they known, they would not have crucified the Lord of Glory. But as it is written: "Eye has not seen or ear heard, nor have entered into the heart of man the things prepared for those who love Him." But God has revealed them to us through the Spirit.

Here are just some of the details about the "hidden wisdom" revealed to us as we pray in His Spirit:

- God has wisdom greater than any worldly wisdom we see.
- Powers and principalities do not have access to this wisdom.
- The authority of demonic forces is limited.
- There is wisdom that has been hidden since the beginning of time, for His glory.
- Through the redemptive cross of Jesus Christ, we have access to this wisdom.
- God is prepared to release this wisdom to us as we get to know Him intimately through prayer.

- This wisdom will overthrow high places and release captives.
- Wisdom dismantles demonic structures and dethrones thrones of iniquity.

When the Lord showed this to me, I knew any demonic force holding a territory captive could not withstand the wisdom that God will release to His people. I knew that if the Spirit of the Lord burdened me to pray for a city, I had authority to gain the keys for the release of its inhabitants. This is a day when the Lord is extending a fresh call of prayer to His people. There is a purpose-filled urgency. He will show us a specific territory to conquer as it really is and say to us, *"Overcome every obstacle that is keeping these people from coming to know Me. Open the door for My House to be built within them so that they may experience My Love throughout eternity. Through prayer, gain wisdom that will dethrone the thrones of iniquity wherever they have been established. Then establish My Throne that many may worship Me and gain life everlasting!"*

This is how entire cities will experience salvation. This is how we will overthrow thrones of iniquity and see God's covenant plan for whole territories flourish in days ahead. In Daniel 10, we find Daniel seeking God with intensity for 21 days. At that point, the Ancient of Days sent the aid of Michael, the Archangel. Revelation was then released into the earth realm—revelation that we are walking in today.

Daniel's vision is recorded in 7:21-22: "I was watching; and the same horn was making war against the saints, and prevailing against them, until the Ancient of Days came, and a judgment was made in favor of the saints of the Most High, and the time came for the saints to possess the kingdom." In this passage we see that the Ancient of Days is going to favor us (the saints) in days ahead. Make no mistake, the time *will* come for the saints to possess the kingdom. That means we *will* take dominion, govern, prevail and dominate the world powers around us.

However, in verses 24 and 25 we find this:

The ten horns are ten kings who shall arise from this kingdom. And another shall rise after them, He shall be different from the first ones, and shall subdue three kings. He shall

speak pompous words against the Most High, shall persecute the saints of the Most High, and shall intend to change
times and law. Then the saints shall be given into his hand
for a time and times and half a time.

Notice what Scripture says the enemy does. He will attempt to
change both *times* and *law*. There will be a great struggle in days
ahead as Satan attempts to persecute the saints by getting us out of
God's timing or controlling us so that we can't enter into God's
timing. One of his tactics will be to change the laws around us. Many
laws are being and will be developed to stop or constrict God's children from operating in freedom. This is why it is so critical for us
to understand God's timing and the spiritual boundaries He has
given us through His law, not the world's. If not, deception will easily enter into our lives.

Trial by Fire—and Lions

Daniel teaches us another important lesson through his revelation
experience with the Ancient of Days. Notice that prior to his grand
vision came his lions' den experience. The thing I most like about
Daniel is his consistency in praying and seeking the Lord in the
midst of adversity. In truth, what often got him in that hard and
trying place was his consistent prayer life. He prayed three times a
day. When decrees and governmental shifts occurred that forbade
seeking a Higher Source, he did not change his communion with
God but kept his consistency in seeking revelation. When jealousy
and devised evil came against him, he consistently prayed. When he
was in the lions' den, I do not think he changed his consistent praying. Therefore, God sustained him in the face of what could have
been catastrophe. Consistent praying overcomes our adversary!

Daniel's lions' den experience shows us the war that all of God's
saints will have in days ahead. We will have to maneuver our way
past ungodly decrees that attempt to stop our communication with
a holy God. I believe it's important to understand that Daniel did
not defy the governmental decree. The decree actually stated that
citizens could not pray in public or request a specific blessing from

another god. Daniel went to his room and prayed. The ungodly authorities then worked this against him in an attempt to overthrow God's covenant man who had been positioned for a time such as this. I actually believe God came down as the Lion of Judah and shut the mouth of the other lions that could have martyred Daniel for his faith. Daniel's faith overcame in the pit. Therefore, God gave him access to a greater revelation of Himself. He also showed him in chapter 7 that all of God's people would be persecuted in the future and the enemy would try to "wear down their minds." But eventually, we would prevail.

The Political-Religious Handshake

Daniel was an influencer in the political arena. His faith never once kept him detached from his governmental duties. I believe God's people can follow his example. We should be right in the middle of politics and should influence the government. With the wisdom of God at our disposal, we can look at the past to understand the present. Yet we must always understand that we are from a Kingdom above all kingdoms. Although earthly kingdoms can reflect the kingdom of God, we as His people must always demonstrate our Kingdom identity no matter what earthly citizenship we hold. Ultimately, we serve a higher purpose.

Judas had a major problem with this. He wanted Jesus to change the earthly kingdom to benefit the people of that day. Jesus kept saying, "But My kingdom is not like this kingdom." Judas could not grasp this, and as a result, his political ambition and unrestrained zealous attitude caused him to betray the One who came to redeem him from the prison of this world. Judas was the perfect example of what I term "the handshake between the political and religious arenas." His desire was to use religious power for political means, and vice versa.

I believe this is why Jesus said, "Take heed, beware of the leaven of the Pharisees and the leaven of Herod" (Mark 8:15). This was one of Jesus' major warnings to us as His children! There is a fine line between taking dominion in the sphere of authority that God has placed us in and falling into the snare of the ruling system of the day. Judas fell into this trap, as have countless others.

How do politics and religion come together to stop the kingdom of God from freely advancing in the earth? That is the heart of this chapter. The ungodly union of politics and religion is one of the greatest wars we face. We must always remember that Jesus never once gratified the Pharisees who longed for Him to validate His identity with signs and miracles. Their motive was impure because their ultimate goal was to ensnare Him. Religious forces long to ensnare the move of God in the earth. They want to have control over it rather than yielding power to an unseen, higher force. Jesus was grieved over the hardened hearts of these people. Religion hardens our heart. When a religious group of leaders refuses to keep moving in what God is doing, they become political. In this case, Herod was also desirous to see miracles wrought by Christ. When Jesus did not satisfy either side, the two forces joined together to stop what Christ was doing.

Jesus was trying to present the Father's plan to the people. He wanted to show them the wonderful kingdom of God that turns every earthly reign upside down. But I doubt the disciples of Jesus' day understood what He was really trying to teach them. Likewise, I am not sure today's disciples understand the principle of how religion will always come dangerously into agreement with governmental forces to stop the move of God.

The Church Loses Power by Yielding to Government

This handshake between religion and politics always creates a loss of power in the earth. In June 2005, I saw this firsthand when I traveled to the "Three Romes": Moscow, Istanbul/Constantinople and Rome. The purpose of this trip was to retrace, pray and break the structures associated with the lost power of the historical Church so that the Church today can enter into a new power. In Moscow, the Russian Orthodox Church called itself the "Third Rome." The church embellished its status as the Third Rome and brought all Christianity into the realm of Russian control. The belief was that Moscow was chosen by God.

The second leg of our journey led us to Istanbul, the Second Rome. Istanbul is a beautiful city that blends several cultures. Once known as Constantinople, Istanbul was declared the "New Rome" when Constantine established the city as the headquarters of the Roman Empire in the fourth century. In its early history, the streets of the capital were sometimes decked with flowers and drenched with blood on the same day. Such clashes were usually a result of conflicts between religious and governmental structures. Constantine, who became the sole master of the Roman Empire, determined to make this city the future capital of the world by producing a unity of religion and blending worship with culture. As you enter the city today, you see mosques surrounded by minarets across the skyline. Altogether there are 2,400 mosques around the city, some of which are the largest in the world. Yet our guide informed us that although the population of the city accepts the religion of Islam, the vast majority does not practice this (or perhaps any) form of organized worship. Most do not gather as ritually prescribed.

It was from Constantinople that the official "paganization" of the Church was carried out, resulting in hundreds of thousands of believers dying for their faith. For this reason, one of the main places we purposed to visit was the Church of Hagia Sophia (Holy Wisdom), which was a perfect picture of what happened in the Church during this time. This enormous structure was originally built by Constantine as the showplace of his new church, and was later reconstructed by Justinian. For its construction, the builders used huge marble columns from the temple of Diana in Ephesus, along with other items from a pagan temple in Pergamum (which John called "the seat of Satan"). This was a physical picture of how elements of paganism were incorporated into the Church, resulting in a new religion that had worldly power but lacked the presence and power of God.

The domed Hagia Sofia is physically impressive, standing 175 feet high with a dome of 102 feet in diameter. In fact, this was the largest church in the world for almost 1,000 years. Justinian hoped this immense church would turn a new page for the Church in that region. However, we discovered that the church ended up as a mixture of various religions. In 1453, the Hagia Sophia was converted to a mosque with the arrival of the Turks. In fact, most of the other mosques in the city were patterned after this world-renowned "Christian" structure.

A Loss Through Unity

As the architect behind this city's fusion of religions, Constantine was arguably the most influential figure in the Church's inclusion into politics. A history shaper, he made Christianity, which had suffered bloody persecution until that time, the religion of the empire. His goal was to blend the monotheistic worship systems of Judaism and Christianity with the worship of the sun, the veneration of Mithras (which we will discuss later) and other pagan forms of religion. He longed to produce a unity of religion.

Consequently, this combination of worship removed the persecution of the Christians—but only for those who were not extreme in their worship. Constantine not only protected Christians, but he also protected the heathens' rights. He suppressed any divination or magic that was being using privately in homes and declared that any practice of heathen worship would be done on public altars and in sacred places. In general, he prohibited family sacrifice and made everything public, which formed a so-called "unity of religion."

In actuality, what this did to the Christian Church was slowly dilute its foundational beliefs and God-ordained practices. Most of the early believers were strongly rooted in Jewish culture. Acts 15:5 speaks of church members who were still actively involved in the party of the Pharisees. In Acts 21:20, James boasts that in Jerusalem there were many "tens of thousands" of Jews who believed in Jesus yet remained zealous for the Torah. Repeatedly, we see Paul and other members of the church still taking Nazarite vows, practicing Jewish rituals, observing Sabbaths and feasts and bringing offerings to the Jerusalem Temple (see Acts 21:23-26; 24:14-17). Paul never spoke of his Judaism in the past tense. He proudly proclaimed, "I am a Jew!" (22:3) and "I am a Pharisee!" (23:6). In the very last chapter of Acts, Paul meets with Jewish leaders in Rome and assures them that he still identifies himself with Judaism and has done nothing to violate Jewish customs.

Yet Constantine's tossing of Christianity into a great melting pot of religion led many believers to incorporate pagan practices into their faith, while abandoning their Jewish roots. Persecution may have lessened for the Early Church, but there was a great loss to God's original intent of influence and power that He desired for us to display in the earth. What exactly was lost?

- The ability of Christians to gather in vibrant worship
- The Hebraic attitude toward God
- The Hebraic attitude toward Scripture
- A loss of the emphasis on the home
- A loss of the Hebraic approach to life
- A joyful Christianity, as instead poverty and suffering were seen as virtues
- A loss in the biblical cycle of life

The God-given Jewish celebrations were designed to teach God's children the principles of life with Him. God instituted the feasts so that His covenant people would always be reminded of who He was and what He had done in the past. These feasts were also given to remember God's great acts of salvation, deliverance and healing grace. He knew that if we would remember His power displays of the past, we would have faith to see Him move today and in the future. By participating in the prescribed feasts (Passover, Pentecost and Tabernacles), Israel's worship would remain fresh, vibrant and properly aligned with its Maker.

Outwardly the Church as an institution continued to grow. Conversions had once been proven through manifestations of God's power. Beginning with Constantine, conversions were now obtained through economic incentives, as well as governmental and military power and alignment. This brought entire nations into "Christendom." The Church gained wealth and prestige, but lost its true identity.

Rome: The Original Shift Away from God's Best

If Constantinople saw a persecution-less yet diluted Christianity, Rome was where the Church's "Great Compromise" was made under Constantine. One of the most interesting places we visited during our travel to the "Three Romes" was the Cathedral of San Clemente. In the basement of this church, excavators have discovered a Mithras temple. Mithras was the god worshiped by Constantine, and it was from Mithraism that many pagan concepts were brought into the Church. In the Basilica of San Clemente, the Mithras temple was literally the foundation of the church. What a picture of what happened to the Church in Rome in the fourth century! Constantine divorced the Church from its biblical foundation and married it to a pagan one—and the Church accepted this to avoid persecution. Yet as long as the Church had been willing to endure persecution, it moved with great spiritual power and had overcome the Roman system. When the Church compromised, it immediately came under the Roman system, changing its makeup from that time on.

I share this because of the lesson we find in Daniel's life. Daniel endured persecution from three other leaders who devised a law to rob him of religious freedom. As he persevered and held fast to his convictions, the Ancient of Days revealed Himself to him. Persecution entails the wearing down of our minds and emotions by the enemy. This is exactly what will occur and begin to intensify in the future. The snare for us will be to join in a political handshake with government versus continuing to be on the cutting edge of God's reformation plan in the earth.

Breaking the Fear of Persecution

During our time in Rome, we knew that to reverse what had been done and break the Church's compromise with pagan religions, we needed to identify with places where persecution and imprisonment had occurred. We asked the Lord to order our steps, to send us to key places where we could unbraid the religious cord that seems to be choking out the power for God's Church today. Sometimes we are unaware of how religious influences of our past keep us from being free in the present to worship and operate in boldness. We also remain in the dark as to how principalities hold religious structures in place. Our goal was to change that.

We began our first day by visiting the Mamertine Prison. This is a rock-hewn, cave-like underground prison where both Peter and Paul were likely held for their faith. While there, we prayed for an anointing to be released to the Body to persevere under persecution and to finish the course in victorious faith. We began to clap, sing and praise. Despite the officials' protest, we continued. Sincere praise is always hated by the religious-political structure.

We then went to Circus Maximus, where much of the martyrdom of the Early Church took place. We asked the Lord to redeem the blood in this earth through worship, and to teach us how to partner with the blood of the martyrs. *Let the sound that is in the ground precede us so that the sound of heaven is released!* As I have written in other books, every time persecution of faith results in bloodshed, the ground cries out until the earth is reconciled back to God and the enemies of the gospel are dealt with.

As you visit many of the churches in Rome, it becomes easy to spot the power of religion in operation. One place that stands out in my mind is Santa Maria Maggiore. The ceiling of this building is covered in gold patterns, and in the front quadrant's ceiling section, there is an image of a bull. It is no coincidence that the bull god, or Aipes, was a Mithraic image. We stood under that image and declared that the influence of Mithraism in the foundation of the Church would be broken. We also broke lines of communication between the living and the dead. Throughout the building you could see symbols of spiritism that were aligned to hold the Church captive. We asked the Spirit of God to confuse the communication between the Queen of Heaven and religious systems of the earth, and we declared that many who are held captive by these confused religious forms would be set free.

We also visited the baptismal room, which features the symbol of the evil eye overlooking the baptismal. In front of the baptismal is the skull and cross bones aligned with the head of a cobra. These were all symbols used to produce fear in individuals so that they would repent. We asked God to unlock the defilement that holds individuals captive even from infant baptism and that keeps them from ever experiencing a true relationship with the living God.

Another strategic place we visited was the Cathedral of St. John Laterano. As we entered this large structure, we noticed that the inscription directly above the entrance read "Christ the Savior Church." This was the same name of the large cathedral recently built in Moscow. The Cathedral of St. John Laterano was originally built by Constantine and is still the Basilica of the Pope. This cathedral has statues of each of the original apostles. We began to decree that a restored true apostolic foundation would arise in the Church. We also asked the Holy Spirit to move mightily on the Catholic leadership, which will produce great confusion and division. Many times the Lord brings the sword of division to produce His will. There at St. John Laterano, I prophesied of a major division in the Catholic leadership that would be in the news by October 2005. (Pope John Paul II died on April 2, 2005, which called for a new pope to be elected.)

As we left, we noticed a tile mosaic in the floor picturing the dove returning to Noah in the ark with an olive branch in its mouth. This was the Scripture reference from Genesis that the Lord had given me at the beginning of the year—that by the tenth month we would begin to see the new foundation. All 10 of us circled around that dove and decreed that at the end of October there would be a noticeable change in the Catholic religious structure.

We ventured to the famous St. Peter's Square, where the Pope comes out to speak before massive crowds. In the center of this grand square is an obelisk, which has Egyptian origins. When the Pope comes out to speak, many times the shadow of this obelisk overshadows him as he communicates. I find it interesting that Isaiah 30:1-3 says, "'Woe to the rebellious children,' says the LORD, 'who take counsel but not of Me, and who devise plans, but not of My Spirit, that they may add sin to sin; who walk to go down to Egypt, and have not asked My advice . . . and trust in the shadow of Egypt!'" The Pope's voice is heard throughout the world.

This produces a system of communication that holds countless people captivated to a wrong structure of worship.

We declared that the shadow linked with Egyptian idolatrous worship would be removed from the communication system of the Catholic Church. We felt like this was the place for true communion to be restored, and so we stood around the obelisk, took communion and declared that the lines of communication that produce false worship around the world would begin to be broken and confused. There is also a place in St. Peter's Square where you can stand and, no matter what point you look at, all the columns on that side of the square are perfectly aligned. We each stood on that spot and made a declaration of realignment concerning the authority of the Church. This was a powerful time of intercession.

A Foundation of Mithraism

Our last place to visit was the Basilica of St. Clemente. As I mentioned above, this particular cathedral was built on the ruins of the cult of Mithras. The Christian Church compromised and, as part of Constantine's "unity of religion," allowed much of this cult's beliefs to infiltrate the minds of believers. Because it has such a stronghold in the history of the Church, I feel it's important that we understand the beliefs involved in Mithraism to expose the counterfeit attempts of the enemy.

Mithraism was a foundation of Constantine's worship, as it was for thousands of his warriors who spread their beliefs as they expanded the Roman Empire. The god Mithras was originally a Persian deity considered to be the mediator between humanity and Ahura Mazda, the god of light. Mithras overcame evil and brought life, both animal and vegetable, to humankind. Statues of this god characteristically show him holding a bull by the nostrils while plunging a knife into its neck. The Romans identified Mithras with the sun god and held three conflicting theories related to his birth: (1) He was born of an incestuous relationship between Ahura Mazda and his own mother; (2) he was born of an ordinary mortal; (3) he was born from a rock. Only males were allowed to worship this god, and those who were initiated formed associations bound together by secret rites and symbols peculiar to their cult. These associations met regularly with a designated leader, sometimes in houses. More often than not, however, the worshipers of Mithras met in a structure called a Mithraeum, designed to imitate the cave in which Mithras killed the bull, which was the central act of this cult's mythology.

Having no professional clergy to conduct ceremonies, the cult would initiate new believers through seven stages that supposedly prepared the initiate for ascent to the god of light. (Male children were even allowed to participate in the lower stages.) In ancient rural settings, part of this initiation actually included slaying a bull. The initiate was placed in a pit covered by an iron grate. The bull was then slain on the grate, while the initiate attempted to catch its sacred blood with his tongue.[3]

Of all the "mystery religions," as they are classified, Mithraism became the strongest rival to Christianity. This was primarily because of the virtual mimicry of Mithraism's major belief components to those of Christianity. Like Christ, Mithras was supposedly born of a virgin (obviously proving two of the birth theories wrong) in a stable around the time of the winter solstice, and was attended by shepherds who brought gifts. Interestingly enough, the emperor Aurelian declared December 25 to be the official birthday of Mithras around 270 AD. However, in 313 AD, Constantine, despite being a follower of Mithras, declared December 25 the official birthday of *Jesus* and adopted the "cult" of Christianity as the state religion.

Sunday was the holy day of Mithraism, and followers ate a sacred meal on the day. After his redemptive work on Earth was finished, Mithras partook of a last supper with some of his devotees and then ascended to heaven, where he continues to assist the faithful in their struggle against demons. Mithraism also held a belief in a final judgment. Those who worshiped Mithras believed in eternal life for the righteous and punishment for the wicked. The world would finally be destroyed by fire. The belief was that Mithras did not die, but instead ascended to heaven. From there he would return at the end of time to raise the dead in a physical resurrection for a final judgment, sending the good to heaven and the wicked to hell. Often in artistic renderings Mithras is shown with a nimbus, or halo, around his head. The head leader of Mithraism was called a "papa" (pope), who ruled from Vatican Hill in Rome. They also celebrated *sacramenta* (a consecrated meal of bread and wine), in remembrance of the last supper of Mithras.[4]

Why am I sharing this and focusing on so many details? Because we must realize the degree to which false religions will try to duplicate the power of God that is found in His people. When we lose the power of God and choose form, we develop a foundation of operation that is contrary to the will of God and instead embrace demonic hosts that lead us astray from God's purpose. First Timothy 4:1-5 explicitly states:

> Now the Spirit expressly says that in latter times some will depart from the faith, giving heed to deceiving spirits and doctrines of demons, speaking lies in hypocrisy, having their own conscience seared with a hot iron, forbidding to marry, and commanding to abstain from foods which God created to be received with thanksgiving by those who believe and know the truth. For every creature of God is good, and nothing is to be refused if it is received with thanksgiving; for it is sanctified by the word of God and prayer.

First John 2:18,22 states:

> Little children, it is the last hour; and as you have heard that the Antichrist is coming, even now many antichrists have come, by which we know that it is the last hour. . . . Who is a liar but he who denies that Jesus is the Christ? He is antichrist who denies the Father and the Son.

And 1 John 4:3 says:

> Every spirit that does not confess that Jesus Christ has come in the flesh is not of God. And this is the spirit of the

Antichrist, which you have heard was coming, and is now
already in the world.

By looking deeper into the ancient Mithras cult, many alarms
should go off in our spirits about our worship forms today.
The Roman cult shifted the Church far away from God's original
intent of power and His ascended life for us in the earth. When we
move from His plan of governing His people and choose an earthly form, we lose power and enter into captivity. We shift from a
heavenly pattern to an earthly pattern that reflects an earthly government. We lose the power of God and are left with form invaded by demonic hosts!

This is not a new ploy of the enemy. Actually, this is the same
thing that happened to the Israelites when they came out of Egypt
and were unwilling to wait for the Lord to establish His law as their
guiding worship boundary. They made the golden calf and went
with a different form. We must wait carefully for the Lord's justice
this hour. Our problem is that we have given over so much power
to the enemy that we are no longer being ruled in a society governed by God's authority.

Which Way Is It?

Governments are shifting. We currently find an ongoing worldwide political battle over which way administrations will lean: left
or right. The *Britannica Concise Encyclopedia* links the political left
to egalitarianism in its desire for the people to control every major
state institution. "Leftists tend to be hostile to the interests of tra-
ditional elites, including the wealthy and members of the aristoc-
racy, and to favor the interests of the working class. They tend to
regard social welfare as the most important goal of government."[5]

On the other extreme is the right, which in the United States
is synonymous with conservatism. As *The Columbia Encyclopedia*
explains, "Conservatives value the wisdom of the past and are generally opposed to widespread reform of society."[6] They generally
prefer a limited means of social welfare.

So which is right—*correct*, that is—and which is wrong? Left or right: Which way should we lean? We must remember, the nation of America was not birthed out of conservatism, despite what many Christians believe. Nor was our faith birthed out of a conservative philosophy. Leftist governments usually fall into rebellion and drift from the moral justice of God. Yet given the history of both sides, I am not sure that either of these is right or wrong in practice. And here is where Kingdom people many times get mixed up: They model God's kingdom after civil structure, and, as a result, go to war with the left or the right. However, we are a people with a different foundation.

Both the left and the right contain philosophies that draw us both closer to and away from God's kingdom plan. What we must realize, however, is that the key to Kingdom rule is adhering to the Word of the Lord and biblical absolutes as our final authority, not the structure of one political party or system. For instance, while leftist governments speak to the needs of the working class and poor, the Bible has, for generations, addressed the issue of poverty and giving to those in need. In fact, in the Torah, the first five books of the Hebrew Scriptures, Moses relates that there was to be no poverty in the land:

> There shall be no needy among you—since the Lord your God will bless you in the land that the Lord your God is giving you as a hereditary portion—if only you heed the Lord your God and take care to keep all this Instruction that I enjoin upon you this day. For the Lord your God will bless you as He has promised you; you will extend loans to many nations, but require none yourself; you will dominate many nations, but they will not dominate you (Deut. 15:4-6, *JSB*).

From the establishment of God's people in the wilderness, there was an understanding that the Lord intended there be no poverty in Israel. He knew, however, that it would exist and has many instructions that address the treatment of the poor. Rashi, a

famous Jewish rabbi of the eleventh century, explains Deuteronomy
15:4-6 eloquently by writing, "At a time when you perform . . . the
will of the Omnipresent . . . there are destitute among others . . . but
not among you. And when you do not perform . . . the will of the
Omnipresent . . . there are destitute among you."[7] In *Everyman's
Talmud*, rabbinic sages teach that giving to the poor is not "an act of
grace on the part of the donor, but a duty. By giving alms he is merely practicing righteousness, i.e., performing a deed of justice."[8] In
other words, the Omnipresent One expects His children to care for
the needs of those around them.

In the New Testament, Jesus discusses doing charitable deeds
in the Sermon on the Mount (see Matt. 6:1-4). His main point in
this text was to show that giving was to be done in secret. If you give
in secret without ostentation, the Father will reward you openly.
Jesus also chided Judas by reminding him that the poor will always
be with us (see Matt. 26:11). I believe He was also revealing the
Father's heart to us over the need for extravagance at times.

The key to the Early Church was that its government ruled
their gatherings, and from their gatherings they influenced society. Their apostolic rule that we find in Acts 2:44-45 reflected the
way they operated in their deeds. That Body of believers provided
for all who were in need in their assemblies. It appears that they
made a concerted effort to provide for the poor.

A Lean to the Left

Throughout history there have been countries where social movements, voting or revolution have changed the government. Many
of these changes have been born out of economic depravation and
collapsing economies. During the last century there were numer-
ous instances when nations moved to the left as a result of national leaders who brought great harm to their nation.

One such country where this occurred was Germany. After
World War One, the German economy experienced many financial difficulties. France invaded a part of the nation to seize coal
deposits and cover unpaid reparations. To pay the workers at
these mines, the German government devalued the Reichsmark.

This backfired dramatically, as from July 1922 to the end of 1923, the mark went from 493 to the dollar to 4.2 trillion to the dollar! The government eventually stabilized the economy, only to have the Great Depression of the 1930s hit. The German people soon became disillusioned with the status quo and turned to the National Socialist German Workers Party, otherwise known as The Nazi Party. Hitler became Chancellor of Germany in 1933, and the rest is history.[9] Through him, the antichrist system seized control of the country and attempted not just to annihilate God's covenant people, the Jews, and seize their resources, but to take control of the world. It was not his time.

In the last few decades, Latin America has seen a move toward the left. Nations such as Venezuela, Uruguay and Bolivia have all moved toward more socialist governments. In an article concerning the shift to the left in this area of the world, journalist Benjamin Dangl writes, "These leaders, whose victory in office is due largely to these social movements in the street, have pledged to fight poverty and prioritize the needs of the people over the interests of Washington and international corporations."[10] Leaders such as Hugo Chávez and Evo Morales are promising to help the poor. In fact, Venezuela's Chavez has even offered to assist the poor in the United States with cheap heating oil.[11]

Change Can Be Good

I am not a political analyst, and I don't intend for this chapter to dissect the various governmental movements of the world. My point is simply this: Governments change. Some governments can even take a radical, structural, 180-degree turn within a matter of years given an extreme condition. Often those changes are necessary for the survival of the country. Yet the main problem does not lie in policies, presidents or political structures; it is in a continual disregard for the heavenly government of the Ancient of Days.

Israel went through its share of governmental changes in the Bible. One reason for these changes was the character and performance of the leadership, as was the case during the transition from Eli to Samuel to Saul. This was also true during the changeover from

Solomon to Rehoboam/Jeroboam, when the kingdom was split into the 10 northern tribes (Israel) and the two southern tribes (Judah).

In the early chapters of 1 Samuel, we find Eli serving Israel as both priest and judge (see 1 Sam. 2:27-30; 4:18). Eli's sons were given authority as priests; however, they were found to be corrupt before the Lord, and Eli did not correct them. God spoke to Eli through a servant and said, "Why do you kick at My sacrifice and My offering which I have commanded in My dwelling place, and honor your sons more than Me, to make yourselves fat with the best of all the offerings of Israel My people?" (1 Sam. 2:29).

These sons of Eli are described as not knowing the Lord (see 2:12), taking offerings meant for the Lord and for the people (see vv. 13-17), and having relations with the women who served at the entrance to the Tent of Meeting (see v. 22). In chapter 2 verse 12, these priests are referred to as "sons of Belial" (*KJV*), though some translations simply say they were "corrupt." The term *Belial* means "without profit, worthlessness; by extension destruction, wickedness."[12] *The Interlinear Bible* translates the phrase as "sons of worthlessness."[13] These sons did not know the Divine and had no reverence for Him. They were greedy and took that which was dedicated to the Lord and that which the Lord had determined was the property of the one giving an offering. Eli's sons were not content with the share prescribed for them. It is not surprising, then, that the Scripture states, "Nevertheless, they did not heed the voice of their father, because the Lord desired to kill them" (1 Sam. 2:25). During times of transition, godly leadership, with a mind to holiness, is imperative. Governing authorities should always be conscious of the needs of those they are shepherding, as well as the requirements the Lord has placed upon the flock.

God sent two prophetic words of warning to Eli. One came in the person of a man of God and the other through Samuel. In the first, the man of God prophesied to Eli and caused him to understand that he was about to lose both of his sons in a day, his lineage would be cut off from the priesthood, God would raise up a faithful priest for Himself, and those left in his house would come and bow down to this new anointed priest (see 1 Sam. 2:27-36).

In a second warning that confirmed the first prophetic word, the Lord spoke to Samuel: "For I have told him that I will judge his house forever for the iniquity which he knows, because his sons made themselves vile, and he did not restrain them. And therefore I have sworn to the house of Eli that the iniquity of Eli's house shall not be atoned for by sacrifice or offering forever" (1 Sam. 3:13-14). Since Eli knew what his sons were doing and did not correct them, his family suffered the consequences forever. The nation transitioned to a government ruled by a judge/prophet/priest (Samuel), and Eli's family did not participate in that leadership.

Leadership Issues

Sadly, Samuel repeated the cycle with his own children. In 1 Samuel 8, we read that Samuel's sons, Joel and Abijah, desired "dishonest gain, took bribes, and perverted justice" (v. 3). According to one Old Testament dictionary, "dishonest gain" means to "take a cut . . . greased palms and expenses padded."[14] Samuel's sons lacked the moral character qualities required for priesthood. The writer of 1 Samuel relates the following immediately after the description of the sons: "All the elders of Israel assembled and came to Samuel at Ramah, and they said to him, 'You have grown old, and your sons have not followed your ways. Therefore appoint a king for us, to govern us like all other nations'" (1 Sam. 8:4-5).

The sins of the leaders caused the people to request a different form of government. This request might seem appropriate, except for the fact that they were essentially rejecting the Lord as their King. Put in terms I previously mentioned about governments making an about-face, Israel simply went from one wrong extreme to the other. The people needed a change in structure but went too far—I believe, too far left—and ended up with a structure God never intended.

A king was going to cost the Israelites. First Samuel 8 continues by describing what the new king would require of them: a tithe of their grain and vintage, along with the best of their fields, vineyards and olive groves. Nevertheless, Israel still wanted a king.

Then there is the history of Solomon. Solomon was known for receiving from God unsurpassed wisdom. The Queen of Sheba came from her native land to see this great wise man. However, he turned his heart away from the Lord and built shrines to Chemosh and Molech. Scripture says this:

> The Lord was angry with Solomon, because his heart turned away from the Lord, the God of Israel, who had appeared to him twice and had commanded him about this matter, not to follow other gods; he did not obey what the Lord had commanded. And the Lord said to Solomon, "Because you are guilty of this—you have not kept My covenant and the laws which I enjoined upon you—I will tear the kingdom away from you and give it to one of your servants. But, for the sake of David, I will not do it in your lifetime. I will tear it away from your son. However, I will not tear away the whole kingdom; I will give your son one tribe, for the sake of My servant David and for the sake of Jerusalem which I have chosen" (1 Kings 11:9-13, *JSB*).

This prophecy was fulfilled by the hand of God. He sent a prophetic word to Jeroboam. Ahijah revealed to him that he would be the leader of the 10 tribes being taken away from Solomon's son, so Jeroboam waited in Egypt until the death of Solomon. After Solomon's son, Rehoboam, ascended the throne, Jeroboam led the people of Israel to Rehoboam and asked him to relieve them of the burdensome service that his father had placed on them through all of his building projects. Rather than listening to the wise counsel of the elders who spoke to his father, Rehoboam listened to "the young men who had grown up with him, who stood before him" (1 Kings 12:8). Rehoboam denied their request, which caused the people to rebel and throw off his leadership. The tribes were adamant about their decision: "Now when all Israel saw that the king did not listen to them, the people answered the king, saying: 'What share have we in David? We have no inheritance in the son of Jesse. To your tents, O Israel! Now, see to your own house, O David!' So Israel departed to their tents" (1 Kings 12:16).

The 10 northern tribes cast off the entire Davidic dynasty because Rehoboam refused to lighten their burden. Thus, what God had spoken prophetically was accomplished in the earth. The Lord was not pleased when the leadership of the nation stepped away from His Law. In fact, the king was to copy the Law with the implication that it was a guide to rule by. He removed leaders from their positions of authority when there was a major violation of His Word. This removal manifested in sudden death (Eli's sons), in a request for a change in government (in the case of Samuel), and in a refusal to be governed by the Davidic dynasty (in the case of Jeroboam and the 10 northern tribes).

It is interesting that in each of these cases, the general public disliked leadership that did not have godly character. This character was evident in their treatment of the people and their lack of obeying the Lord and loving His Word. Remember that people usually opt for a leftist government when they see that their leadership is not working for the country's good but have become selfish, greedy, self-serving and, in many cases, too powerful. It is then that people will tend to try to overhaul the status quo and force a change in government. Leftist governments have a reputation for being concerned for the working class, the average person on the street. When people have been under a government that does not appear to be that way, they look to leftist political parties for help. As we have already discussed, this can serve as a snare.

The Real Kingdom

These are wonderful but dangerous times. The Body of Christ is maturing, but it's not yet mature. Perhaps more than at any other time in history, the Church is in a crisis of competition for harvest with other organized religious forces, including Islam, Buddhism, Hinduism and a host of other -Isms. Confrontations with demonic forces behind opposing belief systems will be the norm for the future, and God is calling His Body to prepare for the warfare we are entering even now. Part of our preparation is to develop an understanding of our role in the future establishment of governments. Both the Body of Christ and the governments of nations are already changing drastically. Through these changes, however, our most important understanding is how we are aligned in Kingdom government.

Kingdom rule is different. The Kingdom is *good news*! In the Kingdom, Christ accomplishes His mediational authority. He rules in the earth realm *through* His heavenly Kingdom, with His subjects responding to Him from both an individual and a collective identity. In other words, we respond to Him as both a single citizen of His kingdom and through the corporate Body. This is essential to understand if we are going to affect a territory.

Every kingdom has a king. This king has ultimate authority over the rule of his kingdom. Yet through the Lord's divine plan, we as His subjects have been given Kingdom power. We can enter and rule *with* Him. We find this unique system of governmental rule expounded upon in Ephesians 4:11-16:

> And He Himself gave some to be apostles, some prophets, some evangelists, and some pastors and teachers, for the equipping of the saints for the work of ministry, for the edifying of the body of Christ, till we all come to the unity of the faith and of the knowledge of the Son of God, to a perfect man, to the measure of the stature of the fullness of Christ; that we should no longer be children, tossed to and fro and carried about with every wind of doctrine, by the trickery of men, in the cunning craftiness of deceitful plotting, but, speaking the truth in love, may grow up in all things into Him who is the head—Christ—from whom the whole body, joined and knit together by what every joint supplies, according to the effective working by which every part does its share, causes growth of the body for the edifying of itself in love.

We also find the order of God's kingdom listed in 1 Corinthians 12:28: "And God has appointed these in the church: first apostles, second prophets, third teachers, after that miracles, then gifts of healings, helps, administrations, varieties of tongues." In Ephesians 2:20, the foundation of this Kingdom government is once again mentioned as "having been built on the foundation of the apostles and prophets, Jesus Christ Himself being the chief cornerstone."

The Kingdom is made up of people who have submitted themselves to be ruled by God. His kingdom is *not* made up of law but is governed by grace. His kingdom has an administration. There are ways that He "does ministry" in His kingdom. Every kingdom has a culture; so does this Kingdom have a culture. I believe this is the most difficult concept for us to understand. Many times we become a part of the King of kings' kingdom, yet we continue to operate in the culture of this world. No!

The Lord's kingdom is *not* based just on needs. He has ways to take care of all the needs in His kingdom. It is *not* based on worldly patterns. When King David deviated from the Lord's pattern, he found himself in trouble or creating trouble. It was the same way with Moses; when he struck the rock the second time instead of speaking to it, he deviated from the pattern of heaven. This caused him to lose the right to enter into the promise that he was pressing and leading the people toward. We can never forget that God's kingdom cannot be comprehended by the natural mind. Our mind is in transition until it is fully overcome by the Spirit of grace. Until then, the carnal mind remains in enmity with God (see Rom. 8:5-8).

One final thought on God's kingdom: It cannot be obtained by ambition. This is what Judas had to learn. It is easy to point the condescending finger at Judas, but we must remember that John and James, the Sons of Thunder, had to learn the same lesson. Jesus said to them, "You do not know what manner of spirit you are of" (Luke 9:55). The Kingdom cannot be postponed. It is here and now within those who have submitted to the King. It is filled with glory. And it is God's intent for the ambassadors of that Kingdom to carry His glory throughout the world until the whole world has experienced true transformation—the kind that brings *real* life and freedom to all!

Be Like Daniel!

Considering all that we've talked about in this chapter—the fight for power, the interweaving of religion and politics, the shifting of governments, the basis for real earthly authority—most readers will probably be left with one question: *What is my role in all this?* It's a great question, one that we must always ask of our King. *Lord, what would You have me do for You?*

One of the best examples I can think of to answer this question is once again Daniel. This young man, who possessed wisdom far beyond his years, lived in a civil kingdom but represented another Kingdom. He ministered to the king of Babylon, yet he served the King of the Jews. He ruled in the midst of exile and captivity. Earlier in this chapter, I talked about the Ancient of Days. Daniel declared of the Lord, "He reveals deep and secret things . . . light dwells with him" (Dan. 2:22). It is no coincidence that when this prophet viewed the Ancient of Days, he observed that "his eyes were like torches of fire" (10:6). When the apostle John saw the throne of God and the Lamb, the apostle observed one with "seven eyes" that he identified more than once as "a flame of fire." Zechariah declared that these seven flames of fire are the "eyes of the Lord, which scan to and fro throughout the whole earth" (Zech. 4:10).

When we look *into* the eyes of the King, that which is carnal within us melts away. When we look *through* the eyes of the King, we see the world as He sees the world. We see the nations as He sees the nations. We see our assignments differently. When we look through His eyes, we see how to rule and take dominion.

We need to be like Daniel if we are going to make it in days ahead. Daniel had an excellent spirit. We develop excellent spirits by allowing our minds to be transformed to reflect the Kingdom culture that we are a part of. Daniel allowed his character to be tested. He understood how the Kingdom that he was a part of operated in revelation and information. And he developed prophetic interpretation skills that gave him a greater understanding than anyone in the earthly kingdom around him. In other words, he received Kingdom revelation. He was separated unto God. Therefore, the supernatural atmosphere around him was not a threat to him. He knew that he could gain revelation from God and triumph over the occult. He understood past prophecy so that he could prophesy into the future. He had an uncompromising, disciplined prayer life. He did not fear the future but simply predicted it. He saw into a different spiritual dimension and then recorded what was being revealed to him. He had a Kingdom understanding. He understood how to operate in the earthly kingdom he was a part of, called Babylon; but he operated from a holy God who ruled heaven and Earth.

If we desire to represent the Lord well in this earthly war over power, we must gain a Kingdom perspective just as Daniel did. God is greater than any earthly king or kingdom. He sees the hearts of religious leaders who manipulate their flocks for political purposes. He is aware of governmental shifts and is far above the latest political leaning. He establishes thrones and brings them down. And in His glorious wisdom, He has invited His people to rule and reign on this earth with Him!

CHAPTER 7

The Wealth War
Defining Your Boundaries

The first war humanity ever faced was in the Garden of Eden. There, the serpent approached Eve and convinced her to want something she could not have. Adam came in agreement with his wife, and the couple was immediately introduced to "greed and unbridled ambition," as one Bible commentator says.[1] By listening to the cunning serpent and then admiring the fruit, Eve acquired a desire that was so strong that it countered the expressed will and purpose of God. Together, she and Adam entered into a whole new world of unholy, unintended and unfulfilled desire that put them at war with their Maker.

I have talked about desire more than once in this book. In chapter 2, I made a connection between desire and the mind. I established that desire, in its basic, neutral form, prompts you to seek something to possess. What you desire becomes that which is most precious to you. Given that definition, we can safely say that desire ultimately leads to an appraisal of value. In the last chapter, I alluded to the link between power and desire. When desire goes awry and remains unchecked, there exists an open door for manipulation and compromise. Warfare is soon to follow. Without godly desire, we will remain in conflict with God, just as Adam and Eve came to be in the Garden.

Mention the word "desire" in a room full of people and you will undoubtedly get a varied response of associated words: "ambition," "lust," "power," "sex, "want." Yet what has been the one common thread through the majority of history's wars, divorces, arguments, conflicts and scandals? Money. The desire for material goods. In short, *wealth*.

It is human nature to want more. Yet in America, we have reached an all-time materialistic high—or should I say low? For decades, American culture has known nothing but plenty. We are a nation bursting at the seams with a belief in the almighty dollar— and why not? Those who can recall the lean years of the Great Depression are literally a dying generation. We have enjoyed abundance for so long that we now equate happiness with a fully loaded 401(k) and a diversified financial portfolio. That, of course, and a comfortable piece of real estate, the latest shiny SUV and all the high-tech gadgets a credit card can hold.

Clearly, our desire is out of alignment.

The Root of All Evil?

What is the Church to do in a culture enamored with possessions? Christ explicitly and repeatedly taught about the dangers of the love of money. In fact, we have all probably sat through enough sermons on tithing, giving or financial stewardship to know that money is a big deal to God. It is the one subject Jesus spoke about more than any other. And yet, as Christians, we have typically responded one of two ways to money throughout history: We have either looked down on it, holding up poverty and meagerness as the higher path to Kingdom living, or we have fallen in love with it, using an assortment of biblical misinterpretations to justify a lifestyle of excess.

It is time for us to align with God's thoughts on money and wealth. We must reformat our beliefs with His truth, not our own stigmas and misconceptions. Though it has become almost cliché to say this, we seem to forget again and again: *Money* is not the root of all kinds of evil—the *love* of money is (see 1 Tim. 6:10). I believe wealth is an essential element to the kingdom of God. And why not? He is, after all, the Creator (and therefore the Owner) of all things. He is the Master, the Giver, the Supplier; we are simply stewards. As Psalm 50:10 says, He owns "the cattle on a thousand hills"—and then some!

So why is wealth such a tough subject for the Church to grasp? If it is essential as a tool to expand influence and effectiveness—and ultimately to bring the harvest in—why are there so many conflicting thoughts and theories? Will the people of God finally understand His plan and position themselves to receive the wealth transfer in the future? Why have so many who at one time kept a proper perspective on money now fallen into its trap? What kind of power lies behind this undeniable force?

These are the questions we'll address in this chapter. Understand that I am merely scraping the tip of the iceberg in this chapter when it comes to addressing the issue of wealth and the Church. In fact, it is such a deep subject that I plan to write another book to go with this series that is primarily about the war over wealth. For now, however, we must grasp certain elements to adequately prepare ourselves for that war, which I believe will be one of the fiercest battles in the future.

Let the Boundary Wars Begin!

I grew up among the oil millionaires of Texas. My father was never one of these men, but we were surrounded by those who had hit the oil jackpot. One of the first things you learned when you lived around land that potentially held oil was the concept of boundaries. Owners took the boundaries of their land *very* seriously—and why wouldn't they, given the potential it held for changing their lives overnight? An established, legal boundary made the difference between who got rich and who didn't. From a more biblical perspective, it declared dominion and authority to both sides over their respective properties—which obviously became a bigger deal when oil or gas was discovered.

On the land my family owned, we not only had possession of the land, we also had the rights to the minerals of that land. If our land was ever sold, we still kept the mineral rights inside those boundaries. This was not uncommon in our area, which meant not only were there boundary wars, but there were wars to maintain the rights of what was underneath the surface of the land. Though our family lost the boundaries that encompassed the land we once owned, I still have the rights to many of the minerals underneath the land and inside those boundaries.

Dominion is always linked with boundaries. The question is, How will you occupy and rule in your sphere of authority? You see, boundaries are the personal property lines that each of us has been given. These come in all different forms. Henry Cloud and John Townsend, in their book *Boundaries*, share with us that boundaries can be physical: These help us to determine who may touch us and under what circumstances. Boundaries can be mental: These give us freedom to have our own thoughts and opinions. They can be emotional, helping us deal with our own feelings, attitudes, beliefs, behaviors, choices, values, limits, talents, thoughts and desires, and allowing us to disengage from the manipulative emotions of others. Boundaries can also be spiritual: These help us to distinguish God's will from our own and give us a renewed awe for our Creator. Spiritual boundaries also protect our beliefs and faith.[2]

There is and will continue to be a great war over boundaries. Individuals, people groups and entire nations will be jostling for authority through expansion of their boundaries. Yet what we must realize is that most often the greatest impetus behind this is not a need for more *land*; it is the want of greater *supply*. It is easy to grow dissatisfied with the supply lines established within our own boundaries and decide that we want to take something from someone else's boundary. This is how dominion wars began ages ago, and how they will continue to rage in the coming days.

As I mentioned earlier in this chapter, desire, if not sanctified, manifests as covetousness and leads us into lust and war, especially over what belongs to our neighbors. Desire is linked with the deepest longing we have. What we wish for and what activates our appetites are linked with desire. Even what begins as a godly pursuit of something can become evil if we ignore God's will for our lives. That desire turns into lust. Lust leads to covetousness. Covetousness leads to delusion. Delusion leads to murder. Murder leads to death and ungodly rule. Not only have we seen individuals go down this destructive path of misplaced desire, but also nations do the same.

The desire for material wealth drives the human race. However, this desire can become a destructive force in the earth if not channeled and submitted to God's rule. Even within the Church, if this current message of wealth transfer is not communicated properly, there will be many pitfalls that occur.

In days ahead, we will see many changing boundaries in the earth. There will be an attempt to illegally rearrange the boundaries of nations. Governments will align to overtake lands that were never destined to be overtaken. We must watch these wars carefully in the natural earth realm because they are linked with a quest for wealth.

An Eye for Every Dollar

Have you ever really examined a dollar bill? Right there, on the flip side of every George Washington, is an evil eye imbedded in the paper. To fully trace the history behind this would be difficult. However, there is a thread that goes from Nimrod to Horus to the contractor of Solomon's Temple, Hiram. This thread then weaves into the fabric of our nation's history via the royal society of English scientists and engineers dedicated to the wonders created by the "Great Architect of the Universe." In colonial Savannah, Georgia, we find the practices and order of the Grand Lodge making their way onto American soil. These were then propagated through the Freemason-dominated Founding Fathers of our nation and those associated with them. As the United States matured, this "secret society" based upon ancient Egyptian ways began to manifest its philosophy within American culture.

George Washington, our first president, took his oath of office on the Masonic Bible. In 1792, Washington laid the foundation of the White House. This was the same year the dollar was adopted as the unit of currency for the United States of America. In *The Hiram Key: Pharaohs, Freemasons, and the Discovery of the Secret Scrolls of Jesus*, Christopher Knight and Robert Lomas trace the lost secrets of Freemasonry from the beginnings of Egypt to and through our culture today:

The symbol for the dollar is an "S" with a double vertical strike-through, although, in print, it more usually appears today with a single vertical line: $. The "S" was borrowed from an old Spanish coin, but the two vertical lines were the Nasorean pillars of "Mishpat" and "Tsedeq," better known to the Masonic founders of the United States as "Boaz" and "Jachin," the pillars of the porchway to King Solomon's Temple.

Today the dollar bill bears the image of a pyramid with an eye set within it, which is the most ancient of all images in daily use because it has come down to us from before the time of Seqenenre Tao, escaping the purge of Egyptian motifs of the king-making ceremony caused by the prophet Ezekiel during the Babylonian captivity of the Jews. It represents God (in the form of Amen-Re) having an ever-present eye, casting His gaze over His people to judge every action they make in life, so that they will receive their just deserts in death. The whole basis of Ma'at was a measurement of the goodness done in life as seen by God. On the obverse of the one dollar bill is Brother George Washington, and on the now-defunct two dollar bill was the image of another famous Freemason, Brother Benjamin Franklin.[3]

Mammon in the Land

To reclaim our nation from the hold of these ancient spirits, we will have to be like the people of Israel when it was time to go into the Promised Land. We must recognize that we are up against occult forces that are holding the wealthiest nation of the world captive.

In Deuteronomy 8:18, we find that as the Lord prepared His covenant people to enter the land He promised, He told them that He would give them the power to get wealth. However, He also knew this would entail a spiritual war with Mammon. When you study Canaanite history, you find that the ruling god of the Canaanites was Baal. Baal's greatest ruling force in the earth was Mammon. The assignment or mission that Joshua and the tribes of Israel had to accomplish was transferring the wealth from all of the inhabitants of that region into God's covenant, Kingdom plan. Therefore, Mammon had to be defeated and the wealth held by its false worship transferred.

There are two economic systems on the earth. God has one economic system, and He teaches the necessity of being a good steward in this system. Satan has another economic system that is ruled by Mammon. This god, through demonic forces, controls the administration, transfer and distribution of wealth within this system. Matthew 6:24 refers to the complete difference between the two: "No one can serve two masters; for either he will hate the one and love the other, or else he will be loyal to the one and despise the other. You cannot serve God and mammon."

Mammon controls the world's finances, especially the issue of *supply* and *distribution*. He is assisted by other demons in the relay of wealth. Linked with the Babylon system, Mammon is both a prince of economics and of religions. Again, Scripture makes an allusion to the connection between these two forces when it says that we can transfer the *chayil* of sinners to the righteous (see Prov. 13:22). This Hebrew word means "wealth" or "riches." And yet it also has a militaristic connotation in its meanings of "army," "strength," "power" and—most fittingly for our future times—the spoils of war or fruits of warfare.[4] Placing this verse in the context of our war with Mammon, we have a promise that we will gather the spoils of war after triumphing over this earthly prince. There will be a transfer of wealth from his tight grip on the world's economy into the hands of God's kingdom army.

Avoid the Trap

This transfer of wealth into the hands of the Church sounds easier than it is, however. Not because God cannot bring it about (which He will), but because we all must be careful not to fall into the trap countless other believers have succumbed to. There is a subtlety to Mammon's ways, and he is excellent at enticing those who have a hidden love of wealth. This will be especially true in the future for those who will be handling the financial reaping from the transference.

Because the evil eye is involved in our money system, we must guard ourselves against the *love of money* (see 1 Tim. 6:10). *Philarguria*, the Greek word used for the phrase in that verse, refers to avarice (an inordinate desire to gain and possess wealth[5]) and to covetousness (an eagerness to possess something and an extreme greed for material wealth[6]). If we are not careful, this is the fruit that money can produce in our hearts.

We must also beware of what Mark 4:19 calls the "deceitfulness of riches." This deals primarily with the perceived power that comes with money. This produces a heart attitude that seeks to manipulate through false pretenses and appearances. Money is good when it is a servant to us. However, when we become a slave to its dominion, we are in trouble. The Word highlights several people who were cursed by wealth or had impure motives to gain wealth, such as Judas, Esau, Gehazi, Ananias, Sapphira, Lot and Achan. All of these individuals were trapped by impure desires. As we move forward against the enemy, we must renounce every issue of covertness that is tied to Mammon.

Wealth Can Become an Idol

Obviously, we all need material things. Provision is necessary for our lives to be functional in the world we are part of. However, the Lord says to be *in* the world but not *of* the world (see 1 John 2:15-17). When the Israelites left Egypt, God prompted the Egyptians to give them all kinds of goods. Exodus 12:36 says, "And the LORD had given the people in the sight of the Egyptians, so that they granted them what they requested. Thus, they plundered the Egyptians." Imagine these former slaves having their hands filled with silver and gold—from their masters! This is an example of what the Lord still wishes to do for His children as He breaks us out of the system we are in and points us toward His covenant blessings.

God gave Moses a detailed plan for His people, but the people did not wait on Moses. Instead, they grew impatient. They took all of the provision that had been given to them and, in their discouragement, wandered back to the same gods from which they had just been liberated! Exodus 32:4 says, "And he [Aaron] received the gold from their hands, and he fashioned it with an engraving tool, and made a molded calf. Then they said, 'This is your god, O Israel, that brought you out of the land of Egypt!'"

Not only was this molded calf a familiar god that had been in Egypt, but this bull calf was also worshiped in Canaan through the religious system that had been erected in Canaanite worship. When we do not offer God His portion and make our provision holy before Him, we open ourselves to the operation of the evil eye working over our finances. The evil eye aligns with our idolatry, and our idolatry is aligned with Mammon. As a result, we fall under the control of this false god.

Covetousness and Envy: A Green-Eyed Monster

Besides turning wealth into an idol, there are other ways we can veer from the plan of kingdom riches that God intends. Jesus said in Luke 12:15, "Take heed and beware of covetousness, for one's life does not consist in the abundance of the things he possesses." These words are particularly hard to swallow for us Americans who define ourselves by what we possess. We are used to coveting. To covet means to have a strong desire for something to the point of envy. This sin is linked with uncontrolled, inordinate, selfish emotional desire. That is why the enemy loves to lead us into illicit forms of idolatry. Idolatry misdirects our desires from a holy God to flesh-filled, demonic-inspired forms of lasciviousness. This is what James is talking about when he says, "Where do wars and fights come from among you? Do they not come from your desires for pleasure that war in your members?" (4:1).

It is essential during these times that we stay in God's covenant timing. When we acquire wealth out of God's timing and out of His way, we will get the curse that is on that wealth. Money can often have curses attached to it. If you don't believe this, I invite you to research all the mega-dollar lottery winners who, after winning, faced nothing but problems. Sickness. Betrayal. Family deaths. Divorce. Bankruptcy. If we don't know how to break the curse before we get cursed money, it's a sure thing that we will wind up with the same curse that money has carried through the years.

As Malachi 3 tells us, one way to break the curse off of money is to tithe and give offerings.

Covetousness and envy are not to be taken lightly, especially for today's believers. We must pray for the Body of Christ in this area. Envy is linked with the evil eye. When we look at something or someone else with an unholy desire, we fall into the power of this demon's grip. Envy is not just another form of jealousy—it is an open door for the enemy to work in our lives. Proverbs 27:4 underscores just how powerful envy is: "Wrath is cruel, and anger is outrageous; but who is able to stand before envy?" (*KJV*). Envy cannot be an acquaintance of any believer. It must be kept out of our lives at all costs. We must sanctify what God gives us and be satisfied with our portion.

Prospering Within the Boundaries

Being satisfied with our portion can be difficult when that portion amounts to barely scraping by. I have known many believers who believed that to "get closer to God," they needed to strip themselves of all possessions and live as the poor do. Their basis, as you might guess, is when Jesus told the rich young man, "If you want to be perfect, go, sell what you have and give to the poor, and you will have treasure in heaven" (Matt. 19:21). "Jesus always seemed to favor the poor," they add. It hasn't helped that since the first monk swore off material possessions, the established Church has held up the vow of poverty as a higher calling.

Let me set the record straight: Poverty was never in the heart of God, nor was it in His plan for humanity. When the Lord planted the Garden of Eden, He placed humans within its boundaries to cultivate and watch after that domain until it was multiplying and increasing. There was not to be *any* lack in the land. God continued to express this mindset in the earth when He called Abraham from Ur of the Chaldeans and promised him prosperity.

Abraham, in turn, proved himself a faithful steward. We see this first when he defeated those who had kidnapped his nephew, Lot, and responded by releasing his booty to Melchizedek the priest. In fact, I advise you to read the account in Genesis 14, which is one of the most important transitional chapters in the Bible. This chapter integrates war, giving, prosperity and a covenant alignment that is perpetuated through the ages.

Abraham is a model for believers of what to do with riches. More than once, the Bible makes mention of the tremendous extent of his wealth. In the showdown with his nephew's captors, Genesis 14:14 relays that he took with him 318 of his *trained* servants—who knows how many *total* servants he actually had! Yet Abraham's wealth never seemed to get in the way of his faithfulness to God and his obedience to the Lord's calling. Just as important was that Abraham understood the boundaries God had established in his life. Within those boundaries, he prospered. When he stepped out from those lines (such as when he lied to Pharaoh about Sarah being his sister), he didn't prosper.

God never allowed Abraham to make a covenant with Pharaoh in Egypt, yet in Genesis 21, we see him making a God-ordained covenant with Abimelech of the Philistines. As expected, he prospered in that covenant relationship. It is interesting to see how the blessings of this covenant even poured down to Abraham's son, Isaac, who later ventured to Gerar. There, in the midst of famine, Isaac stood out with his fruitfulness. "Then Isaac sowed in that land, and reaped in the same year a hundredfold; and the LORD blessed him. The man began to prosper, and continued prospering until he became very prosperous" (Gen. 26:12-13). This was not the Promised Land where Isaac was to prosper, yet it shows how God allows us to flourish even within the boundaries of our captivity, as long as He has determined those boundaries.

Abraham transferred his success and prosperity to his children. In fact, many of the prophecies linked with his children had to do with wealth. Generations later, Asher, the son of Jacob, received a blessing of abundant wealth. According to Moses' words, found in Deuteronomy 33:24, Asher would dip his feet in oil. In the same chapter, we see that he was to share this wealth with his brothers, and the family would continue a lineage of abundance. Verse 28 states, "So Israel will live in safety alone; Jacob's spring is secure in the land of grain and new wine where the heavens drop dew" (*NIV*).

Part of Asher's prosperity was his possession of Tyre and Sidon, key cities on major trade routes. These trading cities were filled with iniquity. In fact, Jesus addressed both of the cities because of their iniquitous patterns. Yet when you receive a prophetic blessing from God and your boundaries have been determined by Him, you have authority even over iniquity. You have a right to all that the iniquitous structure is ruling. This is how the transference of wealth will occur in days ahead. God will have individuals take dominion over cities ruled by iniquity.

We find this promised by Jesus in the parable of the minas, found in Luke 19:11-27. Many points could be made from this parable, but in terms of understanding the concept of boundaries, the lesson is simply this: Those who operate in godly stewardship with what was given in the boundaries they were assigned will inherit the rule of cities. What a promise for those willing to war righteously in the coming days over dominion, authority and the transfer of wealth!

A Fierce Opponent in a Fierce Battle

As we have already seen, money is not inherently evil. It is anything but a sin to be wealthy; in fact, in God's timing He is searching for those pure-hearted stewards who can be showered with His riches—and know how to handle them accordingly. However, money will always be connected with the forces of evil as long as it is of this world. The reason for this, as we have mentioned, is Mammon, who controls the world's finances. Yet as the earth's treasurer of sorts, he works for someone who holds a higher office: Satan, the prince of the power of the air (see Eph. 2:2).

I believe it is important for us to understand just why the war over wealth will be so fierce in coming times. We are talking about a transfer of riches from earthly minded, pride-filled, demonically influenced kings, presidents, CEOs and moguls to heaven-bent believers, many of whom will come from a past of modest means. We can expect more than a little opposition! And we must realize this opposition will not be just from the richest men and women on the planet, it will be from Satan himself. The prince of darkness will do everything he can to thwart God's plans on earth—including His plan to bestow on His children the riches necessary to bring in the harvest of souls. Let's look at what Scripture has to say about the connection between Satan and money. Ezekiel 28:13-18 says:

> You were in Eden, the garden of God; every precious stone was your covering: the sardius, topaz, and diamond, beryl, onyx, and jasper, sapphire, turquoise, and emerald with gold. The workmanship of your timbrels and pipes was prepared for you on the day you were created. You were the anointed cherub who covers; I established you; you were on the holy mountain of God; you walked back and forth in the midst of fiery stones. You were perfect in your ways from the day you were created, till iniquity was found in you. By the abundance of your trading you became filled with violence within, and you sinned; therefore I cast you as a profane thing out of the mountain of God; and I destroyed you, O covering cherub, from the midst of the fiery stones. Your heart was lifted up because of your beauty; you corrupted your wisdom for the sake of your splendor; I cast you to the ground, I laid you before kings, that they might gaze at you. You defiled your sanctuaries by the multitude of your iniquities, by the iniquity of your trading; therefore I brought fire from your midst; it devoured you, and I turned you to ashes upon the earth in the sight of all who saw you.

In this chapter we see that Tyre had a prince. The first half of the chapter is addressed to this prince (28:2); the second, to the king of Tyre (v. 12). While these passages can certainly be read literally as a word from the Lord to these two royal figures, the common interpretation considers the prince as a false messiah, while the king is Satan himself. With that in mind, we see that one of the reasons Lucifer was cast out of heaven was because of "the iniquity of [his] trading" (v. 18). As a sinless angel made perfect for God's holy presence, Satan held the highest position of anything ever created. This position apparently also involved some type of trading. Yet I find it fascinating that God does not call this mercenary trait out as his sin; instead, it was the fact that Satan became violent and envious of God "by the *abundance* of [his] trading" (v. 16, emphasis added). Satan, the one who lures his victims into the *love* of money, fell into the very trap he now sets for others. It seems he was never satisfied with what he had—he always had to have more!

It was through this that the seed of iniquity entered the Garden. The voice of this bad seed influenced the woman to be moved from the spiritual boundaries God had placed upon her. Man (Adam) willfully shifted. The serpent planted the seed of iniquity in the woman and the man so that they would have the capacity to make judgments as to their own welfare. These choices would be made independently of God. Since then, any time we defy the law and boundaries of God, we remove the path of freedom in our lives and the lives of those around us. This is what creates war.

Notice also that the issue returns once again to boundaries. When we operate within the boundaries and authority God has given us, we will find success. When we venture outside those boundaries, we set ourselves up for conflict and failure. This is a universal principle that God established, one that I cannot stress enough. In the Bible, we find that within each boundary that is mentioned there are key societal structures that are developed. These structures allow us to rule and reign in the civilization that we have been positioned within. When we read Genesis 4, for instance, we can gain insight into how civilization developed. More specifically, we see the order in which civilization developed: agriculturally (including the breeding of livestock, sheep and cattle), urbanistically, pastorally, musically and religiously. I believe all wars attempt to undo the development of a society in this order as well. War affects our land, what we eat, our urban development, the way we are taken care of, the way we rejoice and express joy through sound, and the way we worship. Can you see now how Satan attacks from each of these angles? He wants us roaming outside our God-appointed boundaries!

It's About the Harvest!

The war over the transfer of wealth is one of the most crucial of the coming days. If we hope to have unprecedented Kingdom influence throughout the world, we must have the necessary supply lines. And if we hope to have access to those supply lines, we must first take possession of them. As we have discussed, that requires an understanding of our appointed boundaries—those in both the earthly realm and the spirit realm.

We cannot forget, however, the ultimate reason behind this war over wealth. It is not to personally gain as much riches as possible. Yes, God desires to bless each one of us, and His infinite abundance will leave us astounded for all of eternity. But in these times, our primary goal *has to be* the advancement of His kingdom. We must have a vision to see the harvest come in! If not—if our vision is for ourselves—then we lose the purpose and blessing of the Father, who, as James 1:17 says, is the giver of "every good gift and every perfect gift."

Essentially, the war over wealth is not about wealth at all. It is about the harvest. People. *Souls.* We all know that we are to pray for the Lord of the Harvest to send harvesters into the harvest fields. But we also have to understand our own harvest fields and call forth harvesters who are specifically meant for those fields. Times are changing. We cannot send harvesters with old methods into today's harvest fields. Many of the fields are filled with AIDS and homosexuality. Perversion rules in other fields. Some are controlled by Mammon, while others have been captured by Islam, Buddhism or Mormonism. We must learn to define our harvest fields and understand the enemy that is holding each one captive.

In Matthew 12:25-30, the Lord said:

Every kingdom divided against itself is brought to desolation, and every city or house divided against itself will not stand. If Satan casts out Satan, he is divided against himself. How then will his kingdom stand? And if I cast out demons by Beelzebub, by whom do your sons cast them out? Therefore they shall be your judges. But if I cast out demons by the Spirit of God, surely the kingdom of God has come upon you. Or how can one enter a strong man's house and plunder his goods, unless he first binds the strong man? And then he will plunder his house. He who is not with Me is against Me, and he who does not gather with Me scatters abroad.

Jesus knew how the religious world thought, so He gave those who were listening to these words a spiritual principle. He said that unless you bind the strong man, you cannot take back his goods. It is no different when relating to the coming harvest on this earth. Once we define the harvest fields and understand the strong man that is guarding and keeping those fields intact, we can then bind him and take back the field. Once the field is under our authority, we can begin to plow differently, cultivate that field and even raise up a new crop in days ahead.

Mandates for Victory

The truth of the matter is that we will overcome! Revelation 12:10-12 says, "Then I heard a loud voice saying in heaven, 'Now salvation, and strength, and the kingdom of our God, and the power of His Christ have come, for the accuser of our brethren, who accused them before our God day and night, has been cast down. And they overcame him by the blood of the Lamb and by the word of their testimony, and they did not love their lives to the death. Therefore rejoice, O heavens, and you who dwell in them! Woe to the inhabitants of the earth and the sea! For the devil has come down to you, having great wrath, because he knows that he has a short time.'"

Daniel 11:32 adds, "Those who do wickedly against the covenant he shall corrupt with flattery; but the people who know their God shall be strong, and carry out great exploits." Our future may be filled with conflict, but the Lord has developed an overcoming anointing in us. I define overcoming like this: *The ability to receive a supernatural power or strength to conquer or defeat anything that*

is distressing you or attempting to stop you from advancing on your path.
We all want to advance on our path, not only as individuals, but
also as a corporate Body. To do so, here are six mandates that I
believe the Lord would give us.

1. *We must understand authority.* Authority is the key to
   power. No greater faith had Jesus seen in all Israel than
   that of the man who understood authority (see Matt.
   8:5-13). The Lord showed me that if I would begin to
   understand and analyze every authority that had influence in my life, I would begin to operate in a new level
   of faith. To the extent that we submit to the authority
   God has placed in our lives, our faith has the opportunity to be stretched and strengthened. Faith is the overcoming agent that God's people have on this earth (see
   John 14:12); therefore, if the Church is to overcome, we
   must understand and submit to proper authority.

2. *We must deal with our greatest fears.* The spirit of fear creates an unsound mind, weakens power and negates
   love. The Lord showed me that at the end of each 10-
   year period, a new move of holiness would begin to
   emerge among His people that would unleash a gen-
   uine fear of the Lord. He also showed me that a new
   administrative move of God had to come into each
   time frame. The fear of the Lord releases wisdom, and
   wisdom will unlock and dismantle demonic forces.
   You cannot shout down principalities and powers—
   they are a structured hierarchy that forms a government, and governments have to be dismantled.
   Wisdom causes false governments to topple. If we will
   tear down the spirit of fear that is hindering us and
   move into a new fear of the Lord, we will topple iniquitous patterns that allow principalities and powers to
   blind unreached people groups, cities and even entire
   nations to the light of the gospel.

3. *We must increase our discernment.* Every time I receive a vision of the future, the Lord has also spoken words that have given me courage. "But Lord, I do not have the ability to discern at this level," I have often said. And each time, it was as if the Lord said I did not have a choice. *"Discipline yourself in the Word and exercise My Spirit within your spirit,"* He said, *"for it will take both Word and Spirit to cause the reality of Me to be seen in days ahead."* If we quench the Holy Spirit in our lives, or if we do not wash ourselves with the written Word, we fall out of spiritual balance and open ourselves to delusion. Under those conditions we can never reach the level of discernment we will need for the critical times ahead.

4. *We must know who labors among us and who comes into our sphere of authority.* June Rana has worked for me for more than 15 years now. She is my office manager. However, she is also the watchman who keeps post at the door to see who comes in and out, what they are bringing in, and what they are attempting to receive once they come into my sphere of authority. Without her, our sphere could be penetrated by adverse forces trying to lead us astray. I have said it previously, but I will say it again: It is imperative that God's people communicate necessary information to one another efficiently during these times. The Lord showed me that He was going to start building true unity of purpose and function within His Body from territory to territory. I began to see a network that would form a net. When this net was completed, He would begin to drag it through cities and nations, collecting a great harvest. I saw that everyone in the regional Body would need to be connected to each other, with everyone working to accomplish God's purposes for that territory. One reason we will need to know each other and be linked together is to help discern when infiltrators attempt to undermine God's purposes.

5. *We must not allow the world to conform us to its blueprint.* However, we must not fear the world, either. The prince of the power of the air rules this earth. Satan loves to find places in our human nature where he can ensnare us to do his will. To prevent this, Christians often distance themselves from the world—they become separatists, and the root of their actions is fear and religious pride. When we get cleaned up, we are always a little afraid that the temptations of this world will get us dirty once again. But we are to be like Jesus: in the world but not "of this world" (John 8:23). The Lord is planning for the glory that He is about to release in His Church to permeate the earth. We cannot spread His glory if we hide out.

6. *We must understand this wealth transfer that is being prepared for the kingdom of God.* We have talked about this throughout the chapter, but let me reiterate that I believe the Lord is disciplining us so that He can send us forth without being trapped by Mammon. We must allow purification to come into our lives wherever money is concerned. God is planning a great transference of wealth to His people. Wealth does not just mean having money but also having strength and the spoils of war (in this case, a harvest of souls). I believe God wants us to understand money and finances so that we will be good stewards to advance His kingdom in the future. If we allow God to purify us and make us holy, He will then be able to trust us with great wealth.

When the Lord is on your side, you cannot be silenced or stopped in your quest for taking dominion. Sin will have no authority over you! Evil will not be able to reign in your atmosphere. Troubles will not overwhelm you when you are walking with an overcoming strength in your spirit.

Refuse the enemy's voice. Do not allow him to wear down your mind and convince you that you are defeated. He will try many different ploys to oppress you, get you depressed and prevent you from fulfilling your destiny. There will be rumors of wars and visible conflicts as nations rise against nations and the ungodly attempt to gain territorial dominance. But God! He has a prevailing, overcoming people. We will win this war over wealth, divide the enemy's spoils and be able to agree with what our Lord said in John 16:33: "These things I have spoken to you, that in Me you may have peace. In the world you will have tribulation: but be of good cheer, I have overcome the world."

CHAPTER 8

The War of the Nations

Will the Real Ruling Nation Please Rise

These are intense but glorious times throughout the world. Turmoil is escalating as nation rises against nation. Of Ishmael, Jacob and Esau, who will prevail? Of Persia, Iran, Elam, Egypt and Philistine, who will awaken and who will go to sleep? Does Babylon have a fighting chance to rule in the days ahead? Is there a Magi who is seeking the Christ Child today? Will the nation that rages the loudest rule the longest? These are the pertinent questions of our day.

Meanwhile, the Church from nation to nation is arising. I see a new hunger for prophetic revelation so that the vision of what God is doing in this hour can become more and more clear (see Prov. 29:18). Without prophetic revelation in this hour, we will lose our way. The Church must have revelation for how to war against a growing antichrist force in the earth. We must have a new move of the Holy Spirit in the Church to prepare and strengthen us for the times ahead. And we must realize that the Holy Spirit is the only restraining force against evil.

Why do we bother praying for the nations if it seems they will always rage and wage war with each other? Why should we even be concerned about the ever-present conflicts surrounding us? The main reason is found in Psalm 2. Because of the issues addressed in this chapter, I feel it's important that we examine the entire text:

> Why do the nations assemble with commotion [uproar and confusion of voices], and why do the people imagine (meditate upon and devise) an empty scheme? The kings of the earth take their places; the rulers take counsel together

against the Lord and His Anointed one (the Messiah, the Christ). They say, Let us break Their bands [of restraint] asunder and cast Their cords [of control] from us. He Who sits in the heavens laughs; the Lord has them in derision [and in supreme contempt He mocks them]. He speaks to them in His deep anger and troubles (terrifies and confounds) them in His displeasure and fury, saying, Yet have I anointed (installed and placed) My King [firmly] on My holy hill of Zion. I will declare the decree of the Lord: He said to Me, You are My Son; this day [I declare] I have begotten You.

Ask of Me, and I will give You the nations as Your inheritance, and the uttermost parts of the earth as Your possession. You shall break them with a rod of iron; You shall dash them in pieces like potters' ware. Now therefore, O you kings, act wisely; be instructed and warned, O you rulers of the earth. Serve the Lord with reverent awe and worshipful fear; rejoice and be in high spirits with trembling [lest you displease Him]. Kiss the Son [pay homage to Him in purity], lest He be angry and you perish in the way, for soon shall His wrath be kindled. O blessed (happy, fortunate, and to be envied) are all those who seek refuge and put their trust in Him (*AMP*)!

Why should we continue to pray for the nations in the midst of their wars? Because they are the Lord's inheritance! That is also why the above questions must be answered.

Haggai, that wonderful restorative prophet, portrayed the Lord as the "Desire of All Nations." Indeed, He is more valuable than all of the valuable possessions of the heathen. All the gold and silver in the earth cannot match the cost of Him in our midst. He will shake the nations and produce His desired effect in them. He will do whatever is needed until His Temple is filled with glory. He is the "wealth of all nations" (Isa. 60:5), and though they war and rage, He will have the ultimate say in the affairs of the earth.

A World Aligning

In this chapter, I will deal specifically with the nations and regions the Lord has spoken to me about. I believe there are major shifts about to occur in the alignment of power throughout the earth. We know from the Bible that nations will align and realign themselves according to whom they are serving. More important, each nation will be ultimately judged by God for its actions and alignments.

There are two elements that factor into God's judgment. First, Matthew 13 and 25 make it evident that nations will be judged by their relationship with the One True God. That judgment also factors in the Lord's preeminent covenant with Abraham—a covenant that will produce either a blessing or a curse in the earth realm. Essentially, we will be able to put every country on the map into one of two categories: "Goat" or "Sheep." This is how the peoples of the earth who are grouped in political spheres will also be classified in days ahead.

Second, nations will align themselves—and be judged accordingly—based on their love or hatred for God's chosen people, Israel. These alignments will become religious as well as political, stirring up the waters of demonic power that we talked about in chapter 6.

One such nation that will align with others to come against Israel is Russia. She and her children, Gog and Magog, will arise with new strength in days ahead and attempt to rule. Ezekiel 38:3-6 says:

Behold, I am against you, O Gog, the prince of Rosh, Meshech, and Tubal. I will turn you around, put hooks into your jaws, and lead you out, with all your army, horses, and horsemen, all splendidly clothed, a great company with bucklers and shields, all of them handling swords. Persia, Ethiopia, and Libya are with them, all of them with shield and helmet; Gomer and all its troops; the house of Togarmah from the far north and all its troops—many people are with you.

As a result of Russia's newfound aggression, the United States and other nations will begin to distance themselves from Russia. In fact, 2008 will be the defining year for Russia. For a season, a new favor will arise and rest upon Russia so that new alignments can be formed. The nations listed in Ezekiel (obviously with their modern-day names) will begin to align with this power from the north that is seeking a renewed role in world influence. The Cold War is over, and the thaw has occurred. Now these nations will become "hot" in the next 10 years. A new river of terror will begin to flow from the north. But God!

The European Union is well worth watching. There will be a new rise of anti-Semitism among these nations. Their greatest attempt to stop God's plan will be through financial control. Islamic influence in these nations will increase, and eventually they will align with anti-Israel forces in the Middle East. For many EU countries, the reliance on socialism will have created a declining birthrate. By clinging to the attitude of "Let me love my life and be secure with my pension," older generations will have established a stronghold of selfishness that stops the future from being birthed. As a result, the need for family will slowly be removed from these countries' societies. Therefore the need to war will shift. I see a full compromise with anti-God forces in the next 10 years. But God!

England is slowly being bought and controlled. In fact, England will have few original Englanders before long. For the country's economic state to continue and have any major influence in the world, it must realign itself. London will become a ruling Islamic financial center. (More on this later.) But God!

China will become the most influential nation in the future (also covered later). The Dragon and her children, other Asian nations, will arise. They are creating a society in direct competition with God's kingdom plan. These nations will have a great move of God, but then the opposing force will arise and attempt to stop what is being birthed by the Church. Great persecution will arise from these nations. The persecution will come in the form of religious control. China's booming economy will set the pace for the rest of the world. I believe this shift began in 2006, will mature by

2010, will influence all trade by 2016, and put China in full control of other nations by 2026. But God!

Africa will become a model for shifting rule. Nations will continue to war, while governments fold and are quickly replaced. As the Middle East dominates the world financially with its influence, it will seek to control hidden riches in Africa by manipulating the wars in these nations in the next 20 years. At the same time, Africa will be known as a religious hotbed. The greatest influencing forces in the European nations will be the Africans, and because of their passion, Europe will look to these nations to quench its own spiritual dryness.

South and Central America will become financial disasters and adopt a revolutionary mentality. The leftist governments of these nations will align with China and Russia. The conflicts throughout these continents will move north. At the end of 2009 and proceeding into 2010, Mexico will have a great shift and the "border wars" with America will escalate. North American trade agreements will be reevaluated because of terrorism moving from border to border. By 2016, Texas and California may begin to re-create state laws and appear to leave their statehoods to become nations. But God!

Why do I make the statement, "But God!"? Because *He* is in control and has a "strong people" arising in the earth. This people is a "peculiar people," whom God has chosen for Himself, a "nation above all nations" (Deut. 14:2, *KJV*). I am not referring exclusively to Americans or Israelis or any other specific earthly nation—this is a Kingdom people! A people chosen by God throughout the earth to execute His plan of covering this planet with His glory.

The United States of America: Will They Remain So?

It has almost become cliché to say this, but it is nonetheless true: America is at a crossroads. Our country could easily fade from its illustrious glory within the next 10 years. We are caught in an intense battle in the ancient area that was once called Babylon, and any Bible scholar can tell you that despite the name changes and deconstructions over the centuries, Babylon will rise to house the world's final dictator, the Antichrist. Whether we are approaching that time remains to be seen, but it does give an indicator as to with whom America is dealing.

At the same time, we are standing on the precipice of what could be the greatest spiritual awakening this country has ever seen. Whether that occurs in the near future also remains to be seen. What we do know, however, is that we are in a seven-year season of war that has been appointed by God. I believe a dream God gave me on September 24, 2001, sheds some light on our current state:

> I was standing looking at a huge lake that was covered with a coat of thin ice. Every now and then, a puzzle piece would drop from heaven, and I would walk out on the icy lake and put the piece in place. Before long, I recognized that the puzzle that was covering the lake was a map of the United States. I finally laid the last piece of the puzzle—the state of New Mexico—in place. Once I did that, it was as if I ascended three levels into the heavens. The best way to describe this ascension is as a staircase ascending up. On each floor there was a meeting room where I could watch a government-type council convene to discuss their plans. Once these meetings were done, I then walked up to the next level.
>
> The first government council was that of the enemy. His government was unable to see the plan of destiny that was in place over our nation. In this meeting, the council members continued to plot their wicked schemes over how to disrupt and bring chaos. On the second floor was the council of civil governments. These people were able to better understand the present times and issues regarding the United States, and they were discussing how to protect this nation. The third floor held the council of God. His government had been called into council over how to advance His kingdom in the United States.
>
> On this third floor, I was able to walk into the council and see all the key issues regarding the United States

and her future. Because I was at a higher level, I could fully
see the key places in the United States where the Church
needed to reinforce itself. I could also see key cities that
needed to be on watch against the enemy's plan. It seemed
as if I could also see the timeframe that was necessary for
the Church to intercede so that the wisdom of God could
come into full maturity and be executed in the earth realm.
While I was watching from this third floor, someone from
the second floor began to approach the puzzle map that
was in place on the lake. I began to yell, "Not yet! Not yet!"
However, he could not hear my voice and proceeded without caution, which caused the ice to break and the entire
puzzle plan to fall into the lake.

I then awoke, and almost immediately the Spirit of God began
to speak to me and give me a portion of the interpretation of the
dream. He said, *"I have a clear plan for America. I am calling the Body
of Christ into a new, mature strength. I am calling My people into intercession now. This plan will produce victory in days ahead and will bring justice that will affect the world. I am calling My people to pray for the civil
government of this land. I am a God who puts leaders in place. I have positioned the leadership of this nation for such a time as this. Even though the
civil government is gaining a clearer direction of My purpose, the plan that
is forming and maturing is on very thin ice at this time. The civil government of this nation has developed a unity and is gaining timely wisdom.
Unless my people pray, this plan will not be in firm place to advance, and
much destruction can occur. If My people, who are called by My name, will
pray, not only will I heal and secure their land, but from their land I will
touch the world in an incredible way, reveal My glory and call forth My
inheritance in every nation. I can foil the plans of the enemy that are set
against cities in this nation and cause many cities to experience a sweeping
move of My Spirit. However, the civil government of this nation must move
in My perfect timing."*

I believe this dream was linked with the War on Terror that we
have been propelled into during this seven-year war season. Even
though this dream could have several meanings and be applied to

several situations in our nation, I believe it was most significantly about moving forward in Iraq to dethrone a strongman who could have worked great destruction in the world. But after uprooting that tyrant, our plan to rebuild and restore was weak at best and non-existent at worst.

Because of how the Iraq War has progressed, the United States will lose credibility among the nations. This will release great political and financial compromise in days ahead. Politically, the United States will realign herself with the nation that seems to be gaining the most control and influence in the world: China. The U.S. will not be trusted by the nations of the Middle East. She will promote peace in an attempt to regain credibility with the nations of the world, and while doing this, will greatly compromise her relationship with Israel. This will also be her downfall with God, though it will not stop the awakening He has planned for this nation.

Veering from the Past

The America that was defined by pilgrims, patriots and pioneers—all of whom were propelled by the covenant of God to find a place of freedom to worship—is not the same America we live in today. The multi-ethnicity of America has redefined our way of operation and the actual fruit of our nation. Many Christians believe the same root of godliness remains, but in actuality, so many tolerant belief systems have been grafted into this once great tree that it's anyone's guess as to what type of fruit is now being produced. The cultural revolution of the 1960s changed the thinking process of our nation, and the fruit of that revolution has now come into fullness. Can the produce of that matured generation be harvested? Is this fruit edible and will it nurture our future? Only if a serum of absolute truth is re-injected, one that can revive the original seed of faith that created this great land.

We must remember that moral absolutes create faith and establish a demonstration of integrity and character that leads to wholeness. When a nation loses its moral absolutes, the actions of its people shift. Morals are redefined. Poor choices are made. And overall lawlessness rises. To control lawlessness, therefore, more laws must be established. And eventually, the freedoms that were an original driving force of life in the nation must be restricted and controlled. This is the dilemma America will face.

Sexual freedom creates an unhealthy womb. We as a nation have but one choice at this time in order to sustain a future: We must go and sin no more. This will take a revolution that is greater than any revolution we have known. The next seven years will determine whether our nation becomes healthy again or loses its virility to produce a vibrant generation. But God!

The female gender, their rights and their leadership are keys to the future of this nation. Mothers nurture. I am not proposing that all women stay home and have children. However, I am encouraging women to become the nurturers of the next generation. How women view families and lead the family unit into the future is critical to the armies of the earth. How women are allowed to influence the kingdom of God will be key to winning the war against the forces of evil.

I also feel that the African descent in America's heritage is key to its future. The civil rights movement in the 1960s was pivotal to the reversal of oppression in this nation. The danger now lies in the hands of the younger generations: Will they choose to make the same mistakes, lash out in revenge and oppress the next minority group? Or will they take the lead, champion justice and equality, and release the strength of endurance that is so key to our nation's foundation?

These generations may well be the serum of faith needed in this nation. They represent more than a generation—they represent the hope of the family structure. Tragically, we have come to a time when family must be reinvented. Because of our iniquity, our children now face the challenge of overthrowing the idols we have erected. Recently at an annual gathering of the prophetic prayer movement in Denton, Texas, Dutch Sheets shared that he felt the ruling spirit in America was that of Baal. Baal was the demonic ruler of Canaan, the most prominent idol mentioned throughout the Bible. In Judges we read about God calling Gideon (probably at a young age) to destroy his father's altar to Baal. This was no small task. To overthrow the altar of Baal in Gideon's day was not only an offense to those who worshiped this god, but it was also a direct slap in the face to the ruler of that land—who, coincidentally, held authority over Gideon's own father. Destroying the altar of Baal meant that the ruler of that land was dethroned. Essentially, Gideon was putting a death sentence on his entire family, including his father. After offering a few excuses (and putting out a couple of fleeces), Gideon obeyed and led a people to realign with the God of their father, Abraham. The entire nation of Israel moved back into a place of restoration because of a single young warrior.

We need a generation of Gideons to arise in America today. To change this nation's course, the arising generation must have a counter-revolution fueled by the Spirit of God. The iniquities of the father must be overturned for the next generation to advance. If we go to war against the forces of darkness without recognizing our fathers' iniquity, we will be weakened in the heat of battle.

The Church must be on full alert at this time. This is a time of revelation, and the Lord is calling together spiritual councils to release wisdom and direction into the earth realm. Apostolic leadership in cities across our nation must rise up, and it is essential that these leaders have full communication with those walking in God's intercessory prophetic dimension.

We as a Church can come into agreement with the throne room of heaven and release revelation to the earth so that civil government will gain clarity of God's purposes of justice in the earth realm. These are times to fully find our footing so that we will know how to stand in the future. If we gather the revelation God is releasing from heaven, we can see God's plan shifted into place. We must develop a Kingdom mentality.

God also has a plan to release the watchman anointing in every key city in our nation. I see the Church standing! Yet if the Church does not find its firm footing at this time, we will see civil government continue to move outside of God's timing. I mentioned the importance of this in chapter 6, but let me repeat the key verse: Daniel 7:25 says, "He shall speak pompous words against the Most

High, shall persecute the saints of the Most High, and shall intend to change times and the law." God has a perfect plan of victory, but we must re-evaluate how we are watching and what we are seeing. We must surround God's plans with prayers and intercession. We must renew our prayer life for this nation.

The Middle East: Will There Ever Be Peace?

There is no region of the world that receives more media attention than the Middle East. At the same time, there is no area that is in such a perpetual state of conflict. We continue to look for peace in the Middle East, but peace will only come when the purpose of God is completely fulfilled. Around the world, people remain divided by their staunch loyalty to either Israel or the Palestinians. Governments remain at odds based on whether they are pro- or anti-Israel. This perspective can even divide homes and families.

Many have overwhelming mercy toward the Palestinians, and for good reason. Their occupation and societal growth within the present-day boundaries of the State of Israel prior to 1948 made them to appear to be a nation deserving of its own land. Meanwhile, Israel appeared to be nothing but usurpers as they reoccupied and developed their God-given boundaries beginning in 1948 and accelerating until 1967. Until the last days, wars will forever escalate over these boundaries.

On the other hand, many sympathize with what seems to be an Israeli nation battling terrorists from within who use methods of fear to create chaos throughout the land. As Jews, they have become a besieged nation surrounded by Islamic extremists who would rather see Israel completely exterminated than compromise or yield the land they believe is theirs.

The Bible is explicit that Israel is God's chosen people. But does loving the Jews inherently mean that we as the Body—Messiah-believing Jews, Gentiles *and* God-fearing Jews—believe that all Muslims should be rejected? The answer is a resounding *No!* God has as much compassion for the Arabs as He does the Sudanese,

Kenyans or Irish. As a matter of fact, God will establish a house of prayer for every ethnic group. God will have a remnant that comes to His holy mountain.

The real issue of dissension and conflict comes from the spirit, Allah, that drives a people to hate God's covenant plan. When people worship this spirit, this evil force devoid of grace, they become bound and motivated with a deep-seated hatred for God's plan and for the law of love that Jesus came into the earth to bring.

We must respect the heart, desire and purpose of a holy God to set aside a people and a land for His purpose. How we, as nations, choose to relate to this land and its people determines our future standing with God. Whether we are sheep or goat nations revolves around our relationship to the preeminent covenant He extended to Abraham, Isaac and Jacob.

The Consequences of Encroachment

Pam and I both come from the oil and gas world. Pam actually worked for years in the Department of Rates and Regulatory Affairs, analyzing contracts that dealt with the Federal Energy Regulatory Commission. This agency regulates what crosses boundaries and how harnessed energy is transferred to destinations that need energy. Pam would petition this agency on behalf of major energy companies for permission to move needed resources from one area to another. Companies could acquire energy from one place, but it could not cross a boundary without permission.

I also dealt with physical boundaries in the workforce. Before I finished my undergraduate degree in college, I pipelined during the summer. Not only did we lay new lines for gas transportation, but we also did maintenance on an extensive network of gas lines around the South. One of my jobs was to see if anyone had encroached on the pipeline right of way. I would report this, which then prompted an analysis of the original legal contract. If needed, the "squatter," as they were known, would then be asked to move whatever had entered the boundaries of the land. Yes, it seemed hurtful and heartless at times, but if trespassers remained within a boundary where they did not belong, they were in danger.

These are two examples of the need for boundaries and the authority that boundaries bring. God establishes boundaries. Deuteronomy 19:14 says, "You shall not remove your neighbor's landmark, which the men of old have set, in your inheritance which you will inherit in the land that the LORD your God is giving you to possess." Once God determines a boundary, that boundary is intact in heaven. Earth must reflect the boundaries in heaven. When He planted the Garden in Genesis 1, He determined boundaries. When He made covenant with Abraham, He determined the physical boundaries of that covenant. He promised Abraham and his descendents victory over every enemy within that boundary and made them stewards over all the resources within those boundaries. Even through the unfaithfulness of these descendents, God has remained faithful to both His established boundaries and resources. However, the earth realm has been in conflict with God's purposes. At the core of the boundary wars in the Middle East is the question of who really has authority.

In 1948, God began to restore His boundaries in heaven back in the earth realm. However, those following a spirit in direct opposition to God contest these boundaries, even refusing to recognize the legality of established official documents. An online newsletter from Koinonia House offered this take on the conflict:

In 1947, when both Jew and Arab were offered their own states, only the Jews accepted. The original British Mandate included land on both sides of the Jordan River, but the area now known as Jordan was given to the Arabs. By the time the carnage of the Holocaust became fully known, the Jews and Arabs had been fighting over Palestine for decades and British efforts to reconcile the sides had not succeeded. In 1947, the United Nations stepped in and voted to partition Palestine into two separate states—one Palestinian and one Jewish. The Jews were not happy with the partition plan but agreed to the compromise. The Arabs, however, maintained an all-or-nothing position and refused to accept the U.N.'s plan. Had they agreed, the Palestinians would have had their state in 1947. Now that which was agreed upon and legally acquired by the Jews is longed for and coveted by the Arabs.[1]

The problem with many radical Islamic groups is that they will only accept peaceful terms if the nation of Israel is destroyed and the city of Jerusalem is under their control. Obviously, these are not "peaceful conditions," yet the condoning of terrorism to create and weaken a people is a major philosophy upheld in the many extremes of the Muslim culture. This mindset does not only target Israel but also anyone who blesses and aligns as an ally.

The War Against Israel

In *From Iraq to Armageddon*, Keith Intrater, a highly respected Messianic leader and friend of mine, writes the following:

> The satanic strategy to stop the return of Yeshua has, by its very nature, three lines of attack: The terrorism of Islamic fundamentalism against Israel, the lusts of the secular humanistic world to weaken the Church, and the rejection of Yeshua by rabbinic Judaism against the movement of Jewish believers in Yeshua. I am not speaking here of militant Islam, liberal humanism or rabbinic Judaism per se, but rather of certain spiritual forces operating through them. Those three spiritual enemies are suicide terrorism, the lusts of this world and religious rejection of Yeshua.[2]
>
> When we speak of the physical descendants of Abraham, we must recognize not only the Jewish people, but also the other "seed" of Abraham: the Arab people. They are the physical descendants of Abraham through Ishmael. Ishmael was born of Hagar, Sarah's servant. Yet he and the nation born of him are blessed because they are also Abraham's seed. . . . We should have a great love for the Arab peoples. As a Jew, I see them as our cousins in the Middle East. Despite the horrible conflicts that our two peoples have experienced in this century and throughout

history, we should maintain the hope of reconciliation and
peace is available through Yeshua. . . . Both Isaac and
Ishmael were Abraham's physical seed. Both of them were
blessed because of God's favor on Abraham. In order to protect the lineage of the Messianic seed, God had to separate
the descendants of Ishmael and Isaac (see Gen. 21:12).
However, that does not restrict God's love for the Arab peoples. All of the blessings of Abraham are for the Arabs, except
for two specific aspects of the Messianic covenant: The lineage of Yeshua and the ownership of the land of Israel. . . .
All of the spiritual blessings of Abraham are available to
Arabs through faith in Yeshua. Not all Arabs are Muslims.
Some of them have maintained their faith in Yeshua in the
midst of a hostile Muslim world. . . . It is God's will for Arab
and Jew to be reconciled through the cross of Yeshua (see
Eph. 2:14-15). Ultimately, it is God's destiny for Israel and the
Arab nations to be united in His kingdom. . . . Let us pray for
a mighty revival of faith in Yeshua in the Arab nations, just as
we pray for Israel to be saved.[3]

God loved Ishmael, but He hated Esau (see Mal. 1:2-3). There
are two different spirits driving the Muslim people. God will
redeem one stream, and the other will choose never to serve Him.
One stream will find itself within His boundary of grace. The other
stream will be outside of grace, embracing hate and greed and
always attempting to take back what it gave up in the beginning.

Many nations will converge to encroach on God's land and the
resources He has given Abraham's seed. In the Day of the Lord, He
will go forth and fight against the nations that embrace this attitude. He will send natural disasters to work on His behalf. This
brings us back to the question originally asked: Will there ever be
peace in the Middle East? I believe that Zechariah 14 offers the
answer. There will be many nations that stream to the Mount of
the Lord to participate in the Feast of Tabernacles. Those nations
will be saved in the days ahead. Others will stream to God's
covenantal boundaries while harboring the intent to overtake and

rule in His stead—but they will be destroyed. Peace will come, but at the cost of agreement with God's boundaries.

Lebanon: Watch for War

On January 29, 2006, I was ministering at Jubilee Church in Camarillo, California, when the Lord began to speak to me about Lebanon. One of the things they do at Jubilee is pray for the nations each Sunday. When I saw the flag of Lebanon, the Lord began to quicken a prophetic word to me. *"Watch Lebanon,"* He said. Not only was He speaking to the people of that church for them to watch over the nation of Lebanon, but I felt like He was speaking to all of us as His people that Lebanon would become a real prayer focus and issue this year. I was hesitant to interrupt the service and give this word because I was not confident if anyone in the service would understand the concept of Lebanon today. However, I am glad that I heeded the Lord's voice that He was calling us to pray for Lebanon this year.

I heard the Lord say the following:

In the midst of the summer, at the hottest point, you will begin to see the snow of Lebanon melt. Watch as Palestine and Syria form an ungodly alliance with Lebanon, for Lebanon is at a fork in the road of change for the Middle East. Lebanon will become an issue that causes the Middle East to go one way or the other. In the midst of the beauty and grandeur of this place I will begin to write a new script over how the nations will realign. Out of Lebanon a new wineskin will form and a new river will begin to rise. I will bring conflict into Lebanon because it is the boundary that I will deal with this year concerning My promised land of Israel. The warlike tribes of Lebanon will once again arise. But in the end I will win this war, and the riches that have been withheld from My kingdom plan will be released. Watch and see, for there is a new vision. For in the days ahead you will hear a cry arise from the deep affliction and mourning that comes out of Lebanon. Out of the ancient city of Damascus, you will see a caravan arise. I, the Ancient of Days, will create a conflict in Damascus. My power will be displayed to the world when I break the confederation of demonic hosts that are aligned against My covenant plan. Out of Damascus will come a new move of My Spirit. Many conversions and miracles will occur in the region that surrounds Damascus. Watch because I am realigning the nations of this region. I will send angelic forces to guard My plan. No matter how Syria arises against that plan at this time, I will have warring angelic forces that will counteract the plans of men that are aligned with evil forces to create havoc. Sing the songs of the Ancient of Days, for it is those songs that will create the sound of victory over the lands of this region.

In June 2006, just as this word prophesied, Israel and Lebanon entered into war. Israel was surprised at the strength of Hezbollah that had developed underground over the previous 40 years. Though no one "won" the war, Israel was stunned. This proved the strength of the enemy mounting against Israel in days ahead. We must watch Syria now! Since biblical times, she has never fully shown her animosity against Israel. However, as she is backed by Iran and Russia, this will soon be seen.

Iran: Is There Another Magi Looking for the Christ Child?

One of the greatest studies in the Word of God is of the nation of Iran, which is fully represented in the Bible. In the early 1990s I began to look at Kurdistan and found how the hope to this region was the revival and awakening in the Kurds. It's possible that the "wise men" that came to the birth of Jesus were from Persia because the same term was used in Daniel 1:20; 2:27 and 5:15.

We also find references in the Bible to Persia, Medes and Elam—all of these referring to modern Iran—and Persian kings such as Darius, Cyrus the Great, Ahasuerus (Xerxes the Great) and Artaxerxes. All of these were sympathetic to God's covenant plan. This will occur again. However, a great antichrist spirit has always risen in this land. Presently we find this happening. This area of the world, its people and politics will be in great conflict over the next 10 years. However, God will enter these lands and once again resurrect the favor He has for His people, Israel. There will be a great revival among the Kurdish people.

England: Your Time Is Now—Awaken!

I love England. I have been privileged to visit there and minister several times. The last few times I have gone, while ministering, the Lord has spoken that now is the time for the country to arise. In May 2004, the Lord exhorted the English as follows:

Prophets in England, you've got your work set out before you. You are in a difficult time. This is a season when prophets need to meet together, worship, cry out and press into revelation. The enemy has a plan to suppress the vision of God in this land. Do not get discouraged. You need to keep saying what needs to be said, even if it seems no one in this land is listening. There is an unholy alliance being negotiated now in this nation. This alliance will be devastating to this nation in the days ahead. This is a very formative time for the future of this nation. I have worked in times past to prevent this nation from forming this type of alliance. However, now it will be your choice whether you align wrongly or align with Me. I say to the people of England, you will be contending concerning this alliance. Prophets need to contend. Intercessors need to contend. Apostles need to rise up.

This is a time of choice. I will ensure that My message is heard in this land so that the choice is clearly determined. Two prophets in this land will go into high places of governmental authority to tell them the dangers of this wrong alignment. For if this alignment takes place, in five years you will be overtaken by false gods. You are on the verge of being overtaken now. However, there is still time to choose Me. You have three years of choice that will set your course and determine your direction for the next seven years. I am raising up the intercessory call in this nation. Watchmen must have a single eye in the land. This is not a time for divided minds and double-mindedness. I will offer an opportunity for this land to align with My covenant people, Israel. However, if they reject this alignment they will find another alignment with Germany and France at their door. Syria will also be a part of this wrongful alliance and coalition.

*England, you have a choice . . . I am calling My people in
this nation into a time of worship to create portals that My glory
and favor can enter into the nation and bring My choice of life.
There is a sound in England that is like none other in My people.
Join that sound with My sound from heaven now, and this sound
will begin to cover and permeate into high places in this nation.
If you will allow worship to develop in a new way in this nation,
My presence will begin to rule in a new way throughout the land.
Join your present sound of intimacy and exaltation of Me with My
sound of war. Do not just sing these songs with your mouth but
allow the message of these songs to pierce and activate your spirit-
man for war.*

*I am forming doors in heaven. As you worship, these doors
will move into the earth realm and give you opportunity to enter
in and present My message to this land. I am calling you to celebrate in a way that your enemies come to My table. I am preparing a table before you and anointing your shield for war. Do not
resist in this season of war. Raise your shield of faith high. Do
not become complacent and sympathetic with the enemy that is
in your land. If you do, your land will be overtaken. Watch the
key banquets that are occurring in this land. Governmental and
social banquets should be watched carefully. Prepare the way for
Me to enter in and move during these banquets. I will give
prophets and intercessors and the watchmen of this land favor in
these eighteen months. From the center of this land a gate is being
formed. Determine at this gate whether hell will rule or I will rule.
The rulership at the gate of England is being determined now.*

The Sword in the Sky

I returned to England briefly on May 29, 2005. As I was waiting in
London for a flight to Nigeria with my travel companions, we
looked out the windows and saw an interesting pattern in the
clouds. There was clearly a sword emblazoned in white across the
sky. We knew the Lord was communicating about the sword that
had come into the atmosphere over London and England. Not
only did we see this when we were coming through England on

our way to Nigeria, but also when we arrived back in London for our overnight stay. And when we got to our hotel and looked at a picture over the desk in our room, the sky over London in this picture was the formation of a sword where two jets had intersected their contrails!

Sharon Stone, a dear friend and key prophetic leader in England, initiated a prayer effort similar to what Dutch Sheets and I did in America as we went from state to state in our nation. God sovereignly ordained us to be in England for a layover so that we could be a part of the historic Middlesex County gathering in London. (We met in the heart of this area, which hosts the financial and governmental capitals of the United Kingdom.) While speaking to those gathered to pray, I said, "I see a structural weakness that God is addressing in the system of government in the U.K. If God does not intervene now, England will be absorbed by the European Union." I explained that we "saw a sword in the heavens over London and England." I then led the people to ask God what that meant at this time and explained prophetically that any vision or supernatural phenomenon must be interpreted in light of the Word of God.

In the Bible, a sword can have the following meanings: war, pending judgment, a malicious tongue bringing division, the power of truth, a weapon linked with the armor of God or a piece of armor used in warfare to produce victory. I shared with the group various scenarios from the Word of God linked with the sword. In Matthew 10:34, Jesus stated, "Do not think that I came to bring peace on earth. I did not come to bring peace but a sword." I shared that this was a time that the sword was being awakened in the atmosphere over London.

One Scripture passage of importance that began to surface was Numbers 14. This is the chapter in which Israel refuses to enter Canaan and Moses begins to intercede for the people. I concentrated on two verses. In Numbers 14:3, the congregation cries out, "Why has the Lord brought us to this land to fall by the sword, that our wives and children should become victims? Would it not be better for us to return to Egypt?" They actually tried to elect leadership that would take them back to their familiar captivity. The other Scripture was Numbers 14:43: "For the Amalekites and Canaanites are there before you, and you shall fall by the sword; because you have turned away from the LORD, the LORD will not be with you."

I shared that the Lord was saying this was a critical time, that the next 40 days could determine the reversal of the power of unbelief that was holding the Church captive in that nation. This is the chapter in which we read that the people were punished after they were unwilling to go to war when they saw the giants in the land. I sensed the Lord wanted to take a sword and cut from the British the power of unbelief and passivity and the fear to war for their inheritance. I ended with Joshua 5 and saw a tremendous pattern that God was trying to bring forth. This chapter includes:

1. The concept of crossing over to advance toward your inheritance
2. Circumcision, or cutting away, of the reproach linked with your past captivity and unbelief
3. The provisional change from eating manna to eating the produce of the new land
4. The visitation of the Man of heaven with the drawn sword

When we saw the sword in the heavens over London, the hand holding and guiding the sword that would determine the future of this nation was not seen. I believe this is the situation in many nations around the world today. What hand will guide and rule each nation? This is the key question for a remnant in each nation to ask the sovereign Lord who rules the nations.

In England I decreed that tradition would not guide the Church, nor would false religion (the sword of Islam) be able to become the guiding force over England. From this passage I felt like God was saying, *"I want to take charge over England and London for this hour. I want to be the commander in chief over how you progress forward from this day on. I want to transfer a new power over you so that you can face that which has been invincible in your past. Contend for My sword to lead you in victory against the giants that you have been unwilling to face in the past. This is your time."* I declared that if the people of England did not prevail now, the sword of Islam would fall upon the nation.

The Time Has Come!

On July 7, 2005, I was awakened at 4:30 A.M., unable to breathe. Around 5 A.M., the Lord told me to turn on the television and watch the news. I had been praying about a trip to England and was excited to return there with Dutch Sheets and a ministry team. I knew that the 40-day period that had been prophesied was now!

When I turned on the news, I saw Tony Blair making a statement that London had been attacked by terrorists. The underground transportation network and bus network in central London had been suspended due to several bombings. Actually, one of the buses that had been attacked—the one shown on the news—was directly in front of the hotel that we were scheduled to stay in. *It was the fortieth day!* When we arrived in England, the Lord said, *"Do not resist in this season of war. Raise your shield of faith high. Do not become complacent and sympathetic with the enemy that is in your land. If you do, your land will be overtaken."* He again reminded me that we needed to keep a careful eye on governmental and social banquets.

In 2007, I returned to England with a team and gave another word. Sharon Stone, Julie Anderson and Pastor Sam Onyenuforo co-hosted an incredible prophetic gathering. They expected 400 people, but almost 1,000 came. You could feel the atmosphere change when the worship began. God began to release a prophetic anointing. I talked to the group about how England would become an Islamic center for finances, and how situations would arise in their nation that would cause them to align with the Muslim world in a different way. This would then create an opportunity for them to touch the Muslim nations. I shared that if they were going to redeem their call as an apostolic nation, they must see a shift now! I also shared that there was a difference in what God was doing in the nation and how He was calling forth His kingdom people for this hour. Here is the prophecy:

> *There is a sound in England from My people that must come forth now. I will use national situations and forces to cause your voice to*

rise up to Me. I am going to reshape the economic structures and government systems of this land. I have determined this year to bring you to the end of the open window that I have rested over you. This nation will not survive without the voice of My people rising in this land. I want to remember My covenant with you; I want you to share in My covenant blessings with Me, but I must hear your voice.

The sound of the voice of My people must come forth now. You are carrying that sound within you. Do not be afraid to allow a cry to arise in the midst of this land. I am doing one thing in this nation and another thing in My people. I will use adverse circumstances in this nation to bring forth the covenant sound that has been held captive. When My people were in Egypt, they did not cry out to Me while they were building until I removed the straw that they were using. The circumstances ahead will cause My people to arise and come forth beyond the political correctness that they have walked in the past. [Interestingly enough, the next day news broke about 15 British troops captured for "trespassing" in Iranian waters.]

I say to this nation: Alliances, divine alliances! How you align now determines the change in this nation as the world knows you. Be careful not to allow the North, those of the Russian government, to influence you wrongly. If you make alliance with the government of the North, this will be contrary and work adversely to the will of My people in this land. Watch very carefully for hidden meetings with hidden agendas that could cause this land to be captivated and become a stronghold of the antichrist plan. Do not allow the enemy to threaten you as My kingdom people and persecute you in the financial arena.

You have been a land that has used the sword many times, but this is the year that My eye is upon you. I know your comings and I know your goings. I see the sword that is hovering above you. However, I am offering My sword to you. If you receive My sword, then My voice will be heard in this land. There is a generation that has never heard the sound of My voice that is rooted so deeply in this land. Reach up now and I will cause My sword to be put in your mouth, and the world will hear My voice from England.

If you feel like this prophecy is part of your inheritance, or if it touches a root in you, receive this word for yourself and pray for England in a new way. Unless England becomes a warrior again, it will be controlled and influenced by others.

China: The Sleeping Giant Awakens

In 2006, I took a historic mission trip to China with Peter Wagner, Ché Ahn and a wonderful intercessory team. We met with key leaders representing all the movements in China. During our time in Hong Kong, we spoke at a conference with thousands attending the night rallies. I also gathered with intercessors from all over the city. In Beijing, we convened with many of the Christian leaders in that area. There is hunger for God in China. This is the nation of worldwide influence in days ahead.

It was amazing to be in this country. I had waited years for this moment. When the Lord visited me at the beginning of 1986 with a profound vision (the one I shared in the introduction to this book), much of the revelation He gave me was about China. Peter asked me to be the first to speak to the leaders that had assembled from all over the nation, and I felt led to tell them about the vision and prophecy I had received in 1986. In this vision, the Lord clearly revealed to me what would happen in the next 40 years in 10-year increments. Much of what He showed me revolved around this nation, its leadership and its people. Here are the details from my vision that involved China:

- *1986:* This will be the turning-point year. The government of the land will arise, and from its oppression much change will begin to occur in the people. (This was the year of student revolutions forming. The Tiananmen Square protests then occurred in 1989, resulting in a massacre.)

- *1996:* In this year, the government of the Church will begin to arise in a new way. An apostolic awareness will enter the earth, and leadership with a mind for change will arise across the earth. (This was the year Peter Wagner convened the National Symposium on the Postdenominational Church at Fuller Seminary. Bishop Bill Hamon regards it as the historical turning point for public recognition of the new apostolic movement, of which the International Coalition of Apostles—leaders from around the world aligned in a network to hear what the Spirit is saying to the Church—is now a central part of this move. Even though God did not show me the apostolic church arising in China, I feel like the context of the overall vision timeline included China. When we arrived in China for our visit in 2006, the leadership of the Church there gave a loud "Amen!" as I shared the overall vision. They also informed me that their greatest "leadershift" began in 1996.)

• *2006:* China will come into the world picture. This will be the year China will take its rightful place in the new season. (As the trip approached, those involved could all see why our Chinese Summit was not held in 2004 or 2005, dates we had previously worked on, but in 2006. I also shared privately with Ché Ahn that this vision would be sealed with a Chinese mayor of Los Angeles. Ché mentioned that in March 2006 a Chinese woman was elected mayor of Temple City in Los Angeles County.)

• *2016:* By Rosh Hashanah (September/October), China will take its place as the most influential nation in the world economy. Its economy will be second to none. At this point the United States will realign itself with China and they will be allies.

• *2026:* The Chinese people will be the most dominant and influential people on Earth, and China will have the principal role of bringing in the world harvest. (During our trip, Peter shared with me that for some years he had been prophesying that by 2025 China will be sending more Christian missionaries to other countries than any other nation.)

During our assembly with the Chinese church leaders, David Wang, a key apostolic business leader, noted three significant observations: (1) the de-Christianization of America, (2) the kingdomization of the Chinese church, and (3) the Christianization of China.

In 2005, China passed its first law regulating tax-free charitable giving that went into effect in March 2007. More recently, the Chinese Ministry of Civil Affairs approached David to serve as a government consultant for formulating the laws regulating charities in China. He has also been appointed to a government committee comprised of 100 delegates who will advise leaders on the lifestyle of China's youngest generation.

Interestingly enough, David also shared with us five emerging themes among the Chinese people that would contribute to the historical process I had prophesied:

1. A youthful population
2. A spiritual revival with a focus on outreach
3. Higher education
4. Economic power
5. A strong spirit of venture

The Church Is Rising in China

The Christian movement in China has three broad segments: the Three-Self churches (these are the only churches registered with the government), the house churches (those that are unregistered) and the Third Church (those currently in formation). The Tiananmen Square massacre of 1989 caused the Third Church to be birthed overnight. This is a white-collar, hard-working, elite constituency of businesspersons and professionals numbering probably one million families. There are many Third Church groups across the cities of China, but they have virtually no communication among themselves. They, of course, do not meet in formal church buildings. Their leaders are bright and passionate to serve God, but they have virtually no understanding of Church government. They have access to enormous quantities of material resources, but they have no way of systematically deploying these resources. The Third Church is focused on equipping its leaders and must decide if it is to become a closed church or an open church that will change the society in China.

While we were in China, the Lord impressed Peter Wagner to commission one of the leaders as a horizontal apostle to the Third Church. This was a turning point for this leader, followed with a personal prophecy. As Peter began to take the authority to release the apostolic movement on the leaders of that nation, I realized that the fulfillment of the vision God had given me 20 years before was happening. Peter began to decree: "The Third Church in China will come into unity, not in an ecumenical form, but in an apostolic form for the transformation of this nation."

At this point, I began to prophesy:

> For I have chosen you for such a time as this. The leaders of the Third Church will be like the Mordecais at the gates of city after city after city. You will begin to hear the plots of the enemy that are working in entire cities. I have caused the Third Church to arise because this is the third day. You will be ushered into political arenas to open the gates for My glory to come in. You will understand My times and seasons. I am going to remove the trauma of your birth. For the trauma in the Third Church in its birth will now become the foundation of its destiny to change the political course of this nation. Fear not, for those enemies of your past will not become an entryway to your future. It is the resource structure of your influence of this church that will redirect the course of the Middle East. This will be the church leadership that forms a path through hostile nations and paves the way back to My city, Jerusalem. Today I am putting the anointing of David upon you. Stake your claim for the future!

America Meets the New Superpower

In *The Independent*, Clifford Coonan provided the following assessment in April 2006:

When President Hu Jintao of China shakes hands with President George Bush in Washington tomorrow and gives one of his fixed grins for photographers, it will not be just another meeting between the leader of a large developing country and the chief executive of the richest nation on earth.

China is rising fast and is expected to eclipse the United States economically in the future—its gross domestic product is tipped to overtake that of America by 2045. While Mr. Bush has only given Mr. Hu an hour of his time for a state lunch, the global balance of power is changing and in future meetings, the Chinese will set the timetable. The rise of China is posing awkward questions for the U.S., along with the realization that its days as the world's economic superpower are numbered.[4]

As America declines economically, thanks in part to a debt-ridden, bloated middle class, China has managed to help its poor. China has contributed more to global growth than any nation over the last few years. Now the most populous nation in the world wants its accomplishments to be recognized by the other world powers. Although Japan is a driving force in Asia, China is increasing its economic growth rate each year at a greater rate. China has already overtaken Britain and France to become one of the world's largest economies.[5]

Coonan goes on to say, "China, the emerging Asian superpower, is ruled with an iron fist by the Communist Party, which has transformed a once centrally planned economy into a free market one—'socialist with Chinese characteristics.'"[6] China is not a democracy, and many are angered over its attitude toward human rights and the Communist Party's treatment of organized religions. The West sees China as favorable to nations such as North Korea and Iran. Also, China plays favorites to the oil-rich pro-militant-Islamic nations of Africa and central Asia.

Says Coonan: "The war in Iraq or Iran's nuclear ambitions are side issues compared with the question about China's 'peaceful rise' and what to do when it decides to flex its muscles. Keen to keep the spin positive, senior Chinese foreign affairs officials said Mr. Hu's visit would 'provide an opportunity for Americans to better understand China's policy of seeking sustainable development and peaceful growth.'"[7]

This is what I saw in the vision God gave me in 1986. This is what is now becoming a reality.

My son, Daniel, had a recurring dream that he communicated to me:

> I was in a camp leading an army. We were positioned on top of a mountain. We were staying in old-style, canvas tents. It was night, and I recall looking up at the moon, which was shining through a tree. The tree was one that you would see in Oriental pictures and carvings. I moved to the edge of a cliff, with my army standing behind me. Below in the valley was an encampment of enemy soldiers. I knew I was viewing into the Chinese army. There were far more of them than there were of us. However, I had a sense of peace. I knew the army backing me could defeat them. I also knew that we could not move forward until the dawn broke forth!

A new day is breaking in the Church. There are harvest angels that are being sent to back the army of the Lord and His covenant people. China will be "the Nation of Dichotomy." It will have an army set against the purposes of God and His People. At the same time, China will send forth the greatest army of harvesters the world has ever known. Be at peace—the war ahead is already in the hands of the Lord.

The Time for Fulfillment Is Drawing Nigh!

With every nation and region I have mentioned in this chapter, the same question exists: *Who will rule?* Will countries side with the powers of this world, or will they seek the will of the Lord? Will the kingdom of darkness advance, or will the Kingdom of Light expand? Psalm 24:1 tells us that "the earth is the Lord's, and all its fullness." "Fullness" means that there is a place of abundance (see John 10:10). Fullness occurs when something fills up or comes to completion (see Matt. 9:16; Mark 2:21; 6:43; 8:20). In terms of seeing God's fullness in the nations, we must remember that God's definition of this includes a particular number of Gentile salvations (see Rom. 11:25). According to Paul, that is part of God's requirement for completeness.

Have no doubt: The Lord *will* complete His plan of fullness in the earth. However, much of that plan, as it applies to today, involves who will rule the nations. Governments and leaders will always vie for world power, yet Jesus promised that the meek would inherit the earth (see Matt. 5:5). God will rule, and we will eventually reign. Therefore, fear not! Even with the nations aligning and mounting against the God of heaven and Earth, He will rule. He will see to it that the earth remains His, and it will be made full of His purpose and plan.

Will the nations rage? The answer is *yes*! However, never forget that there is a God on the throne. His Son gave His life to save the people of the earth. He will *always* have the last word! Let's listen and stand carefully.

CHAPTER 9

The Harvest War
Keep Praying and Prophesying!

L ife is full of transition. We are always journeying from one stage to another—from childhood to adolescence, from singleness to marriage, from inexperience to expertise. Each transition presents the opportunity for preparation. When you *prepare* something, you get it ready, put it together, frame it. The word can also mean to get ready for action, to gird, to brace, to fortify or to strengthen. God believes strongly in preparation. Throughout the Bible, we find Him urging His children to be a people prepared for what He has called us to do.

It is no different now. We are currently in a time when preparation is essential. Wars will never be won by those caught off-guard. The more we are prepared for the enemies of our time, the more effective we will be in our battles to further God's kingdom. I believe there are 10 ways we can prepare for war during this season:

1. Know why we are at war.
2. Know who our enemy is and how he operates.
3. Know who we are and how God is preparing us for this future war.
4. Have a strategy for victory.
5. Think prophetically.
6. Stay alert to activity and anything unusual around us.
7. Keep our spirits alive and active so that we discern properly.
8. Know how to get in touch with each other immediately.
9. Learn to understand each other's ways and methods of communication.

10. Avoid letting petty issues distract us—they may be the
     work of religious spirits.

Hopefully by now you have a grasp of the overall picture of the
days ahead. We face a multitude of wars in various dimensions and
from every front. In the next 20 years, all nations will reconcile
around Israel, while some will arise to become dominant on the
world scene. The United States of America will attempt to find its
voice new and fresh but will not be heard as loudly as in the past.
Mammon will be the greatest influencing force of rule in the world.
Bloodlines will continue to conflict with other bloodlines simply
because nations are comprised of people with unredeemed blood.
The carnal mind will continue, as always, to be in enmity with God
and resist His knowledge. Antichrist will continue to have a plan to
rule the earth. However, the earth—again, as always—will still be the
Lord's and the fullness thereof!

The Peculiar Nation

But then there is our role. Throughout this book I have discussed
our response to these coming wars. I have tried to offer insight and
prophetic understanding in hopes that we, as a Body, will be prepared and ready for the times. Strategy is key, but so is a heartfelt
passion to see the world full of the Lord's glory.

With that in mind, let me offer this final chapter as one continuous word of encouragement. Treat this as a commencement of
sorts. Most of us have attended a graduation ceremony. It's a cul-
minating event, a final climactic moment when those who have
labored for years finally walk across the stage with heads held high
and receive their diplomas. And yet, when you think about it, the
primary goal of the day is not to have some long ceremony based
on an official piece of paper being handed over. Nowadays you can
skip the ceremony and just have your diploma sent in the mail!
No, the underlying purpose of a graduation ceremony is to send
out those who have passed every test, who are ready to step into
the next realm, in the spirit of hope, encouragement and victory.

Graduation day is a celebration, a sealing and a breaking—sealing the past and breaking into the unknown future. It is a day of blessing.

I hope these final words come with a similar weightiness. We now know the wars ahead, and we will continue to gain revelation and understanding in an effort to be prepared. Now let the passion for seeing God's kingdom come alive expand in you. Often that starts by being reminded of who you are.

Exodus 19:5 in the *King James Version* says, "Now therefore, if ye will obey my voice indeed, and keep my covenant, then ye shall be a peculiar treasure unto me above all people: for all the earth is mine!" Psalm 135:4 adds, "For the LORD hath chosen Jacob unto Himself, and Israel for his peculiar treasure" (*KJV*). We are a people of God's own possession. In fact, we are a special possession or property that is owned and guarded by the King of all kings. We are a purchased possession that has been bought to reflect a different type of Kingdom. We are a superabundant superpower in the earth realm. We are a private property, an extraordinary possession, treasured by Him. We must never lose this understanding. If we lose the concept of who we are and who we belong to, we lose the war in the heavenlies and in the earth. But when we are assured of the mystery of Christ in us, we can be used by God to master any situation in the earth realm that needs to be brought under His rule.

First Peter 2:9-15 expounds on our identity and charges us to walk in a type of conduct that will give God reign in our life and in the earth:

> But you are a chosen race, a royal priesthood, a dedicated nation, [God's] own purchased, special people, that you may set forth the wonderful deeds and display the virtues and perfections of Him who called you out of darkness into His marvelous light. Once you were not a people [at all], but now you are God's people; once you were unpitied, but now you are pitied and have received mercy. Beloved, I implore you as aliens and strangers and exiles [in this world] to abstain from the sensual urges (the evil desires, the passions of the flesh, your lower nature) that wage war

against the soul. Conduct yourselves properly (honorably, righteously) among the Gentiles, so that, although they may slander you as evildoers, [yet] they may by witnessing your good deeds [come to] glorify God in the day of inspection [when God shall look upon you wanderers as a pastor or shepherd looks over his flock]. Be submissive to every human institution and authority for the sake of the Lord, whether it be to the emperor as supreme, or to governors as sent by him to bring vengeance (punishment, justice) to those who do wrong and to encourage those who do good service. For it is God's will and intention that by doing right [your good and honest lives] should silence (muzzle, gag) the ignorant charges and ill-informed criticisms of foolish persons (*AMP*).

We have been picked and gathered as an eclectic group of heavenly saints. We have been given great power to rule in the earth. We are a dangerous people that the world must reckon with from generation to generation. We recognize who we are and who we represent. We are not a people of fear. We are not unstable or unsound in our representation to society. We are a people filled with the love of God, interacting with angelical forces and decreeing the message of God in the earth realm. We are redeemed worshipers who will fulfill the promises of a holy God. We will grow loud as we shout "Yes!" and "Amen!" to the promises He has spoken. The world will hear our voice.

Our priestly duties continue to unfold from generation to generation. Yet our obedience in fulfilling these duties will always cause war in the earth with a foe who is in rebellion to God and attempting to lead mankind down a similar path. As we worship, we will rule and take dominion in the earth.

We War with Our Prophecies

First Timothy 1:18 says, "This charge I commit to you . . . according to the prophecies previously made concerning you, that by them you may wage the good warfare." To be victorious, a prophetic people must be an interceding, praying band of warriors who know how to use their sword. Like Jacob's son, Gad, we will be a troop that overcomes at the last (see Gen. 49:19). We shall crowd out the enemy's plans and invade his territories and strongholds. We may fall seven times, but we will arise from defeat and change into a garment of victory.

Age will not stop this peculiar tribe. We will be like Caleb and cry, "Let us arise and overcome" (see Num. 13:30). We are a strong people who will be able to endure persecution and suffering, be tempted yet resist until His blood in our veins is once again spilled. We are a people who see that One has broken the curse that ruled our lives, and we will resist any operation of the curse from ruling us now and forever! We are a people who are coming out and "crossing over." We are moving from victory to victory. We are receiving new strength to blossom forth in the days ahead. We will overrun our enemies and all the strategies that are being developed to overcome and entrap us.

Luke 11:22 says, "But when someone stronger attacks and overpowers him, he takes away the armor in which the man trusted and divides up the spoils" (*NIV*). We *will* conquer, overcome, prevail and get the victory when challenged by the forces of the world that would conform and control us. We *will* take our fields and bind the enemy from operating and holding the spoils for kingdom advancement. Romans 12:21 will be our motto: "Do not be overcome by evil, but overcome evil with good." Our latter end will be greater than our former. First John 2:13-14 sheds light on who we are:

> I write to you, fathers, because you have known Him who is from the beginning. I write to you, young men, because you have overcome the wicked one. I write to you, little children, because you have known the Father. I have written to you, fathers, because you have known Him who is from the beginning. I have written to you, young men, because you are strong, and the word of God abides in you, and you have overcome the wicked one.

Again, John adds this qualifier of who we are: "You are of God, little children, and have overcome them, because He who is in you is greater than he who is in the world" (1 John 4:4). And though it has

been given unto the devil to make war with the saints and to overcome us, with power given him over all kindreds and tongues and
nations, *we will be a strong people who do exploits in the earth and prevail
in the end*. For, we, this peculiar nation, represent the Lord of lords,
and King of kings, and they that stand against the enemy are called,
chosen and faithful. As Revelation 12:11 says, "And they overcame
him by the blood of the Lamb and by the word of their testimony,
and they did not love their lives to the death." We will overcome!

We Move in the Suddenlies

Because we are a chosen people, we must choose our wars carefully
in days ahead. There are many conflicts around us that could trap
us as we try to right every wrong. We must allow our General to give
us a directive and then move as skilled warriors to overcome the
enemy quickly.

In *The Art of War*, Sun Tzu says:

> In general, the method for employing the military is this:
> Preserving the [enemy's] state capital is best, destroying
> their state capital second-best. Preserving their army is best,
> destroying their army second-best. Preserving their battal-
> ions is best, destroying their battalions second-best.
> Preserving their companies is best, destroying their compa-
> nies second-best. Preserving their squads is best, destroying
> their squads second-best. For this reason attaining one
> hundred victories in one hundred battles is not the pinna-
> cle of excellence. Subjugating the enemy's army without
> fighting is the true pinnacle of excellence. . . . Thus the
> highest realization of warfare is to attack the enemy's plans;
> next is to attack their alliances; next to attack their army;
> and the lowest is to attack their fortified cities.[1]

We must be a strategic people, wiser than the serpent and gen-
tler than the lamb. We must move in the suddenlies of God, taking our assignments and shifting quickly. We each have been given
a portion of garden to watch after, protect, cultivate and multiply.

Even now, we are advancing in His glory, and that glory is invading other fields. This is the invasion that is threatening the enemy!

Sun Tzu continues with these incredibly relevant and prophetic words:

> When employing them in battle, a victory that is long in coming will blunt their weapons and dampen their ardor. If you attack cities, their strength will be exhausted. If you expose the army to a prolonged campaign, the state's resources will be inadequate. When the weapons have grown dull and spirits depressed, when our strength has been expended and resources consumed, then the feudal lords will take advantage of our exhaustion to arise. Even though you have wise generals, they will not be able to achieve a good result. Thus in military campaigns I have heard of awkward speed but have never seen any skill in lengthy campaigns. No country has ever profited from protracted warfare. Those who do not thoroughly comprehend the dangers inherent in employing the army are incapable of truly knowing the potential advantages of military actions. One who excels in employing the military does not conscript the people twice or transport provisions a third time.[2]

When we exhaust the wealth of an enemy, the enemy must submit.

We Pray with All Kinds of Prayer, But Are We Still Praying?

I am so thankful that the Lord orchestrated my path to be with Peter and Doris Wagner. The Wagners, when asked by the AD2000 Movement to find leaders in nations who could mobilize prayer for the 10/40 Window, immediately surrendered to the mission. To pray for this least-evangelized area in the world, they began to rely on the many leaders they had trained in the School of World Mission at Fuller Theological Seminary.

This shift laid the groundwork for how prayer would be viewed in the global Body of Christ. Global Harvest created what became known as "the prayer movement." Individuals and teams went on prayer journeys to all the nations inside this window of the world and learned about spiritual warfare, prayer walking, confronting the enemy, and watching and interceding for harvest in a new way. This changed the way we viewed the enemy of God who was controlling the harvest fields of the world. Doris even took a team to the highest of high places, Mt. Everest, to command the enemies of the gospel to "let go" of the harvest.

This task of praying for the 10/40 Window had a target date of 2000 to complete the assignment. In the overall process, Peter and Doris scheduled an event known as Celebration Ephesus to gather a prayer army at the ruins of the amphitheater in Ephesus for a four-hour praise and worship celebration. More than 5,000 participants from 62 nations gathered to worship and praise the King of kings for all He had done during the decade. During this prayer mission, the number of unreached people groups went from 1,700 to around 500! Amazing!

At the end of 1999, it seemed the prayer movement was not ending but just beginning. Peter and Doris called us to shift our prayer focus from the 10/40 Window to the 40/70 Window, an area that begins in Iceland, encompasses all of Europe, crosses northern Asia and reaches to the northern tip of Japan. This covered a region where the gospel had once had an impact but that was now cold and gripped by religion. Teams entered all 64 nations of this window. However, the prayer movement had matured from the 1990s. These teams were not just prayer walking, but they were now also searching and connecting with the churches of the "New Apostolic Reformation" in the area. The question was being asked: "Where are the intercessors, apostles and prophets, and are they connected and praying?" As if heeding the call, intercessors were suddenly awakened to the need to connect with prophets and apostles in territories. If prophets and apostles did not exist in certain territories, the intercessors' assignment was to bring them to birth.

By the end of this assignment in 2005, Global Harvest had matured tremendously. The ministry was hosting global gatherings each year. Peter was leading the Body of Christ into a renewed understanding of our need for apostles and prophets today. This was causing the prayer movement to change drastically. The next assignment or prayer target would become what Peter named the 9/11 Window—the area of the world where most Muslims live and the regions where Islam is advancing rapidly.

During this same timeframe, Dutch Sheets and I heard the call to visit each state in America and evaluate the army of God in this nation. You can read about that incredible journey in *Releasing the Prophetic Destiny of a Nation*, the only known prophetic history book of the entire United States. The prayer army has made a great shift. No longer are we a group of intercessors trying to find our way; we have become prayer warriors who are aligning in a new way.

New Wine Coming into the Wineskin

From state to state in our nation, mobilization has begun again. However, this time the connections are different: Apostles are praying, prophets are prophesying with clarity, and intercessors are birthing the future.

Not too long ago, the Lord clearly said to me that *"the prayer movement needs to be the wine for the wineskin that is forming."* He revealed to me that as the apostolic government of the Church matures, the prayer movement has to stay fluid and remain new as a drink offering to their region. He showed me new people in every state who are to be involved. He showed me how many of you had been faithful in the past season, but how you will need to expand your connections. An apostolic governmental anointing in the prayer movement has now emerged. As we draw closer to the end times and see spiritual warfare intensify, we need to pray in such a way that we may receive revelation for the battle and live in such a way that we withstand the schemes of the enemy.

The Lord sovereignly positioned me with Mike and Cindy Jacobs at the beginning of the 1990s. I was a prayer warrior, and Cindy was an intercessor. She has had great influence in my life.

I listen closely when she prophesies to the prayer movement. Recently she spoke the following: *"It is time to shift the prayer movement. We must become apostolic in our expression. We must find the intercessors and the prophets and align them with the apostles in each state. If each leader of the present movement will shift, their state will shift. If this shift does not occur, the Lord's kingdom will not be established from state to state and a nation will suffer greatly."*

The Current Movement

So where are we as a Body? Get a sense for the wonderful movement of God through the following (and it's only the tip of the iceberg!):

Mike and Cindy Jacobs are presently leading an initiative to pray for the highways of our nation, focusing on Interstate 35. Apostolic prayer thrusts are arising throughout our nation. Dutch Sheets has developed the National Governmental Prayer Alliance to align those interested in the area of governmental intercession for directed, precise prayer. I continue to surround our nation as I did when I visited its major port cities in 2005. (We are now seeing more clearly the reason the Lord said to go to all these key ports.)

One of the greatest models of corporate praying has developed in Oklahoma, where John Benefiel and Jay Swallow have seen a revival among the Native American people as they connect with the movement of God for this season. Kansas and other states have joined with Oklahoma to advance the prayer army in that region. Apostles John and Jay, along with Jean Steffenson, have stood faithfully to see the host people of our land restored, and they are trusting the Lord for the Resolution of Apology to the Native Peoples to move forward. This resolution recognizes and honors the importance of Native Americans to this land and to our nation—in the past and today—and offers an official apology to the Native peoples for the poor and painful past choices our government sometimes made to disregard its solemn word. It is a step toward healing the wounds that have divided us for so long—a potential foundation for a new era of positive relations between tribal governments and the federal government.

Another initiative that has begun is to pray for the river systems throughout various states. Venner and Bill Alston of Wisconsin, Regina Shank of Missouri and many others across the nation are pioneering this. James Nesbitt led a group to pray for the Great Lakes. Barbara Yoder has led many initiatives in Michigan, including a 40-day watch for the city of Dearborn, where Islam has its greatest concentration in our nation.

New York and New Jersey have two of the most vibrant territorial movements that are focused on praying the prophecies over their states. California has a great grassroots movement and has been leading teams to pray for the district court system. In Tennessee and Alabama, Tammy Alsup developed the first State Apostolic Councils to move forward and see a region transform. Prayer centers are developing in Chicago and Las Vegas, and we are establishing a Watch Center in Denton, Texas. Truly, the remnant in every state of our nation continues to rise and mature in the midst of the enemy's raging influence over our culture.

Changes have been made within the prayer movement's communications. With wars increasing and warfare intensifying, we must become more "intense" in our praying. God is leading us into new levels of strategic praying so that the enemy does not overtake and defeat us in days ahead. This is a season of building for our future. We are maturing into the revelation that the apostle Peter declared—that Jesus is the Christ, the Messiah. Once Peter gained that true revelation, then the Lord could say, "Upon this revelation I will build My church" (see Matt. 16:18). In Hebrew, the concept of building actually means to add sons and daughters—exactly what we want! Jesus added, "The gates of Hades shall not prevail against it [the Church]. And I will give you the keys of the kingdom of heaven" (v. 18). If the Church is built properly, then we have the authority to unlock His kingdom purposes in the earth.

Praying for Transformation

The prayer movement must move into the next dimension of influence in each state of this nation and other nations throughout the world. As we pray, we must make "social transformation" more than just a buzzword. It must become a reality. Divine connections must occur for the army to communicate efficiently and effectively. Communication comes from our *connections* and *commitments*. Transformation comes when we align with the mind of Christ and have a common purpose in each territory to reflect His specific will for that territory. We must know what communication networks are operating in a region and what audiences we are influencing.

Prophets must mature in their prophesying. Here is a question I have asked many: Are you *wine* or a *wineskin*? Do you flow predominately in the category called wine (revelation), or are you developing a wineskin for others to pour into? If you are *wine*, what are you being poured into? Where are you being poured? If you are a *wineskin*, who pours into you?

God is raising up a Kingdom army full of prayer warriors who know their sphere of authority. We are being sent again! We must embrace the shifting paradigms that are being communicated this hour from heaven. We must assist in the development of strategies to unlock the nations of the earth.

God will use this peculiar people in the earth to change the way His kingdom advances. *Are we still praying?* The answer is a loud *yes!* The army of God is growing stronger and stronger daily.

Ask the Lord to renew your prayer life. Pray with words and pray the Word! Travail and pray without words. Pray in the Spirit with words unknown. Commune with your Maker and be bold in the earth realm where you have been positioned as a witness to His love, grace and power. Speak and decree the Word. War with your prophecies. Do not let the confusion around you create a veil of darkness that stops you from moving forward.

The Veil of Darkness Can Be Overcome!

Our son Daniel is a policeman. When he was seven years old, he and I went to a missions conference at Christ for the Nations in Dallas, Texas. We were looking at exhibits and he glanced up at a map that included nations in the Middle East. They were painted in black because at this time in history they had not really been penetrated by the gospel. He then looked at me and said, "Daddy, you are called to those dark nations."

I struggled with this word, but I knew it was right; I was called to pray for those nations. I could see past the map and notice the veil of darkness over those nations and how it was holding back harvest in that part of the world. Out of the mouth of babes . . .

I now have visited some of those nations and will continue to ask the Lord to remove the veil in that area of the world.

Recently, John Mark, another of our sons (the bowler) was in a bowling contest. In this contest, they dropped a black veil in front of the lanes. There was only one foot of lane visible and then the curtain hid the remaining 59 feet. For a bowler who bowls well, this is a great test to throw a ball without being able to see down the lane.

During the practice time, I saw that John Mark was struggling. He was relying upon his mind to give him a strategy to overcome. I finally said to him, "Don't let the veil of darkness create fear and cause you to change your game plan. This is a spiritual issue."

His first thought, of course, was, "Dad, do you have to see something spiritual in everything?!" However, he listened. Before long he was throwing as if the veil were not there. After his seventh strike in a row, I knew he had mastered the veil and was hitting the mark.

We are to do the same. No matter how dark society around us gets, we must stay focused and "hit the mark" with our prayers. We must not change our game plan. The outcome is already known: the Lord wins in the end. We are simply collaborating with Him in the victory. As the war unfolds, we must be prepared and open to trying new methods of warfare to gain victory.

The war *will* continue to unfold. But we are a people who continue to mature into the peculiar treasure that will have the greater influence in the earth today.

Introduction: The Changing Structures of War

1. Chuck D. Pierce and Rebecca Wagner Sytsema, *The Future War of the Church* (Ventura, CA: Renew Books, 2001), pp. 28-32.
2. Chuck D. Pierce and Rebecca Wagner Sytsema, *When God Speaks* (Ventura, CA: Regal Books, 2005), pp. 83-84.

Chapter 1: Becoming a Warrior in a Season of War

1. Norm Chomsky and Carlos Peregrín Otero, *Radical Priorities* (Montreal, Quebec: Black Rose Books, 1981), p. 157.
2. Chuck D. Pierce and Rebecca Wagner Sytsema, *The Future War of the Church* (Ventura, CA: Regal Books, 2001), p. 54.
3. Cindy Jacobs, *Women of Destiny* (Ventura, CA: Regal Books, 1998), p. 153.
4. Pierce and Wagner Sytsema, *The Future War of the Church*, pp. 54-62.
5. *American Dictionary of the English Language,* (San Francisco: Foundation for American Christian Education, 1987), "violence."

Chapter 2: The Mind War

1. William Morris, ed. *The American Heritage Dictionary of the English Language*, New College Edition (Boston: Houghton Mifflin Co., 1976), "critical."
2. Stephen J. Gerras, "Thinking Critically About Critical Thinking: A Fundamental Guide for Strategic Leaders," June 2006. http://www.au.af.mil/au/awc/awcgate/army -usawc/crit_thkg_gerras.pdf (accessed May 2007).
3. Kathleen McAuliffe, "Life of Brain," *Discover Magazine,* Spring 2007, p. 5.
4. Victoria Schlesinger, "The Motor Cycle Diaries," *Discover Magazine,* Spring 2007, p. 39.
5. Gerras, "Thinking About Critical Thinking: A Fundamental Guide for Strategic Leaders."
6. Schlesinger, "The Motor Cycle Diaries," p. 39.
7. Dutch Sheets, *Authority in Prayer* (Bloomington, MN: Bethany House Publishers, 2006), p. 172.

Chapter 3: The Blood War

1. Linda Tagliaferro and Mark V. Bloom, *The Complete Idiot's Guide to Decoding Your Genes* (New York: Macmillan Publishing, 1999), p. 254.
2. H. A. Maxwell Whyte, *The Power of the Blood* (Springdale, PA: Whitaker House, 1973), pp. 12-17.
3. Robert Jamison, Andrew Fausset and David Brown, eds. *Jamison, Fausset & Brown's Bible Commentary*, on Hebrews 12:24.
4. Billye Brim, *The Blood and the Glory* (Tulsa, OK: Harrison House, Inc., 1995), pp. 51-52.

Chapter 4: The Time War

1. "Researchers Discover Mechanism That Drives Daily Body Rhythms," *Science Daily,* January 11, 1999. http://www.sciencedaily.com/releases/1999/01/9901140 75249.htm (accessed May 2007).
2. For more on this powerful concept, I encourage you to read *Possessing Your Inheritance* (Ventura, CA: Renew, 1999) by Chuck Pierce and Rebecca Wagner Sytsema.

3. Robert Heidler, *The Messianic Church Arising* (Denton, TX: Glory of Zion International Ministries, 2006), p. 86.
4. If you are interested, there is a wonderful, prophetic Issachar School course on how the Lord orders our steps through each month of the year. *Understanding the Months Prophetically* is available for purchase through www.gloryofzion.org or by calling 1-888-965-1099.
5. *Nelson's Illustrated Bible Dictionary* (Nashville, TN: Thomas Nelson Publishers, 1986).
6. *International Standard Bible Encyclopaedia* (Seattle, WA: Biblesoft, Inc., 2003).
7. Dutch Sheets, *Intercessory Prayer* (Ventura, CA: Regal Books, 1996).
8. *Nelson's Illustrated Bible Dictionary.*
9. Candi MacAlpine, *Take Back the Night* (Lake Mary, FL: Creation House, 2005), p. 1.
10. There are prayer focuses associated with each of these watches. They are included in the book *Reordering Your Day*, available for purchase by calling 1-888-965-1099 or through www.gloryofzion.org.
11. *The New Unger's Bible Dictionary* (Chicago, IL: Moody Press, 1988).
12. *International Standard Bible Encyclopaedia.*
13. "Salah," Wikipedia.org. http://en.wikipedia.org/wiki/Islamic_prayer#The_five_daily_prayers (accessed May 2007).

Chapter 5: The Presence-and-Glory War

1. *American Dictionary of the English Language* (San Francisco: Foundation for American Christian Education, 1987), "atmosphere."
2. Kim Daniels, *Give It Back* (Lake Mary, FL: Charisma House, 2007), p. 168.
3. Dutch Sheets, *Authority in Prayer* (Bloomington, MN: Bethany House Publishers, 2006), p. 20.
4. Geoffrey W. Dennis, *The Encyclopedia of Jewish Myth, Magic and Mysticism* (Woodbury, MN: Llewellyn Publications, 2007), p. 58.
5. Derek Prince, *Blessing or Curse: You Can Choose* (Grand Rapids, MI: Chosen Books, 2005), p. 45.
6. Jeff A. Benner, "Numbers 6:24-27," Ancient Hebrew Research Center, www.ancient-hebrew.org. http://ancient-hebrew.org/40_numbers1.html (accessed May 2007).
7. Matthew G. Easton, "David," *Bible Encyclopedia*, ChristianAnwers.net. http://www.christiananswers.net/dictionary/david.html (accessed May 2007).
8. Leen and Kathleen Ritmeyer, *From Sinai to Jerusalem: The Wanderings of the Holy Ark* (Jerusalem: Carta, 2000) pp. 52-57.
9. John Dickson, personal communication dated April 19, 2007.
10. John D. Garr, *God's Lamp, Man's Light* (Atlanta, GA: Restoration Foundation, 2001), pp. 13-14.
11. Ibid., pp. 16-17.
12. Robert Heidler, *How Is Your Lampstand Burning: Understanding the Seven Churches of Revelation* (Glory of Zion International Ministries CD Series, 2006).

Chapter 6: The Power War

1. Mark Sutton, *Walk Through the Wall, America* (Longwood, FL: Xulon Press, 2005), pp. xix-xxi.
2. Ibid.
3. Information regarding "Mithraism" from Wikipedia.org http://en.wikipedia/wiki/Mithraism (accessed June 2007); Edward Jayne, "Mithra Versus Christ," EdwardJayne.com, http://www.edwardjayne.com/christology/mithra.html (accessed June 2007); J. P. Holding, "Mighty Mithaic Madness," Tektonics.org, http://tektonics.org/copycat/mithra.html (accessed June 2007).
4. Ibid.

5. "Left," Encyclopedia Britannica Online. http://www.britannica.com/ebc/article-9369950 (accessed June 2007).

6. "Conservatism," *The Columbia Encyclopedia*, Sixth Edition, 2001-05. www.bartle by.com/65/co/conservatsm.html (accessed June 2007).

7. Rabbi Nosson Scherman and Rabbi Meir Zlotowitz, ed., *Rashi, The Art Scroll Series* (Brooklyn, NY: Mesorah Publication, Ltd., 1999), vol. 5, p. 161.

8. Abraham Cohen, *Everyman's Talmud* (New York: Schocken Books, 1949), p. 219.

9. "Federal Republic of Germany," MSN Encarta Online. http://encarta.msn.com/encyclopedia_761576917_23/Germany.html (accessed June 2007).

10. Benjamin Dangl, "Latin America's Leftist Shift: Hopes and Challenges," *Upside Down World*, March 13, 2006. http://upsidedownworld.org/main/content/view/225/1/ (accessed June 2007).

11. "Chavez Boosts Heating Oil Program for U.S. Poor; Takes Swipe at Bush," *USA Today*, September 21, 2006. http://www.usatoday.com/news/world/2006-09-21-us-chavez_x.htm (accessed June 2007).

12. James Strong, *Strong's Complete Dictionary of Bible Words* (Nashville, TN: Thomas Nelson Publishers, 1996).

13. Jay P. Green, Sr., gen. ed. and translator, *The Interlinear Hebrew-Aramaic Old Testament*, second edition (Peabody, MA: Hendrickson Publishers, 1985).

14. Willem A. VanGemeren, gen. ed., *Dictionary of Old Testament Theology and Exegesis*, vol. 1 (Grand Rapids, MI: Zondervan, 1997), pp. 694-695.

Chapter 7: The Wealth War

1. Nahum M. Sarna, *The JPS Torah Commentary, Genesis* (Philadelphia, PA: The Jewish Publication Society, 1989), pp. 24, 31.

2. Henry Cloud and John Townsend, *Boundaries* (Grand Rapids, MI: Zondervan Publishing House, 1992), n.p.

3. Christopher Knight and Robert Lomas, *The Hiram Key* (New York: Barnes and Noble Books, 1996), p. 356.

4. *Vine's Expository Dictionary of Old Testament Words*, PC Study Bible, ver. 5 (Seattle, WA: Biblesoft, Inc., 1998-2007).

5. *American Dictionary of the English Language* (San Francisco: Foundation for American Christian Education, 1987), "avarice."

6. Dictionary.com, *WordNet® 3.0*. Princeton University. http://dictionary.reference.com/browse/covetousness (accessed June 2007).

Chapter 8: The War of the Nations

1. "On Behalf of Israel," Koinonia House Online, June 17, 2003. http://www.khouse.org/enews_article/2003/577 (accessed June 2007).

2. Keith Intrater, *From Iraq to Armageddon* (Shippensburg, PA: Destiny Image Publishers, 2003), p. 84.

3. Ibid., pp. 65-67.

4. Clifford Coonan, "America Meets the New Superpower," *The Independent*, April 19, 2006.

5. "List of countries by GDP (nominal)," Wikipedia.org. http://en.wikipedia.org/wiki/List_of_countries_by_GDP_%28nominal%29 (accessed June 2007).

6. Coonan, "America Meets the New Superpower."

7. Ibid.

Chapter 9: The Harvest War

1. Sun Tzu, *The Art of War*, Ralph D. Sawyer, trans. (New York: Barnes and Noble Books, 1994), pp. 173-174.

2. Ibid.

For more information about Glory of Zion International
Ministries and other resources available from Chuck D.
Pierce, please write or call:

Glory of Zion International
P.O. Box 1601
Denton, Texas 76202

Phone: (940) 382-7231
Fax: (940) 565-9264
Email: plantern@aol.com
http://www.glory-of-zion.org

Find Out Which World Events Were Prophesied in 2001 and What's to Come

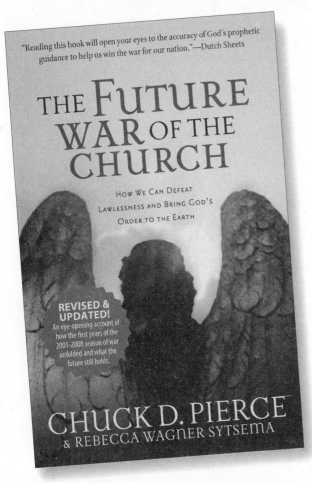

"Reading this book will open your eyes to the accuracy of God's prophetic guidance to help us win the war for our nation."—Dutch Sheets

THE FUTURE WAR OF THE CHURCH

HOW WE CAN DEFEAT LAWLESSNESS AND BRING GOD'S ORDER TO THE EARTH

REVISED & UPDATED!
An eye-opening account of how the first years of the 2001-2008 season of war unfolded and what the future still holds.

CHUCK D. PIERCE
& REBECCA WAGNER SYTSEMA

The Future War of the Church
How We Can Defeat Lawlessness
and Bring God's Order to the Earth
Chuck D. Pierce and Rebecca Wagner Sytsema
ISBN 978.08307.44145

In 2001 Chuck Pierce and Rebecca Wagner Sytsema shared a vision from God, calling on the Church to reestablish His standard of righteousness. Urgent yet hopeful, this call was to arm ourselves for spiritual war against such enemies as moral decay, false religion, hopelessness, apathy and violence. Now they have once again joined forces to tell what has come to pass since the publication of *The Future War of the Church*, and to offer a fresh look into the future that will very soon become our present. In this revised and updated edition, the authors reveal that God is still calling His people to join together to do battle with the forces of evil in this world, empowered by the One whom death could not conquer. "No demonic force, including lawlessness, will be able to stand against a fully functioning Body of Christ. Operating properly in the gifts will lead us back to love where we can work together according to the heart of God." Lay people and church leaders alike can fight against the darkness using worship and prayer, and faith in the strength of the Lord our God. Includes key prayer focuses for standing strong in battle.